❧ Doris Lessing

❧ Doris Lessing

INTERROGATING THE TIMES

EDITED BY
Debrah Raschke,
Phyllis Sternberg Perrakis,
and Sandra Singer

THE OHIO STATE UNIVERSITY PRESS · COLUMBUS

Copyright © 2010 by The Ohio State University.
All rights reserved.

Library of Congress Cataloging-in-Publication Data
Doris Lessing : interrogating the times / edited by Debrah Raschke, Phyllis Sternberg Perrakis, and Sandra Singer.
    p. cm.
Includes bibliographical references and index.
ISBN 978-0-8142-1136-6 (cloth : alk. paper)—ISBN 978-0-8142-9235-8 (cd)
1. Lessing, Doris May, 1919—Criticism and interpretation. I. Raschke, Debrah. II. Perrakis, Phyllis Sternberg. III. Singer, Sandra.
PR6023.E833Z615 2010
823'.914—dc22
                            2010017733

This book is available in the following editions:
Cloth (ISBN 978-0-8142-1136-6)
CD-ROM (ISBN 978-0-8142-9235-8)

Cover design by Melissa Ryan.
Typesetting and design by Jennifer Shoffey Forsythe.
Type set in Adobe Sabon.

∞ The paper used in this publication meets the minimum requirements of the American National Standard for Information Sciences—Permanence of Paper for Printed Library Materials. ANSI Z39.48-1992.

9 8 7 6 5 4 3 2 1

Contents

List of Illustrations   vii
Acknowledgments   ix

Introduction   1
    DEBRAH RASCHKE, PHYLLIS STERNBERG PERRAKIS, AND SANDRA SINGER

PART ONE
Joining the Centuries: Lessing from the Twentieth to the Twenty-First Century

1. Notes for Proteus: Doris Lessing Reads the *Zeitgeist*   11
    ROBERTA RUBENSTEIN

2. "Anon," "Free Women," and the Pleasures of Impersonality   32
    TONYA KROUSE

3. House/Mother: Lessing's Reproduction of Realism in *The Sweetest Dream*   58
    ROBIN VISEL

PART TWO
Engaging the Postmodern Death of History: Redefining Context and Historical Narrative

4. "What Is the Function of the Storyteller?": The Relationship between *Why* and *How* Lessing Writes   77
    ALICE RIDOUT

5. London and Kabul: Assessing the Politics of Terrorist Violence   92
    SANDRA SINGER

6   The Porous Border between Fact and Fiction, Empathy and
    Identification in Doris Lessing's *The Cleft*
      PHYLLIS STERNBERG PERRAKIS   113

PART THREE
Destabilized Genre as Social Critique

7   *love, again* and *The Sweetest Dream*: Fiction and Interleaved
    Fictions
      VIRGINIA TIGER   133

8   Writing in a Minor Key: Doris Lessing's Late-Twentieth-Century
    Fiction
      SUSAN WATKINS   149

PART FOUR
Reflections on Early, Midlife, and Later-Life Lessing

9   Domestic Spaces: Huts and Houses in Doris Lessing's African Stories
      PAT LOUW   165

10 The Challenge of Teaching Doris Lessing's *The Golden Notebook*
    in the Twenty-First Century
      SUZETTE HENKE   183

11 Sex after Sixty: *love, again* and *The Sweetest Dream*
      RUTH O. SAXTON   202

Bibliography   211
Notes on Contributors   225
Index   229

Illustrations

FIGURE 1

Typical African hut in rural Zululand, South Africa. Photograph by Anita de Villiers.   168

FIGURE 2

Samarang: colonial house in Eshowe, Zululand. Photograph by Anita de Villiers.   169

Acknowledgments

We would like to express grateful acknowledgment to *Doris Lessing Studies*. An earlier, shorter version of Suzette Henke's chapter was published in *DLS* 26.1 (Summer 2006) in a special issue titled "Teaching Doris Lessing." An earlier, shorter version of Susan Watkins's chapter appears in *DLS* 25.2 (Winter 2006). Ruth O. Saxton's paper first appeared in *DLS* 24.1 and 2 (Summer/Fall 2004) in a special issue titled "Coming to Age." Phyllis Sternberg Perrakis's chapter is being reprinted by kind permission of Continuum International Publishing Group. It contains only minor corrections from the original version which appeared in *Doris Lessing: Border Crossings,* ed. Alice Ridout and Susan Watkins (London: Continuum, 2009).

We would also like to acknowledge and thank Anita de Villiers, whose photographs of colonial architecture are included in Pat Louw's chapter in this volume.

Introduction

DEBRAH RASCHKE, PHYLLIS STERNBERG PERRAKIS, AND SANDRA SINGER

In the wake of Lessing's winning the 2007 Nobel Prize for Literature, a flurry of discussion began querying her relevance to the twenty-first century. Most notably, Harold Bloom notoriously told the Associated Press, "although Ms Lessing at the beginning of her writing career had a few admirable qualities, I find her work for the past 15 years quite unreadable."[1] He added that the prize is "pure political correctness." By "political correctness," one might assume he's alluding to Lessing's secure place in representing the goals of the women's movement of the 1960s, 1970s, and 1980s. By contrast, *Doris Lessing: Interrogating the Times* demonstrates the continued relevance of her production to a variety of contemporary themes. Wrestling with late-twentieth-century ghosts that continue to haunt our most pressing twenty-first-century dilemmas, Lessing's fiction and nonfiction demand a reformulation of some of our most taken-for-granted assumptions about the contemporary world and how we relate to that world. The three essays in Part One, "Joining the Centuries: Lessing from the Twentieth to the Twenty-First Century," most obviously focus on reading Lessing in light of contemporary concerns.

Roberta Rubenstein's "Notes for Proteus: Doris Lessing Reads the *Zeitgeist*" does what only a lifelong Lessing scholar could do—provide a much-needed overview of Lessing's prolific oeuvre. Identifying Lessing with the mythic figure of the shape-shifting Proteus, Rubenstein, who "followed the author's evolution one book at a time" as each work came into print, traces how Lessing's continual reworking of strategic themes has responded to the changing cultural environment and has been especially important to the lives of women. Expressed in a variety of genres—plays, poems, autobiography, memoirs, polemical and occasional essays, fiction, as well as librettos and sketches—Lessing's vision is difficult to pin down. Giving form to Lessing's protean qualities, Rubenstein unveils how Lessing's writing remains connected to a "global canvas," one in which "relentless wars and aggression between people of different races and ethnicities" threaten annihilation. She demonstrates as well how Lessing's timely fictional renderings of race and sexuality, her candid depictions of vexed mother-daughter relationships, and her prescient commentary on aging shift as new cultural and political contexts demand new solutions. "[T]here is a strong quality of the seer in Lessing herself," writes Rubenstein—Lessing has captured a *zeitgeist* and unveiled "the wounds of *our* times" (emphasis added).

Indeed, if any one literary work captured the imagination of the early women's movement, it probably would be Lessing's *The Golden Notebook*. However, Lessing, called "that epicist of the female experience" by the Swedish Academy that awarded her the Nobel Prize in Literature in 2007,[2] treats gender and sexuality in a way that never lets us rest easy. There is a certain ambiguity for critics and readers in applying a feminist lens to Lessing's work. Although Lessing herself has repeatedly challenged feminist approaches to her work, her very ambiguity toward feminism has allowed her the freedom to reimagine contemporary attitudes toward women in perhaps less restrictive ways. As Tonya Krouse and Robin Visel note in the other two essays in Part One, midlife and late Lessing works offer critiques to gender relations and rework troubling contemporary attitudes and assumptions regarding women's roles. These essays readdress concerns that continue to haunt us—tensions between woman and writer, male and female, body and mind, and the personal and political. In doing so each essay demonstrates how Lessing dares to refashion these binaries in ways at times congruent to, at times challenging to, twenty-first-century thinking. Further, as Rubenstein's and Visel's essays demonstrate, Lessing explores the implications of rethinking these binaries for the older woman.

Likewise, Lessing rethinks the binaries that define female subjectivity, an issue that is foundational to much feminist theory and to Virginia Woolf, who remains an icon to feminist studies.[3] In this light, Tonya Krouse's essay, "'Anon,' 'Free Women,' and the Pleasures of Impersonality," queries the importance of female subjectivity in Woolf, and examines how in *The Golden Notebook* (1962) Lessing's aesthetic also becomes a theory of subjectivity. In particular, Krouse adeptly scrutinizes the predilection for the personal in the formative *The Golden Notebook,* which, as Rubenstein notes, galvanized so many women's personal and cultural lives. Reading *The Golden Notebook* "through and against Woolf's theories in *A Room of One's Own*," Krouse identifies Lessing's portrayal of two crucial issues that continue to challenge the female writer (and feminist theory): how to present an authorial subjectivity that does not imprison the self in a Cartesian, essentially male, mode of being; and how to understand the woman writer's precarious relationship to pleasure.

Robin Visel, in "House/Mother: Lessing's Reproduction of Realism in *The Sweetest Dream*," suggests ways that Lessing further recasts the lingering binary divisions that are the focus of Krouse's essay. Visel resituates the specter of the Victorian "Angel in the House" in the public sphere, where historical and cultural events are never isolated affairs. Visel thus identifies a newly imagined cosmopolitan house that reinvents the British middle-class family, a house that defies the boundaries of empire, patriarchy, and colonialism. Thus, maternity becomes not just a vehicle for reproduction, but a conduit for "revolutionary social change." Reading Frances Lennox of *The Sweetest Dream*—and her predecessors Anna Wulf of *The Golden Notebook* and Martha Quest of *The Four-Gated City*—as haunted by Virginia Woolf's "Angel in the House," Visel investigates the tension between the "homemaker and the woman-who-writes-at-home." In this twenty-first-century work, Lessing "resituates the London house of Anna Wulf and Martha Quest as the home of a new kind of mothering with the potential to resolve some of the ideological binaries and colonialist hierarchies that bedevil her earlier characters." Perhaps the most striking feature of this reinvention is Lessing's attention to politics, especially left-wing politics, as it affects her artist-mothers. Politics and history are "embodied and housed in the Lennox residence. At Frances's capacious kitchen table, Lessing skewers the dangerous naïveté of some of the big ideas of the twentieth century—Communist revolution, anti-colonial nationalism, youth counterculture, and feminism—then reimagines them in more realistic, small-scale, familial terms." Visel claims that in so doing Lessing seems "to make peace with her own ex-husbands and lovers, biological and surrogate children." Thus the painful disjunctions between self and other, woman and writer, male and female, body and mind find a creative refashioning in the process of aging with the "ironic detachment and common sense" that it brings to Frances Lennox and perhaps to her creator.

This decentering of self and world is the focus of Part Two, "Engaging the Postmodern Death of History: Redefining Context and Historical Narrative." As postmodernism emerged as a dominant paradigm in the 1970s, both Lessing and her critics began to engage with reality in new and challenging

Introduction

ways. Previously accepted verities came into question as all narratives became contested. Jean-François Lyotard, perhaps most notably, declared all metanarratives (narratives that previously provided a sense of certainty and guidance) dead.[4] The three essays in this section address Lessing's engagement with this postmodern challenge. Noting Lessing's changed relationship to certainty, Alice Ridout in "'What Is the Function of the Storyteller?': The Relationship between *Why* and *How* Lessing Writes" explores how Lessing's turn from realism to speculative fiction reflects a paradigm shift that sheds light on the contemporary climate of "clashing moral certainties." Comparing "The Small Personal Voice" essay (1957) and *Prisons We Choose to Live Inside* (1986), Ridout contends that Lessing's early realist method of storytelling was driven by a moral vision and by certitudes that define the struggle of good against evil, while her later writings are marked by new uncertainties and the need for critical distance, notably in the form of science fiction and utopia. As Ridout suggests, "self-conscious doubt" supplants "moral certainty."

Exploring Lessing's proclivity for portraying imagined worlds in her later career, Ridout stresses that Lessing is indeed still engaged with the external real, but that her works serve to reveal the shaping narratives of existence while imploding those that prevent us from seeing clearly. Sandra Singer extends the ramifications of this postmodern challenge by taking it into the arena of political violence. Addressing the context of contemporary debates on terrorism in "London and Kabul: Assessing the Politics of Terrorist Violence," Singer poses two key questions: What constitutes terrorism, and is terrorism ever justified? Defining terrorism as "indiscriminate violence" aimed at effecting the maximum shock value, and distinguishing it from legitimate guerilla warfare whose goal is armed resistance, Singer investigates how Lessing explores the problem of terrorism in the fictional *The Good Terrorist* and the nonfictional *The Wind Blows Away Our Words and Other Documents Relating to the Afghan Resistance*. As Singer notes, terrorism for Lessing is motivated by an egomaniacal desire for personal recognition. It is marked further by solipsism and the absence of responsible human agency. It is driven by a delusional, Alice-in-Wonderland-like fantasy that has proved to be truly dangerous. In contrast, Lessing sees the resistance to state-sanctioned oppression as necessary and justifiable. In particular, Lessing cites the Afghan muhjahidin's resistance to Soviet occupation. In this text, Lessing pleads for understanding of Islamic countries, the absence of which fuels the possibilities for further political violence. Reminding us of the historical context of national liberation struggles (including the American Revolution), Singer provocatively asks us to rethink through Lessing's work our assumptions about terrorism.

The concluding essay of this section is Phyllis Sternberg Perrakis's "The

Porous Border between Fact and Fiction, Empathy and Identification in Doris Lessing's *The Cleft*." In this essay, Perrakis keenly identifies the slipperiness of the contemporary historical narrative. No longer a record of fact or even a mimetic representation of cultural ills, Lessing's twenty-first-century historical fable is one that is "porous," oscillating between the unveiling of historical knowledge and the ever-precarious position of the teller of the tale. Evoking contemporary trauma theory, Perrakis contends that Lessing's *The Cleft* dramatizes a reconceptualization of the past that also transforms the present, including ourselves, our personal relationships, and our relations with the global community.

Part Three, "Destabilized Genre as Social Critique," extends how Lessing confronts the perplexities of the postmodern world by examining her changed relationship to narrative and genre. As the representation of what is real has become more labyrinthine, so too have the means used to render that representation, as Virginia Tiger attests in "*love, again* and *The Sweetest Dream*: Fiction and Interleaved Fictions." In this essay, Tiger argues that *love, again* with its "complex comparative structural frame" relays a love story that "turns out to be no 'love story.'" Its competing frames and its complicated windows serve less to tell the story of Sarah Durham than to comment on the lens through which we see romantic love. But even in this most obsessively personal of novels, Tiger points out that Lessing provides detachment not only by the double narrative structure but also by the movement in the beginning from "the omniscient Eye/Voice [narrator] to the writhing, burning intensity of [Sarah's] focalizing voice."

If the structure of *love, again*'s "competing narrative frames" opens up its narrow personal focus, "the competing narrative focalizations" of *The Sweetest Dream* expose "prevailing orthodoxies" and "cant." Set within the political canvas of the "Condition of England" between the 1960s and '80s, Lessing's novel, as Tiger suggests, foresees the "twenty-first-century preoccupations with political correctness and those contrarians who expose its inflexible reductiveness." Narrative as constructed events is a way of thinking, and too frequently a habit of thinking that fuels polarized habits and entrenched ideologies. These narrative dreams are shattered in this Lessing novel, particularly as they are confronted by daily political realities. The novel's resolution, however, in contrast to that of *love, again,* is a life-affirming one in which the novel's three key women "engage in small but sustaining acts of philanthropy" and, in doing so, represent "women who simply get on with it." Thus, *love, again* and *The Sweetest Dream* in addressing the complexities of contemporary narratives and ideologies expand Lessing's assertion in the 1971 introduction to *The Golden Notebook* that "shape" is a narrative in and of itself.[5]

Finally, Susan Watkins in "Writing in a Minor Key: Doris Lessing's Late-Twentieth-Century Fiction" extends the ramifications of narrative to Lessing's career-long concerns with race and colonization. For Watkins, colonialism is a way of thinking that becomes subtly infused in our culture's master narratives. Watkins suggests that Lessing's use of minor genres (the urban gothic, science fiction, and the picaresque) in her later fiction deterritorializes not only language but also the individual's conception of the political world. Narratives purvey vision. If we are, in Susan Watkins's words, "unable to find a safe home in familiar genres" in Lessing's late fabular fiction, we are equally unable in these works to find a "safe home" in anachronistic definitions of race—conceptions of the other as "primitive" and as "animal." Those outworn narratives sanctioned the imperialism and eugenics of the late nineteenth century (and continue to justify forays into the Middle East in order to bring the "enlightened" concept of freedom and democracy to a seemingly less fortunate world). Thus, *The Fifth Child* evokes the gothic to disrupt the narrative of family values that was enshrined in Thatcherite Britain (and which continues to engulf the American imagination). *Ben, In the World* uses the picaresque to critique "the pseudo-Darwinian hierarchies" that "position white masculinity at the apex of an evolutionary chain"—hierarchies which then justify the imperialist narrative as salvific. *Mara and Dann,* in its self-reflexivity, employs a science-fiction disaster narrative to unveil the reactionary and "racist cultural constructs of the animal, the primitive, and the tribe" that so frequently infuse agendas of fear.

Lessing's critiques of our contemporary world, however, never lose sight of the personal. The three essays in Part Four, "Reflections on Early, Midlife, and Later-Life Lessing," interrogate the relationship between Lessing's life and works in three formative periods of her life. Pat Louw in "Domestic Spaces: Huts and Houses in Doris Lessing's African Stories" examines the expression of the colonial tensions of the 1930s in Rhodesian architecture and their inscription in Lessing's African stories. Tying the experiences of the young Lessing to the adult author's art, Louw notes how the Lessing of the 1930s instinctively rebelled against the ideological implications of the settlers' attempt to create a barrier between the house and the outside world. Similarly, Louw interrogates the adult author's use of the structures of the hut and house in her African stories, arguing that they are used not simply as background, but as a conduit for critiquing the entrapments that are inherent to colonial thinking.

Suzette Henke's "The Challenge of Teaching Doris Lessing's *The Golden Notebook* in the Twenty-First Century" examines the attitudes and assumptions of mid-twentieth-century England and midlife Lessing embodied in *The*

Golden Notebook. Beginning her essay by noting the novel's impediments for a generation of students who have no historical memory of the iron curtain or the cold war (and whose experience of the real is filtered through the all-encompassing grid of the present), Henke provides four lenses through which to view "Lessing's epic narrative." Delineating the "'four P's': Global Politics, Sexual Politics, Psychoanalysis, and Postmodern Narrative," Henke braids together in each category Lessing's own comments about what she was trying to do, the attitudes of the time, texts from *The Golden Notebook,* and Henke's own responses when she first read the novel in the early 1970s. The result is an interwoven tapestry of the life and times of midcentury Lessing and midcentury England and America.

Henke then skillfully weaves into this midcentury tapestry the concerns of contemporary life. "It all comes round again," as Henke remarks, with "the ghost of McCarthyism invidiously resuscitated" in attitudes toward contemporary terrorists that are "attended by many of the political dangers similar to those earlier associated with the Red menace of Communism." Henke also suggests the novel's experimental form challenges "formulaic thinking," thereby querying contemporary "cultural dogma." As Henke observes, *The Golden Notebook*'s Molly Jacobs uncannily predicts the backlash and moral conservatism of future generations.

In "Sex after Sixty: *love, again* and *The Sweetest Dream*," Ruth O. Saxton conjoins the issues of women, aging, and sexual pleasure. Saxton suggests that not until *love, again* and *The Sweetest Dream* does Lessing boldly confront the conundrum of female pleasure after sixty, when the world would prefer not to see the older woman or, if it does see her, sees her as a dried peach. What dismays Saxton about Lessing's portrait in *love, again* of Sarah Durham's "eroticized theatrical summer" in which she falls in love twice, each time with a much younger man, is that Sarah "reveals ageist reactions to her own body" and "avoids physical intimacy because of her distaste for her changing body." In contrast, Frances Lennox of *The Sweetest Dream* is able to move beyond the traditional "all-encompassing role of nurturer/caretaker" and to enjoy a second marriage at sixty. In this marriage it is "[t]he big bed, rather than the big kitchen table, [which] is now 'the emotional center of her life.'" Frances is able to "encounter her mirror, recognize change," set "a few limits on her previously unlimited nurturing of others," and experience the death of her mother-in-law and her assumption of the role of older woman without "yearning" for the past or "her younger body" and without "denying herself sexual pleasure" or a fulfilling relationship. Like Henke, Saxton ties the fate of Lessing's two older protagonists to her own responses on first reading the novels and to the author's life, subtlety suggesting that Lessing's refusal to grant Sarah Durham sexual pleasure may be tied to "a profound unmet yearning for maternal love mistaken for 'love' of a man."

If all three essays in this section remind us of the strong autobiographical links between Lessing's fiction and her life, they, and indeed the whole collection, also suggest how Lessing uses her life and art to interrogate the times in which she is living. Never satisfied with easy answers, Lessing continues to play the role of a gadfly, stinging or stirring her readers into questioning contemporary shibboleths and urging them to adopt "the detached, curious, patient, investigative attitude" mentioned in *Prisons We Choose to Live Inside* (qtd. in Alice Ridout's essay, "'What Is the Function of the Storyteller?': The Relationship between *Why* and *How* Lessing Writes," in Part Two). Such an attitude would disrupt rigid constructions of right and wrong, good and evil—what Ridout argues Lessing defines in *Prisons We Choose to Live Inside* as "you are damned, we are saved" cultural habits. In fact, Lessing suggests that our survival depends on moving out of these narratives.[6] As Ridout notes in "'What Is the Function of the Storyteller?'" it is precisely this "you are damned, we are saved" narrative that legitimates the "War on Terror."[7] As rationales such as this one seem to increasingly permeate global venues, Lessing's oeuvre becomes increasingly relevant.

NOTES

1. Harold Bloom, qtd. in Sarah Crown, "Doris Lessing Wins Nobel Prize," October 11, 2007, http://www.guardian.co.uk/books/2007/oct/11/nobelprize.awardsandprizes (accessed July 7, 2009).

2. Press release of the Swedish Academy, October 11, 2007, http://nobelprize.org/nobel_prizes/literature/laureates/2007/press.html (accessed July 7, 2009).

3. This collection updates Ruth O. Saxton and Jean Tobin's edited collection, *Woolf and Lessing: Breaking the Mold* (New York: St. Martin's Press, 1994). See as well Brenda Silver's *Virginia Woolf Icon* (Chicago: University of Chicago Press, 1999); and Roxanne Fand, *The Dialogic Self: Reconstructing Subjectivity in Woolf, Lessing, and Atwood* (Selinsgrove, PA: Susquehanna University Press, 1999).

4. See Jean-François Lyotard, *The Postmodern Explained: Correspondence 1982–1985,* ed. Julian Pefanis and Morgan Thomas (Minneapolis: University of Minnesota Press, 1993).

5. Doris Lessing, *The Golden Notebook* (1962; repr., New York: Bantam, 1971), xiv.

6. Debrah Raschke, "Cabalistic Gardens: Lessing's *Memoirs of a Survivor,*" in *Spiritual Exploration in the Works of Doris Lessing,* ed. Phyllis Sternberg Perrakis (Westport, CT: Greenwood Press, 1999), 45–46, 52–53.

7. See Alice Ridout's chapter, "'What Is the Function of the Storyteller?': The Relationship between *Why* and *How* Lessing Writes," in Part Two of this collection.

Part One

JOINING THE CENTURIES

*Lessing from the Twentieth to
the Twenty-First Century*

Notes for Proteus

Doris Lessing Reads the *Zeitgeist*

ROBERTA RUBENSTEIN

In the early 1970s British novelist Margaret Drabble called Doris Lessing "Cassandra in a world under siege" for her uncanny ability to anticipate social and political trends well before they were recognized as part of the *Zeitgeist*.[1] Four decades later, the observation still holds. One example of Lessing's ahead-of-timeliness is her novel *The Good Terrorist* (1985), which was published nearly two decades before the word "terrorist" became so uncomfortably central to the daily world news and nightly private anxieties.[2] Lessing was frequently mentioned for the Nobel Prize in Literature before the Swedish Academy acknowledged, rather belatedly, her significant place in contemporary letters by awarding her that prize in 2007 at the age of 88, making her its oldest recipient.

A different figure from Greek mythology might also be instructively used to describe Doris Lessing: Proteus, the shape-shifter who, when caught, metamorphosed into multiple other shapes. Lessing is one of the literary world's most accomplished shape-shifters. Few other writers have successfully published in so many different formal "shapes" or genres: plays, poems, polemical and occasional essays, autobiography, memoirs—both factual and imaginative—and, of course, fiction. Even within the last category, the genre for which Lessing is best known, the shapes shift to embrace short stories, novellas, novels, and two multinovel series. These fictions are in turn distributed among diverse literary genres, from psychological realism to speculative fiction, fable, and fantasy. To this eclectic list one can add a graphic novel, a volume of London sketches, two librettos for opera scores, and several collections of pieces devoted solely to the subject of cats.[3]

Further, many of Lessing's fictions themselves unfold through formal shape-shifting, from a novel-within-a-novel to diary and journal entries, parodies, and an assortment of fictional "documents"—correspondence, book reviews, newspaper clippings, lectures, medical charts, and archival reports. Considering the protean Doris Lessing, the contemporary reader might well ask: is this prolific writer one or several? The answer is: if not several, then (at least figuratively) more than one. During the 1980s Lessing published two novels pseudonymously, under the name Jane Somers, to test her premise that it was especially difficult for unknown writers to achieve the publication of "first" novels. Interestingly, her British editor didn't recognize that she was the author of *The Diaries of Jane Somers;* her American editor, who figured out that Jane Somers was Doris Lessing, agreed to support her experiment by publishing the novels pseudonymously.[4]

Even under her own name, for nearly six decades Lessing has continued to surprise her readers by remaining several steps ahead of their expectations. However, the qualities of variety and unpredictability would not by themselves account for Doris Lessing's reputation as one of our era's preeminent living writers. Rather, many of her readers, particularly during the period when her publications coincided with the most active years of the women's movement, have been profoundly shaped not only academically but personally by their engagement with her fiction. Lessing's renderings of the female condition—as expressed through Anna Wulf of *The Golden Notebook* and Martha Quest of *Children of Violence* in particular—are central texts for a generation's thinking about their lives as women (and men): emotional independence; sexuality, the body, and heterosexual relationships; female friendships; motherhood; aging; political engagement and disengagement; psychological development; insanity; unconventional consciousness and spiritual quest; the pathologies of history; utopian and dystopian futures.

The Golden Notebook, Lessing's acknowledged form-breaking masterpiece, remains influential as a compelling imaginative chronicle of a pivotal moment in Western social and political history that appears to have been captured between the covers of the novel almost as it was happening. Since the novel's publication in 1962, Marxist Communism in what is now the former Soviet Union and in Eastern Europe has collapsed. Thus, the sections of the novel that chart Anna Wulf's love-hate relationship and subsequent political disillusionment with the British Communist Party are now perhaps more of historical interest than are other parts of the novel.[5] Nonetheless, it is unsettling to come across certain passages—including newspaper headlines and stories, among the many that the emotionally distressed Anna clips and pastes into her notebooks when she is unable to write—that easily could have appeared in today's newspapers. Two items from the 1950s will suffice as examples: first: "MOSLEM WORLD FLARES. . . . [*Express*]," dated October 17, 1951; second:

> Title II of the McCarran Act specifically provides for the establishment of so-called detention centres. Far from *directing* the creation of such centres, the law *authorises* the Attorney-General of the U.S. to apprehend and detain "in such places of detention as may be prescribed by him . . . all persons as to whom there is reasonable ground to believe that such persons probably will engage in or probably will conspire with others to engage in acts of espionage and sabotage." (emphasis and ellipsis in original)[6]

Although not all newspaper clippings that appear in *The Golden Notebook* are as timely as these examples, together they suggest—from a distance of more than half a century since the decade during which the novel is set—that Anna Wulf/Doris Lessing was symbolically "cutting up history" in order to create, in as direct and vivid a form as possible, both a digest and a deconstruction of the political, social, and moral chaos of the 1950s. Either Lessing was extraordinarily prescient, or the more things change, the more they remain the same. Indeed, some of both.

Fortunately, experiences that were termed the "battle of the sexes" and the "sex war" during the mid-twentieth century no longer rage in quite the destructive ways in which Anna Wulf experienced and chronicled them. However, contemporary college students—particularly women—still find validity in the narrative representations of sexuality and emotional vulnerability in heterosexual relationships that so profoundly distressed Anna Wulf. The ramifying divisions and collisions between the roles of mother and lover, writer and political idealist, along with the brilliant textual mirroring of those divisions, remain invigorating, whether for first-time or returning readers.[7] The sheer ambition of the novel's experimental structure—the form that, to Lessing's dismay, was virtually overlooked when *The Golden Notebook* was first published—has received its due attention and critical understanding, yet it retains the power of its originality. One of my students, reading the novel for the first time, remarked that the narrative and psychological "hall of mirrors" in which she found herself was one of the most exciting, albeit confusing, literary experiences she had ever had.

In *The Golden Notebook* and *Children of Violence,* Lessing incorporated a broad spectrum of ideological, political, and psychological issues, not only those primarily of concern to women. Filtering through fiction her experiences as an idealistic Communist in Southern Africa and later as a disillusioned Marxist in England, she outlined the costs of utopian thinking and overly idealized political engagement, issues that continue to resonate in contemporary experience even though the political picture has changed significantly. Through her depictions of complex mother-daughter relationships—most notably, Martha and her mother, May Quest, as well as the unnamed Narrator and the young Emily Cartwright of *The Memoirs of a Survivor*—Lessing laid bare relationships that may uncomfortably remind some readers of difficult relationships with their own mothers. Long before the subjects of aging and physical decline reached the foreground of scholarly consideration and contemporary cultural analysis, she explored their vicissitudes: Kate Brown of *The Summer before the Dark* (1973) takes a life-altering spiritual journey as her maternal role fades; in *The Diary of a Good Neighbor* (1983), Jane Somers, a woman in the prime of life, must come to terms with her responsibility to the elderly and infirm Maudie Fowler; sixty-five-year-old Sarah Durham of *love, again* (1996) struggles—*again,* in midlife—with the consequences of longing and unrequited desire.

Even Lessing's speculative fiction—from the apocalyptic *Four-Gated City* (1969), *Briefing for a Descent into Hell* (1971), *The Memoirs of a Survivor* (1974), through the *Canopus in Argos* series (1979–83), to two recent novels set on the African continent several millennia into the future—may be read as instructive fables about life on this earth during our own era of relentless aggression and destruction. Although Ifrik, the postapocalyptic African continent where *Mara and Dann: An Adventure* (1999) and *The Story of General Dann and Mara's Daughter, Griot and the Snow Dog* (2005) are set, is metaphorically an even darker place than the Southern Africa of Lessing's earliest fiction, Mara's quest echoes Martha's quest in telling ways.[8] The shape-shifting author is both the optimist who can imagine a more hospitable future and the resolute realist-pessimist who questions whether human nature will ever evolve in ways that might accommodate such potentialities.

There is a quality of urgency to much of Doris Lessing's writing that often overtakes felicities of style; she seems less interested than many writers in the aesthetic qualities of language and narrative form. An observation made by Margaret Drabble more than thirty years ago remains true: she "is not obsessed with form but with content, and she does not care whether the form she finds is new or old, fashionable or unfashionable, as long as it serves her purpose."[9] Moreover, one does not read Lessing for her sense of humor—unless to appreciate her dry, ironic voice. Critics occasionally find themselves perplexed, wondering whether certain stylistic choices are artistically intentional or the consequence of the author's interests lying elsewhere.[10] What some critics regard as aesthetic slackness, Lessing considers authorial freedom. As she has expressed it, "What's marvelous about novels is they can be anything you like.... There are no rules."[11]

Indeed, the rule-breaking *Golden Notebook* represents both thematically and formally the limits of language and of traditional narrative form to capture the complex texture of lived experience. Lessing regards that novel as her attempt to "write a book which would make its own comment, a wordless statement: to talk through the way it was shaped" (*GN*, xix). Through its multiple narrative forms, styles, and perspectives, its disruptions of chronology, and its Möbius-strip-like metafictional structure, the novel brilliantly represents the opposition between aesthetic grace and emotional authenticity: the "raw unfinished quality" that the blocked writer Anna Wulf regards as the most valuable dimension of her life is directly mirrored in the "crude, unfinished, raw, tentative" quality of many passages in the novel (*GN*, 225).

In a panel of writers who gathered in 1991 to discuss the literature that emerged from the women's movement of the 1960s and '70s, Vivian Gornick observed of *The Golden Notebook* that "Lessing's infamous clumsiness as a writer is actually used to brilliant strength. I think she is one of the great so-called bad writers."[12] While not everyone would concur that Lessing is a "bad writer" (or that she is a "great" one), many of her readers would agree that she is not one to whom they go for her craft. At times she can be irritatingly didactic, cranky, blunt, and prolix; there is a side of her that enjoys the soapbox. One only need read *Prisons We Choose to Live Inside*—the published text of the Massey Lectures she gave for the Canadian Broadcasting Corporation in 1985—to come straight up against Lessing the didactic moralist and lecturer.[13] The voice of the polemical Lessing can also be heard in Anna Wulf's repeated, emphatic shorthand phrase "*the point is ...*," to say nothing of the didactic passages in such novels as *Briefing for a Descent into Hell, The Good Terrorist, Mara and Dann,* and *Shikasta.*

Yet a number of Lessing's novels resist the didactic impulse, instead assuming the shape of fables with the author enjoying the position of the traditional oral storyteller whose words are later recorded. In *The Cleft* (2007), she adopts the perspective of a male Roman senator who endeavors to reconstruct the unwritten history of the human race as it evolved from a single (female) gender to the complications and pleasures of heterosexuality.[14] However, just when some readers may begin to wonder what happened to the "shapes" they remember from Lessing's defining realistic novels such as *The Golden Notebook,* she publishes such demonstrably mimetic novels as *love, again* and *The Sweetest Dream*, or a collection that includes stories deeply grounded in realism, such as "Victoria and the Staveneys" and "A Love Child,"[15] as if to remind her readers that the observant social realist has not vanished permanently but merely has chosen to shift shapes once again.

Like Proteus, who in some versions of the myth can foretell the future, there is a strong quality of the seer in Lessing herself. For many years a student of Sufi mysticism, she frequently embeds in her fiction allusions to or transformations of Sufi teaching stories or focuses on emergent strands of the contemporary *Zeitgeist* well before they have reached her readers' awareness. She does not regard her prescience as a quality unique to herself. In an especially revealing image, she has commented that writers who take their profession seriously "place their fingers on the wounds of our times. . . . [T]he author should be something of a prophet, tracing a thing before it is fully apparent, grasping a subject before it becomes a trend, stretching out one's antennae into the universe to sense its most subtle vibrations."[16] Of her attraction to Sufism—which validated preoccupations that were already present in Lessing's fiction, such as her interest in breaking through conventional ways of thinking and being—she has explained, "[F]or people like myself unable to admire organized religions of any kind, [Sufi] philosophy shows where to look for answers to questions put by society and by experience—questions not answered by the official purveyors of knowledge, secular or sacred."[17]

Elsewhere, Lessing has affirmed that writers have an almost collective function, "like a sensitive organ which tends to notice things that other parts of humanity don't. . . . I think writers, without exception, have had the experience of writing as if they were vessels. . . . [Y]ou just plug into a wavelength of some kind."[18] She obviously tapped that experience to explore such ideas through several characters in *The Four-Gated City*. Learning under the tutelage of the clairvoyant Lynda Coldridge and others who aspire to higher forms of consciousness, Martha Quest develops the capacity to "plug into" other people's thoughts. That novel, the final segment of *Children of Violence*, reflects the detailed social and psychological realism that distinguishes Martha's development over the course of the entire series—only, at the end, to shift quite unexpectedly into an apocalyptic appendix set some years into the future. In the more spiritually evolved civilization of that future, a small group of children possess the visionary capacities that Martha struggled to acquire and for which Lynda Coldridge was deemed "crazy" and dysfunctional.

Lessing's prescience occasionally mingles with her literary shape-shifting in another sense. Through the complex narrative structure of *The Golden*

Notebook—its interweaving of fact, fiction, and "truth" and its pressure on the very limits of language to capture experience—the form-breaking metafiction is now regarded as an early expression of the postmodern, a term that had not yet entered the critical vocabulary of literary analysis when the novel was originally published in 1962. Further, Anna Wulf's relentless microscopic analysis of her multiply divided "self" as she experiences psychological breakdown anticipates the now-commonplace postmodern idea of the self as a social construction. *The Golden Notebook* marks a shift from the humanist ideal of wholeness to the poststructuralist/postmodern view of the self as a fiction in which parts or fragments do not necessarily cohere.[19]

Perhaps Lessing's sensitive antennae, her unusual capacity to "notice things" that others miss, developed as a result of her role as an outsider—a position initially thrust upon her by the circumstances of her birth and childhood but one that she subsequently cultivated. She was born of English parents in Persia (now Iran), grew up in Southern Rhodesia (now Zimbabwe), and emigrated to England (still England) when she was thirty. Even these few biographical details regarding Lessing's formative years in areas of the world that were—and still are—in significant political and social transition suggest her fortuitous proximity to some of the major political upheavals of the past and current centuries. A writer who consistently challenges orthodoxies, she is an iconoclast who, ironically—and to her own dismay—has become an icon. Some years ago, she was recommended by England's Queen Elizabeth for a New Year's Honour but refused the designation: when selected for the Order of the British Empire (O.B.E.) in 1977, she politely refused, claiming, "there is no British Empire." Subsequently, she also refused the honor of Dame of the British Empire (D.B.E.), but ultimately accepted the award of Companion of Honour for "conspicuous national service" in 2000 because, as she explained it, "you're not called anything—and it's not demanding."[20]

It is stimulating and gratifying to follow a living writer book by book, an unfolding experience with both intellectual and emotional dimensions that is impossible for Lessing's newer readers to duplicate. Speaking of my own experience, I recognize what a privilege it is to have followed the author's evolution one book at a time. I remember the exhilaration I felt each time I—then a newly minted professor and scholar—began to read Lessing's novels the moment after they arrived in my local bookstore. Those who have discovered Lessing and her sizable oeuvre more recently no doubt have found it quite daunting to contemplate reading several shelves of her books. I say this not critically but as a factual observation: scholars who have come to her work recently inevitably lack the full picture of the complex and protean Doris Lessing. They cannot fully recapture the remarkable sweep, variety, and occasional sheer quirkiness (graphic novel? opera libretto? verbal sketches of London scenes? portraits of cats?) of the author's oeuvre as it has evolved and shifted shapes over six decades, during which it has both anticipated and anatomized the contemporary *Zeitgeist*. On the other hand, recent scholars have established fruitful new avenues of inquiry, including postmodern, postcolonial, and international perspectives.[21]

Yet the self-educated Doris Lessing has never welcomed academic attention to her work and is, for the most part, quite resistant to the idea of scholarly criticism. In her 1971 introduction to *The Golden Notebook,* she sounded a scolding note that she has repeated elsewhere in different ways. Of literary critics, she remarked,

> Why are they so parochial, so personal, so small-minded? Why do they always atomise, and belittle, why are they so fascinated by detail, and uninterested in the whole? Why is their interpretation of the word *critic* always to find fault? . . . That valuable person who understands what you are doing, what you are aiming for, and can give you advice and real criticism, is nearly always someone right outside the literary machine, even outside the university system.[22]

Adding an even more pointed objection to scholars who aspired to analyze and deconstruct *The Golden Notebook,* Lessing protested that "the book is alive and potent and fructifying and able to promote thought and discussion *only* when its plan and shape and intention are not understood, because that moment of seeing the shape and plan and intention is also the moment when there isn't anything more to be got out of it" (*GN,* xxvii, emphasis in original).

The large and diverse body of scholarly and critical writing generated in response to Lessing's oeuvre confirms that readers have ignored her objections to such analysis. Clearly they have not reached the point where "there isn't anything more to be got out of" her work. The critical discourse that her fiction (in particular) has generated is deeply felt, often drawing on each scholar's own personal experience as it intersects with ideas that Lessing has so compellingly rendered. Scholars and nonscholars alike who came of age academically during the 1970s and '80s and read Lessing's fiction as it first appeared in print frequently claim to have been profoundly changed by it.[23]

Those decades were especially transformative years for women in academe, as feminist theory and scholarship blossomed in academic conferences and into print, entered the critical discourse, and transformed (permanently, one hopes) the academic debate along an enormous spectrum from word to action: from the exposure of until-then unexamined gender bias in canon formation and critical analysis to the exposure of the same gender bias operating in the culture that shaped hiring and tenure decisions in departments of literature and other disciplines.

During that era of social and scholarly ferment, Lessing spoke directly and immediately to the condition of many of her readers. Her fiction seemed to capture, explore, and express, realistically and passionately, vital knowledge about where "we" were then—the "we" consisting of a broad audience of academic and nonacademic, female and male, feminist and nonfeminist readers. Although the experience may be difficult for younger scholars and newer readers of Lessing to understand from this later point in time, then it seemed as if everyone "knew," or felt they knew, Anna Wulf and Martha Quest personally. Certainly, no one who aligned herself or himself with the women's movement as it gathered momentum during those years could profess ignorance of *The Golden Notebook*, despite the irony: Lessing objected to the novel's appropriation by feminists, complaining that the narrative was not read in the "right way" when it was published (*GN*, xiv).[24] Regretting that its ambitious experimental design was virtually overlooked in favor of its usefulness as a "weapon in the sex war" (*GN*, xii), she was chagrined that what most seemed to galvanize her readers was her ability to represent so convincingly the vexed intimate relationships between women and men and the important connections between the personal and the political.

The novel's articulation and anatomy of what it meant to be a "free woman" at that historical moment was such a revelation that, looking back from the vantage point of five or six decades (depending on whether one chooses as the starting point the years during which the novel is set or its publication date), it is not surprising that other dimensions of the novel attracted less attention. In a dialogue in the Yellow Notebook between Anna's fictional alter ego Ella and her friend Julia, Ella remarks, "My dear Julia, we've chosen to be free women, and this is the price we pay. . . ." Julia responds, "Free! What's the use of us being free if [men] aren't?" (*GN*, 438–39). To her psychiatrist, Mother Sugar, Anna Wulf says, "I believe I'm living the kind of life women never lived before. . . . There is something new in the world. . . . I want to be able to separate in myself what is old and cyclic, the recurring history, the myth, from what is new, what I think or feel that might be new . . ." (*GN*, 452–53; final ellipsis in original). Similarly, Martha Quest of *The Four-*

Gated City experiments on herself in her quest not only to understand but to gather into herself extrasensory capabilities and a new sense of human possibility.

A good friend of mine who recently reread *The Golden Notebook* and *The Four-Gated City* told me that her first reading of those novels in the early 1970s made so vividly clear what was then termed the "sex war"—an often negative dynamic between men and women that operated not only in the larger culture but in her own private life—that she was galvanized into action: the novels literally empowered her to leave an unhappy albeit "proper marriage" and create a new life. As she put it, "I feel a bit like a Doris Lessing character."[25] Times have changed. Though one should not generalize from one woman's experience to suggest that Lessing's groundbreaking novels functioned as, among other things, the catalyst for uncouplings, it does suggest that reading Lessing was—and continues to be—not simply an intellectual experience but a personal one that directly affects her readers' lives. At a reading of her work in Washington, DC, in 2004, Lessing commented, in response to a question from a member of the audience, that women of the current generation lack a sense of history. In her view, they take for granted what she called "the greatest revolution of our time": liberation from fear of unwanted pregnancy through the advent of effective methods of birth control. She emphasized, however, that credit for this enormous social change goes not to the women's movement but to major advances in reproductive technology, including the birth control pill.[26]

In addition to Lessing's persistence in challenging conventional thinking and orthodoxies of all kinds, a noteworthy element of her oeuvre is her predilection for "reprising" or revisiting explorations of previous themes and characters, as if to suggest that no book can ever be the last word on a given subject, since both she and the world inevitably continue to change.[27] The very idea of a series—Lessing has published two multivolume series—suggests that certain characters and/or themes resist containment within a single volume. For the five-volume *Children of Violence,* Lessing drew directly on her own experience growing up in southern Africa and, later, in England, to chart the life of Martha Quest from adolescence to maturity. During that extended period of time, both Martha and the social/political realities of the world in which Lessing lived and wrote radically changed. Twice during the seventeen years that encompass the publication history of *Children of Violence,* Lessing interrupted her progress on the series to write novels that were not a part of it: *The Golden Notebook* and the largely forgotten, out-of-print *Retreat to Innocence* (1956). Each of these "interruptions" was an essential and pivotal transition in Lessing's literary development.[28]

The second five-volume series, *Canopus in Argos: Archives,* enabled Lessing to develop further the form of social and political extrapolation she had initiated with *The Four-Gated City.* Through speculative or "space" fiction, she created narrative fables that, while participating in the fantastic, can be understood as transformations of realistic themes articulated elsewhere in her oeuvre. As she expresses it, she first imagined *Shikasta* as a "single self-contained book. . . . But as I wrote I was invaded with ideas for other books, other stories, and the exhilaration that comes from being set free into a larger scope with more capacious possibilities and themes."[29] The series is still technically incomplete; at various points, although not recently, Lessing has expressed her intention to write a sixth volume.[30]

In one sense, the *Canopus in Argos* series reprises one of Lessing's earlier ventures into speculative fiction: the "inner space" fiction of *Briefing for a Descent into Hell* straddles realistic and fantastic domains. Inwardly, Professor Charles Watkins may be gifted with exceptional psychic powers and in touch with deeper spiritual understanding; outwardly, he is regarded and treated by medical science as an amnesiac patient who has lost, at least temporarily, part of his mind. Resembling Watkins in certain ways, the emotionally fragile seer Lynda Coldridge of *The Four-Gated City* cannot function in the ordinary world and is regarded as crazy by the medical establishment. However, in *Shikasta* (1979), Lynda reappears in a redemptive role and her extrasensory powers are taken seriously. Indeed, in *Shikasta,* such collisions of worldview are projected, all too presciently, onto a global canvas that features, among other events, an attempt to understand the "Century of Destruction" (the twentieth century) as a record of relentless wars and aggression between people of different races and ethnicities. A "mock trial" initiated by the Combined Youth Armies of the World—the very name suggests generational conflict—also symbolically expresses global conflict as the clash between "White Races" and "Dark-skinned Races."[31] Once again, Lessing anticipated through speculative fiction written in the twentieth century the climate of aggression that marks the twenty-first century. The "war on terrorism" precipitated by the terrorist attack on the World Trade Center on 9/11/01 is only one of numerous wars and conflicts currently raging somewhere on the planet between tribes, races, nations, and generations over ideologies, territories, resources, and religions.[32]

By contrast, in the book that she calls her final one, *Alfred and Emily* (2008), Lessing revisits the subject of war from an altogether different angle, imagining an alternative version of the early twentieth century in which the Great War never happened.[33] In its absence, her father and mother proceeded to live their lives undamaged—rather than, as they were in fact, physically and emotionally damaged—by the "Great Unmentionable."[34] Remarkably, in this revisionist fantasy, Lessing's parents do not marry each other—almost as if she has imaginatively erased herself from their troubled history as well.

Another major theme in Lessing's work, the volatility of heterosexual relationships, is reprised throughout her oeuvre. *Play with a Tiger* (1962), published the same year as *The Golden Notebook,* gives dramatic form to a conflicted, emotionally destructive but ultimately constructive relationship between two characters named Anna and Dave, who reappear in almost the same roles in narrative form in Anna Wulf's struggle with her alter ego Saul Green. In *The Marriages between Zones Three, Four, and Five,* the second volume of the *Canopus in Argos* series, the "sex war" and the vagaries of romantic relationship take the form of a fable with spiritual as well as emotional and political implications.[35]

Three pairs of sequels, each of which began as a single, self-contained novel, demonstrate still other expressions of Lessing's fondness for revisiting ideas first explored in her previously published narratives. Writing as Jane Somers in *The Diary of a Good Neighbor,* she explores the disturbing exigencies of the process of aging and the condition of old age for women, a subject that spills over into a sequel, *If the Old Could . . .* (1984). Similarly, Lessing returns to the story of the anomalous biological and social "throwback" of *The Fifth Child* (1988) with *Ben, In the World* (2000), a sequel apparently prompted by numerous letters and questions from readers who asked her "what happens to Ben?" after the first novel ends. Although the adventures of the siblings, Mara and Dann—who survive their encounters with hostile adversaries and unfavorable conditions for survival in postapocalyptic Ifrik (Africa)—seem to achieve resolution by the end of the eponymous novel, *Mara and Dann,* they continue in the awkwardly titled sequel, *The Story of General Dann and Mara's Daughter, Griot and the Snow Dog* (2005).[36] Even the title and central preoccupations of *love, again* (my emphasis) foreground the author's return to explore "the habit of loving," a subject about which she has written extensively.[37] In the latter novel, the middle-aged protagonist Sarah Durham is several decades older than Martha Quest, Anna Wulf, and the female protagonists of most of Lessing's shorter fiction. In "The Grandmothers" (*The Grandmothers: Four Short Novels,* 2003), Lessing extends the theme in still another—this time, decidedly unconventional—direction: two women whose friendship lasts for decades choose as their lovers each other's sons.[38]

Still another example of Lessing's interest in reconsidering ideas expressed in her own earlier accounts, *The Sweetest Dream* (2001) provides a mellow return visit to the politically and socially transformative decades of the 1960s and '70s, earlier imaginatively rendered in *The Four-Gated City.* Indeed, the novel completes a geographical circle begun in *Children of Violence.* Over the course of that series, Martha Quest develops from adolescence to young adulthood in the imaginary southern African country of Zambesia, reaches maturity in London, and eventually dies—in the apocalyptic coda that concludes not only the novel but the series—in the service of highly evolved consciousness and collective spiritual growth. In *The Sweetest Dream,* also set in London and Africa, the direction of the geographical trajectory is reversed. Middle-aged Frances Lennox finds herself the mother figure for and emotional center of a diverse group that includes not only her own and others' children and assorted friends but also her own mother-in-law, her former husband, his former wife, and his daughter—very like Martha Quest who, during the same time period in London, functions as the mother figure and emotional center of Mark Coldridge's similarly unorthodox family. A member of Frances's extended family—her former husband's daughter, Sylvia—contracts a fatal disease in the service of her idealistic mission as a doctor in Zimlia, an imaginary country in Africa.[39]

It is not that Doris Lessing has run out of new ideas and simply recycles older ones. Rather, she apparently revisits the terrain of her earlier fiction to reconsider and often to shift the emphasis, introduce new perspectives, or draw different conclusions. These reprises may also reflect Lessing's interest in cycles of experience and of history. For example, the Martha Quest–like character of Mara, so central to the first *Mara and Dann* novel, recedes in importance—in fact, she dies early in the second narrative—while her brother, General Dann, literally commands the foreground. In the sequel, Lessing further embellishes the portrayal of postapocalyptic Ifrik, a continent where social and cultural structures have further deteriorated and the primitive law of the jungle is even more evident.

Even in her nonfiction, Lessing has frequently cycled back, whether literally, artistically, or psychologically, to revisit earlier preoccupations and emotionally significant sites. Memoirs such as *Going Home* (1957) established the strand of what might be called the intertextuality of return within Lessing's own writing. *African Laughter: Four Visits to Zimbabwe* (1992), a version of "going home" published more than three decades after the first memoir, traces the author's four visits to Zimbabwe following the cancellation, after more than thirty years, of her listing as "prohibited immigrant" from the country of her emotional, artistic, and imaginative genesis. In 1988, during the second of her four visits to Zimbabwe between 1982 and 1992, Lessing finally overcame a deep inner resistance to revisiting the site of her family home and farm in the bush outside of Harare (Salisbury in her youth).

Although she knew that the earth-and-grass hut of her childhood had succumbed to the elements years before and that "every child who has left home to become an adult knows the diminishing of the first trip home," the visit to the site was nonetheless emotionally wrenching.[40] There, confronting the "magnificence, the space, the marvel" of the place, she understood it as "a privilege . . . a blessing" to have spent her childhood in the idyllic bush country of southern Africa (*Laughter,* 314–15).

Lessing's return visit to the Macheke Hotel outside of Harare, fictionalized in *The Golden Notebook* as the Mashopi Hotel, was similarly revelatory. She discovered that her fictional version of the place had entirely supplanted whatever "true" memories she might once have had. Like Anna Wulf, who struggles with an obstinate "other-self" (*GN,* 130), Lessing discovered that her invented version of the hotel and the people she associated with it were so deeply entrenched in her memory that she could not even recall the proprietor's actual name.

> What happened in Macheke I described, changed for literary reasons, in *The Golden Notebook*. But how much changed? All writers know the state of trying to remember what actually happened, rather than what was invented, or half invented, a meld of truth and fiction. It is possible to remember, but only by sitting quietly, for hours or sometimes for days, and dragging facts out of one's memory. . . . (*Laughter,* 72)

Elsewhere in the memoir of her four visits to Zimbabwe, Lessing observes that "Every writer has a myth-country. . . . Myth does not mean something untrue, but a concentration of truth" (*Laughter,* 35). Since for years Lessing has probed the interstices and overlaps between truth and fiction, memory and imagination, her acknowledgment of the blurred boundaries between them is especially moving and illuminating. In the African "myth country" and other settings, the author has always been interested in examining "what is *real?*" and "What is the *truth?*" She explores such questions both through mimetic realism and through the manifestly *un*real: detours into imaginary environments as diverse as inner and outer space, frozen polar landscapes, altered terrestrial geographies, and mysterious rooms beyond an apartment wall; or by way of characters who possess exceptional mental powers and therefore apprehend quite differently the same world in which we live.

It is illuminating for readers to participate in the spirit of "revisiting" by returning literally to the beginning: to Doris Lessing's first novel, *The Grass Is Singing* (1950). One discovers, already there, both the author's perspicacity and her extraordinary ability to register states of mind and consciousness that can be fully understood only within their specific social, ideological, and psychological contexts. Late in the novel, the narrator describes the final day in the life of Mary Turner, a woman living in racially divided southern Africa who, under the pressures of "the colour bar" and the collapse of her marriage, has slowly lost her sanity. Dimly, she anticipates her imminent annihilation by her black house servant, Moses, whom, over the course of the novel, she has emotionally emasculated and reduced to an object. The omniscient narrator evokes Mary's paranoia and her claustrophobic psychological state, observing that

> it seemed as if the night were closing in on her, and the little house was bending over like a candle, melting in the heat. She heard the crack, crack; the restless moving of the iron [roof] above, and it seemed to her that a vast black body, like a human spider, was crawling over the roof, trying to get inside. . . . She was shut in a small black box, the walls closing in on her, the roof pressing down.[41]

In her African stories in particular but also elsewhere in her fiction, Lessing similarly blends physical and mental domains so seamlessly that the external world mirrors the interior world of her characters in crucial ways. An especially illustrative passage occurs in one of Lessing's classic African stories, "The Old Chief Mshlanga." The fourteen-year-old narrator, the daughter of white settlers, is ignorant of the serious error of racial protocol she is about to make as she treks across the southern African veld to pay an uninvited visit to a native chieftain in his village. En route, she experiences a disturbing "new fear" in a familiar landscape in which, until that moment, she had felt safe:

> I had read of this feeling, how the bigness and silence of Africa, under the ancient sun, grows dense and takes shape in the mind, till even the birds seem to call menacingly, and a deadly spirit comes out of the trees and the rocks. You move warily, as if your very passing disturbs something old and evil, something dark and big and angry that might suddenly rear and strike from behind. You look at groves of entwined trees, and picture the animals that might be lurking there; you look at the river running slowly, dropping from level to level through the vlei, spreading into pools where at night the bucks come to drink, and the crocodiles rise and drag them by their soft noses into underwater caves. Fear possessed me. I found I was turning round and round, because of that shapeless menace behind me that might reach out and take me.[42]

Although for reasons of space I have primarily emphasized Lessing's longer fiction, I should note that she is equally accomplished in the short story form. Another of her classic stories deserves mention here. Few first-time readers of the frequently anthologized story "To Room Nineteen" could anticipate its startling ending from its deceptively understated opening sentence: "This is a story, I suppose, about a failure in intelligence: the Rawlings' marriage was grounded in intelligence."[43] Beginning so coolly, the story ends shockingly with Susan Rawlings sequestering herself in a spartan hotel room on the final day of many such days in which, without explanation, she deliberately absents herself from her life as a wife and mother of four children. The chilling penultimate paragraph reads:

> She had about four hours. She spent them delightfully, darkly, sweetly, letting herself slide gently, gently, to the edge of the river. Then, with hardly a break in her consciousness, she got up, pushed the thin rug against the door, made sure the windows were tight shut, put two shillings in the meter, and turned on the gas. (428)

Of any writer who is both so protean and so prolific, scholars and readers may well ask, how will Doris Lessing be regarded in fifty or a hundred years? Which of her novels and stories will continue to be read—and, indeed, reread—in future decades of the twenty-first century? I speculate that she will be remembered for the sheer scope, breadth, vividness, and depth of her endeavor as a chronicler of major strands of contemporary experience. Certain of her novels—*The Golden Notebook* and the *Children of Violence* series—will endure beyond our own era as vivid renderings of important cultural transitions. As Doris Lessing's protagonists and the forms of her work have shifted shapes and have evolved to address new ideas, she has stretched her readers' imaginations, creating new maps of consciousness and experience. Readers go to her narratives as they go to the great nineteenth-century realists—Lessing's own professed models in the novel form—for the rich texture of their renderings of lived experience, along with their profound psychological insight into the human condition. Her major novels continue to engage contemporary readers because they are, in the best sense of the term—and one that could not be fully appreciated when her early narratives were first published—historical novels. Through Martha Quest and Anna Wulf, Lessing registered for a time beyond her (and our) own the emotional and other dislocations of sensitive, intelligent women as they lived through an especially turbulent era of social change in the mid-twentieth century and stumbled upon, or invented, new paths to self-realization and spiritual maturity. Deconstructing social and political history at diverse turns, Lessing has given narrative form and visibility to patterns, pathologies, and potentialities in the contemporary moments she has observed that remain instructive for twenty-first-century readers, if only for her anatomy of the undertow: the dark side of the liberating assumptions of the women's movement.

In *The Golden Notebook* the blocked writer Anna Wulf regrets that she is incapable of writing "the only kind of novel which interests [her]: a book powered with an intellectual or moral passion strong enough to create order, to create a new way of looking at life" (*GN*, 59). Although Anna Wulf may not have succeeded in her effort, scholars and readers concur that Anna's creator has indeed written several such novels. As Lessing mused about *The Golden Notebook* to an interviewer in 1980, "The idea was that people might look back in 100 years' time, if they're interested, and find a record of the kind of things people thought about and talked about during these years."[44] More recently, she explained to an interviewer, "*The Golden Notebook* will stay because I do think it's a very good report of the time.... [N]o one could write *The Golden Notebook* now, because the time has gone."[45] In fifty or a hundred years, readers will likely still be interested in precisely that dimension of Lessing's fiction—not simply as historical record but as vivid imaginative creations, rendered in varied aesthetic forms and shapes. The author's circuitous imaginative path through the mid- and late twentieth and early twenty-first centuries has taken readers and critics of her work on an extended and remarkable journey: from Africa to England to inner space and outer space and back; to alternative futures for Africa and its fantastic double, Ifrik; and, tracing a different route, back to the possible beginnings of the human race, to say nothing of vital regions of the heart. As the protean shape-shifter has evolved, so also have her readers. May Doris Lessing continue to surprise us.

NOTES

1. Margaret Drabble, "Doris Lessing: Cassandra in a World under Siege" [1972]. Repr. in *Critical Essays on Doris Lessing*, ed. Claire Sprague and Virginia Tiger (Boston: G. K. Hall, 1986), 183–91.

2. See Sandra Singer's chapter in Part Two of this volume, "London and Kabul: Assessing the Politics of Terrorist Violence," in which she discusses *The Good Terrorist* and *The Wind Blows Away Our Words* in terms of current understandings of terrorism [editors' note].

3. Phyllis Sternberg Perrakis takes up the shape-shifting theme in her discussion of Lessing's crossing of various kinds of boundaries, of genre, gender, and species, in her

search for new and appropriate forms through which to express her late-life creativity. See her essay "The Porous Border between Fact and Fiction, Empathy and Identification in Doris Lessing's *The Cleft*" in Part Two of this volume [editors' note].

4. For commentary on the books' reception at publication, see Ellen Goodman, "The Doris Lessing Hoax," and Jonathan Yardley, "Lessing Is More: An 'Unknown' Author and the Success Syndrome," in Sprague and Tiger, 213–14 and 215–17.

5. See Suzette Henke's discussion of the difficulties of teaching contemporary students about the political context of *The Golden Notebook* in her chapter, "The Challenge of Teaching Doris Lessing's *The Golden Notebook* in the Twenty-First Century," in Part Four of this volume [editors' note].

6. Doris Lessing, *The Golden Notebook* (1962; repr., New York: HarperPerennial, 1999), 230 (caps in original) and 233–34. Hereafter cited in the text as *GN*.

7. See discussions of Lessing's depiction of women's sexuality and of the tension between the mind/body, woman/writer, and personal/political dichotomies that women experience in the chapters in this volume by Krouse, Saxton, Tiger, and Visel. See also Henke's discussion of women's sexuality in *The Golden Notebook* in Part Four [editors' note].

8. See my discussion of the parallels in "Mar(th)a Still Questing: Reading *Mara and Dann* through *Children of Violence*," *Doris Lessing Newsletter* 21.1 (Winter/Spring 2000): 10–13.

9. Drabble, "Cassandra in a World under Siege," 185.

10. For example, in a review of *The Story of General Dann and Mara's Daughter, Griot and the Snow Dog* (2005), Geraldine Bedell attempts to justify Lessing's sometimes awkward writing. She observes, "The unwieldy, apparently naive title of Doris Lessing's latest novel gives quite a lot of clues as to what follows. This is a meandering, episodic book, peopled by disconnected characters, told in pared-down, at times, almost perfunctory prose. I think we have to assume that this is deliberate: the apparently uncrafted quality of the novel is crafted to mimic an oral storytelling tradition, reminiscent of ancient epics in which characters had more role than psychology." "Ancestral Voices," *The Observer,* July 3, 2005, http://books.guardian.co.uk/reviews/generalfiction/0,6121,1519819,00.html#article_continue (accessed July 28, 2009).

11. Lessing, "Writing as Time Runs Out," interview by Michael Dean, May 7, 1980, BBC-2, in *Doris Lessing: Conversations,* ed. Earl G. Ingersoll (Princeton, NJ: Ontario Review Press, 1994), 90–91. Hereafter cited as *Conversations*.

12. Gornick, "Opening *The Golden Notebook*: Remembering the Source," part of PEN Panel Discussion, "Thirty Years of Feminism: Literature and the Movement," November 25, 1991, in *PEN Newsletter* 79 (October 1992): 10–11.

13. See Alice Ridout's discussion of the political implications of the vision of the writer in *Prisons We Chose to Live Inside* in her chapter, "'What Is the Function of the Storyteller?': The Relationship between *Why* and *How* Lessing Writes," in Part Two of this volume [editors' note].

14. Lessing, *The Cleft* (New York: HarperCollins, 2007).

15. Lessing, *The Grandmothers: Four Short Novels* (New York: HarperCollins, 2003).

16. Lessing, "Placing Their Fingers on the Wounds of Our Times," interview by Margarete von Schwarzkopf in *Die Welt,* May 9, 1981, trans. Earl G. Ingersoll and Heid-

run Neth, in *Conversations*, 104–5.

17. Lessing, "An Ancient Way to New Freedom," in *The Elephant in the Dark*, ed. Leonard Lewin (1972; repr., New York: E. P. Dutton, 1976), 78. More recently, Lessing has discussed the significant influence of Idries Shah's book *The Sufis* (1964) on her thinking. Although she offers the proviso "I do not believe that one can be changed by a book (or by a person) unless there is already something present, latent or in embryo, ready to be changed," in Shah's contemporary rendering of "a very ancient way of approaching life," she "found what [she] had been looking for." Lessing, "A Book That Changed Me," *Time Bites: Views and Reviews* (London and New York: HarperCollins, 2004), 212–13. See also Müge Galin, *Between East and West: Sufism in the Novels of Doris Lessing* (Albany: State University of New York Press, 1997).

18. Lessing, "An Interview with Doris Lessing" by Susan Stamberg, in *Doris Lessing Newsletter* 8.2 (Fall 1984): 4.

19. See, for example, chapters on *The Golden Notebook* in the following studies: Betsy Draine, *Substance under Pressure: Artistic Coherence and Evolving Form in the Novels of Doris Lessing* (Madison: University of Wisconsin Press, 1983); Molly Hite, *The Other Side of the Story: Structures and Strategies of Contemporary Feminist Narrative* (Ithaca, NY: Cornell University Press, 1989); Gayle Greene, *Changing the Story: Feminist Fiction and the Tradition* (Bloomington: Indiana University Press, 1991); and Magali Cornier Michael, *Feminism and the Postmodern Impulse: Post–World War II Fiction* (Albany: State University of New York Press, 1996).

20. In December 2003, a leaked file that was highly embarrassing to the British government and royalty revealed a list of famous individuals—over 300 since World War II—in many professions who had refused ceremonial honors. See http://news.bbc.co.uk/1/hi/uk/3338583.stm (accessed July 28, 2009). Jan Hanford writes, "December 31 1999: In the U.K.'s last Honours List before the new Millennium, Doris Lessing was appointed a *Companion of Honour*, an exclusive order for those who have done 'conspicuous national service.' . . . The list was selected by the Labour Party government to honor people in all walks of life for their contributions to their professions and to charity. It was officially bestowed by Queen Elizabeth II." Doris Lessing Web site, maintained by Jan Hanford at http://lessing.redmood.com/biography.html (accessed July 28, 2009).

21. See the essays collected in *In Pursuit of Doris Lessing: Nine Nations Reading*, ed. Claire Sprague (New York: St. Martin's Press, 1990) and note 19 above. In April 2004 the First International Conference on Doris Lessing in New Orleans drew scholars from thirteen countries outside the United States—Canada, England, France, Spain, Belgium, South Africa, Australia, Turkey, India, Japan, Korea, China, and Taiwan—whose topics ranged from politics to prophecy, from narrative technique to emotional trauma, from the structures of Southern African dwellings to similarities between Lessing and Asian women writers. A number of essays based on papers delivered at that conference are included in this collection. The Second International Conference on Doris Lessing, held in Leeds, England, in July 2007, featured a similar range of international scholars and diverse approaches to her work. A number of essays from that conference appear in *Doris Lessing: Border Crossings*, ed. Alice Ridout and Susan Watkins (London: Continuum, 2009).

22. Doris Lessing, Introduction 1971 [to *The Golden Notebook*] (1971; repr., New York: HarperPerennial, 1999), xxiii. This introduction is also titled Preface [to *The*

Golden Notebook] and is listed that way in the bibliography to this volume [editors' note].

23. Gayle Greene cites a number of writers and readers—male as well as female—who asserted that *The Golden Notebook* changed their lives. See *Changing the Story,* 52–53.

24. See Tonya Krouse's comparison of *The Golden Notebook* and *A Room of One's Own* as foundational texts in the women's movement in her chapter, "'Anon,' 'Free Women,' and the Pleasures of Impersonality," in Part One of this volume [editors' note].

25. Thanks to S.H. for permitting me to quote her here.

26. PEN/Faulkner reading, Folger Library, Washington, DC, March 19, 2004.

27. Several scholars have also pursued versions of "reprising" through literary analysis of Lessing's work. See Jenny Taylor, ed., *Notebooks/Memoirs/Archives: Reading and Rereading Doris Lessing* (Boston: Routledge and Kegan Paul, 1982); and Claire Sprague, *Re-Reading Doris Lessing: Narrative Patterns of Doubling and Repetition* (Chapel Hill: University of North Carolina Press, 1987). Sprague illuminates a variety of patterns of repetition in Lessing's fiction, from characters' names to larger motifs.

28. For a full discussion of these disruptions, and an analysis of Lessing's first eleven novels in chronological order, see Roberta Rubenstein, *The Novelistic Vision of Doris Lessing: Breaking the Forms of Consciousness* (Urbana: University of Illinois Press, 1979).

29. Re: *Colonised Planet 5, Shikasta,* vol. 1 of *Canopus in Argos: Archives* (New York: Alfred A. Knopf, 1979), ix.

30. As she commented in an interview in 1994, "I want to write volume six, but I always seem to get sidetracked into something else." "Describing this Beautiful and Nasty Planet," interview by Earl G. Ingersoll, in *Conversations,* 240.

31. Lessing, *Shikasta,* 304. See also Katherine Fishburn, *The Unexpected Universe of Doris Lessing: A Study in Narrative Technique* (Westport, CT: Greenwood, 1985), 56–84; Betsy Draine, *Substance under Pressure,* 143–61; and Jeannette Webber, "Doris Lessing's Prophetic Voice in *Shikasta*: Cassandra or Sibyl?" in Phyllis Sternberg Perrakis, ed., *Spiritual Exploration in the Works of Doris Lessing* (Westport, CT: Greenwood Press, 1999), 63–79.

32. With regard to Lessing's prescient identification in *Shikasta* of one aspect of international conflict as that between generations, it is noteworthy that, in a number of countries whose citizens are the most virulently anti-Western, a significant proportion of the population is under thirty. U.S. Census Bureau International Data Base, http://www.census.gov/ipc/www/idb/groups.php (accessed February 23, 2010).

33. Lessing, *Alfred and Emily* (London: Fourth Estate, 2008).

34. Lessing, *Walking in the Shade: Volume Two of My Autobiography, 1949–1962* (New York: HarperCollins, 1997), 253.

35. See Phyllis Sternberg Perrakis, "Sufism, Jung and the Myth of Kore: Revisionist Politics in Lessing's *Marriages,*" *Mosaic: A Journal for the Interdisciplinary Study of Literature* 25.3 (Summer 1992): 99–120; Katherine Fishburn, "The Dialectic of Sex," in *The Unexpected Universe of Doris Lessing,* 85–105; and Roberta Rubenstein, "*The Marriages between Zones Three, Four, and Five*: Doris Lessing's Alchemical Allegory," in Sprague and Tiger, 60–68.

36. See Susan Watkins's discussion of the ideological implications of the minor

genres in which *The Fifth Child*, *Ben, In the World*, and *Mara and Dann* are written in her chapter, "Writing in a Minor Key: Doris Lessing's Late-Twentieth-Century Fiction," in Part Three of this volume [editors' note].

37. Lessing, "The Habit of Loving," in *The Habit of Loving* (New York: Thomas Y. Crowell, 1957), 1–33.

38. Lessing, "The Grandmothers," in *The Grandmothers*, 1–56.

39. See discussions of *The Sweetest Dream* by Ruth Saxton, Virginia Tiger, and Robin Visel in this volume [editors' note].

40. Lessing, *African Laughter: Four Visits to Zimbabwe* (New York: HarperCollins, 1992), 301. Hereafter cited in the text as *Laughter*.

41. Lessing, *The Grass Is Singing* (New York: Thomas Y. Crowell, 1950), 241.

42. Lessing, "The Old Chief Mshlanga," *African Stories* (New York: Simon and Schuster, 1965), 53. See Pat Louw's analysis of the role played by colonial ideas of space and architecture in the African short stories and *The Grass Is Singing* in her chapter, "Domestic Spaces: Huts and Houses in Doris Lessing's African Stories," in Part Four of this volume [editors' note].

43. Lessing, "To Room Nineteen," *Stories* (New York: Knopf, 1978), 396.

44. Lessing, "Writing as Time Runs Out," in *Conversations*, 90.

45. "Doris Lessing Provocateur," interview by Emily Parker, *The Wall Street Journal* online (WSJ.com), March 15, 2008, http://online.wsj.com/article_email/SB120554114603738389-lMyQjAxMDI4MDI1MTUyNDExWj.html (accessed July 28, 2009).

"Anon," "Free Women," and the Pleasures of Impersonality

TONYA KROUSE

Doris Lessing, in her 1971 introduction to *The Golden Notebook,* famously resists the ways in which her novel was "belittled, by friendly reviewers as well as by hostile ones, as being about the sex war, or was claimed by women as a useful weapon in the sex war."[1] In the nearly forty years since she made this complaint, Lessing has made similarly controversial comments in which she has challenged not only the critical reception of her work but also the feminist movement in its entirety.[2] Nevertheless, critics and common readers of Doris Lessing cannot ignore that her fiction offers an incisive critique of gender relations in the twentieth and twenty-first centuries, and they perceive that feminist critical and theoretical approaches may offer the best methodologies through which to examine Lessing's oeuvre. This can leave critics in a difficult position, wherein the author whose texts they so admire seems antagonistic to their approach to her writing. Whether the critic aims to "claim" Lessing for a feminist literary tradition or canon or whether the critic aims to perform a gynocentric reading of Lessing's fiction, the critical enterprise is complicated not only by Lessing's ambivalence about feminism but also by Lessing's resistance against situating her fiction as "feminist" or as embodying a female aesthetic.

Indeed, while Doris Lessing's career develops parallel to the development of feminist criticism and theory, Lessing often resists—if not outright rejects—the ideals that feminist theory and criticism promote at various points in its history. When feminist critics take Virginia Woolf's observation that "we think back through our mothers if we are women"[3] as a call to arms for excavating marginalized texts by women writers, Lessing traces her influence not through literary mothers but through canonical, male, European writers such as Tolstoy and Stendhal.[4] When feminist critics endorse the project common to many women writers of writing women's everyday, embodied experience, Lessing turns to space fiction. Given these tensions, feminist critics have had some difficulty in placing Lessing's writing. Now, in the opening decade of the twenty-first century, with Lessing having been awarded the Nobel Prize in Literature, the task of situating Lessing's oeuvre within feminist theory and criticism takes on great urgency. Lessing's fiction can assist us in finding new approaches to theorizing and critiquing women's writing, and returning to Lessing's aesthetic vision in *The Golden Notebook*[5] can work as a first step in this enterprise.

In this essay, I am particularly interested in situating *The Golden Notebook* alongside one of the foundational texts of feminist literary criticism, Woolf's *A Room of One's Own*. Like Lessing, Woolf famously criticizes feminism, even as, like Lessing, she interrogates patriarchal culture and holds feminist values. Perhaps more significantly, though, Woolf's questions about writing and female subjectivity that ground *A Room of One's Own* seem remarkably similar to those questions that Lessing's protagonist Anna Wulf asks. By considering Woolf's and Lessing's aesthetic values and preoccupations together, it becomes possible to imagine an "impersonal" aesthetic for literature that is particularly rooted in female subjectivity. As Patricia Waugh writes, "women writers, on the whole, have not felt comfortable with an aesthetics of impersonality as it appears in many modernist and postmodernist manifestos. The reason for this is the overvaluation in the first instance of exclusive objectivity, of distance, autonomy, separateness, discrete form, and the disappearance in the second instance of human connection via meaningful affection, communication, or ethical belief."[6] Both *The Golden Notebook* and *A Room of One's Own* exhibit this discomfort, but the aesthetic theory that each espouses investigates the possibility of an "impersonal" aesthetic that avoids the traps of modernist and postmodernist manifestos that Waugh describes.

At the opening of *The Golden Notebook*, Doris Lessing's author-protagonist Anna Wulf has an independent income and a room of her own. She has published one novel, and, as readers learn at the novel's end, *The Golden Notebook*'s opening and subsequent "Free Women" sections are, in fact, her second novel. She writes under her own name: she does not rely on a mask of anonymity, nor does she use a pseudonym to authorize her work as a novelist. Anna is a "free woman," and one might assume that she writes freely as a woman. The story of Anna Wulf in this foundational feminist novel, then, offers one account, albeit a fictional one, of what a woman writer's life might look like if one of Virginia Woolf's theories in her foundational feminist polemic *A Room of One's Own* were put into practice.

Nevertheless, to reduce *The Golden Notebook* to a positive realization of Woolf's initial argument—"a woman must have money and a room of her own if she is to write fiction"[7]—hardly addresses the complexity of *The Golden Notebook*'s narrative; nor does it account for the characterization of Anna Wulf as a woman writer who, throughout most of the novel, is literally and figuratively "blocked." Moreover, such a reading would fail to address the ways in which *The Golden Notebook* engages Woolf's more abstract aesthetic claims about what is required for women to produce art.[8]

A more careful examination of *The Golden Notebook* as it responds to *A Room of One's Own*, in contrast, indicates the ways in which Lessing's text responds to and resists the figure of "Virginia Woolf" as a literary precursor and/or a feminist foremother. In addition, such an examination offers a way into the complicated and sometimes contradictory theory of (women's) writing that *The Golden Notebook* seems to espouse. Finally, this examination accounts for the prominence of both texts as foundational to a canon of twentieth-century women's and feminist literature, as well as for the ambivalence that both Woolf and Lessing express about being co-opted for specific feminist agendas.[9]

This approach allows readers to reimagine the ways in which reading Lessing's representation of the woman writer in *The Golden Notebook* through Woolf's theories in *A Room of One's Own* propels a twenty-first-century revaluation of Lessing's literary achievement. Like Woolf, Lessing 1) demands an effacement of gendered subjectivity in the service of the text, 2) promotes an "androgynous" and diffuse writing subjectivity as central to the creation of great literature, 3) interrogates those binary oppositions that ground Western metaphysics, 4) proposes pleasure as a potential mechanism through which to disrupt those oppositions, and 5) offers a critique of locating the meaning of a text in the body of a unified female subject who authors a text. These features of Lessing's aesthetics, which seem to find a source in Woolf's *A Room of One's Own,* offer a literary version of more recent work by historian of science Donna Haraway and neurologist Antonio Damasio, each of whom offers radical critiques of the reliance on binary oppositions between subject/other, mind/body, male/female, and human/animal since Descartes. In this essay, I will first tease out the relationship between Woolf's theories in *A Room of One's Own* and Lessing's representations of the woman writer in *The Golden Notebook*. As I conclude, I will return to these more recent analyses to demonstrate how such an approach to Lessing's aesthetics confirms their continuing and perhaps even increased relevance in the twenty-first century.

Many critics have performed readings of Woolf's and Lessing's texts alongside one another, and my work here builds on those earlier projects. Most notably, the 1994 collection *Woolf and Lessing: Breaking the Mold* offers perhaps the most comprehensive analysis of Doris Lessing's writings as they relate to Virginia Woolf's. Still, as Claire Sprague incisively notes in the first essay of the collection, the connection between Woolf and Lessing often appears to readers to be a tenuous one. Sprague writes, "Like many Doris Lessing and Virginia Woolf readers, I have always imagined a deep and visible connection between Lessing and Woolf. But that connection was elusive. Was it more wishful than actual? Woolf's name never appears in Lessing's criticism, and verifiable allusions to Woolf in Lessing's work are almost non-existent."[10] While Sprague and the other writers in the volume go on to demonstrate the strong ties between Lessing's texts and Woolf's, to examine these two writers alongside each other still proves a fruitful and not yet exhausted path of critical inquiry. Because Lessing has tended to distance her work from the influence of modernist precursors, to read Lessing's texts through Woolf's still constitutes a demonstrable critical risk.

The project that I propose here—to read *The Golden Notebook* through and against Woolf's theories in *A Room of One's Own*—can seem particularly problematic in light of contemporary feminist approaches to literary criticism. While it is true that *A Room of One's Own* stands as a foundational feminist text, feminist critics have challenged the utility of some of its central theoretical claims, most notably the text's advocacy of androgyny. Near the end of *A Room of One's Own*, Woolf argues: "it is fatal for any one who writes to think of their sex."[11] For this reason, *A Room* advocates an androgynous aesthetic, which explicitly characterizes writing whose purpose is to express the gendered subjectivity of its author—whether male or female—as compromised art. For Woolf, the writer must enact—explicitly and overtly in the text of the literature that he or she creates—a conceptual effacement of the self in which his or her writing subjectivity supersedes his or her gendered subjectivity. This effacement, Woolf's argument implies, should not be a diversion that the writer creates in order to "cover" his or her real motives in the text, but rather the writer's motivation should be to enact this effacement as the prerequisite to producing "great writing."[12]

If readers view Woolf's androgynous aesthetic in these terms, Doris Lessing's *The Golden Notebook* may at first appear to resist Woolf's pronouncements about how to produce great writing.[13] Whereas Woolf seems to endorse the abstraction of the body in and by language, Lessing's author-protagonist Anna Wulf, at least superficially, appears to aim to make sex—her body, the female body—concrete, to specify its effects and to mark its shape in and by language. Whereas Woolf's narrator praises "that curious sexual quality which comes only when sex is unconscious of itself,"[14] Anna Wulf in her four notebooks seeks total consciousness of her sex, which she often equates with her overall identity, and she desires completely to articulate that consciousness in writing. In spite of these apparent oppositions between *A Room of One's Own* and *The Golden Notebook,* I contend that Virginia Woolf's theory of an androgynous aesthetic, which promotes an effacement of sex in the service of great writing, corresponds to the aesthetic vision that Anna Wulf ultimately embraces.

Before beginning to examine the ways in which Anna Wulf's aesthetic vision engages with Virginia Woolf's prescription for an androgynous aesthetic, however, it is useful first to look carefully at the shape of Woolf's claims about androgyny in *A Room of One's Own* and at subsequent critical engagements with the androgynous aesthetic that Woolf advocates. Beginning in this way lays the foundation for examining the important theoretical effects that using Woolf's theory to provide a context for *The Golden Notebook* might produce.

Woolf's detour into a discussion of androgyny as a central characteristic of great writing has complicated and continues to complicate the ways in which feminist literary critics regard and use *A Room of One's Own*. Critics tend to accept the broader material argument of Woolf's polemic, but there has been much less consensus among critics about the utility of androgyny as a vehicle for women's creativity. Within *A Room of One's Own,* as well as in other of Woolf's texts, Woolf appears to engage two competing definitions of androgyny: the first, an idea of androgyny as bisexual or hermaphroditic; the second, an idea of androgyny as a fusion of male and female perspectives. Critics have tended to emphasize one or the other definition, and, as Karen Kaivola notes, the mere consideration of androgyny, whichever definitions critics prefer, has moved in and out of "critical vogue."[15] Critics have tended to approach Woolf's theory of androgyny with a variety of critical, feminist, and social agendas, and the critical reception of Woolf's theory has reflected the feminisms and theoretical affiliations of particular critics in particular historical moments as much as it has reflected the careful reading of Woolf's theory itself. Basically, critics of Woolf's theory tend to fall into three camps: those who see Woolf's androgynous aesthetic as a retreat from the more radical claims about women's writing that *A Room of One's Own* implies, those who see Woolf's androgynous aesthetic as a potentially viable structure for enabling women's creativity, and those who see Woolf's androgynous aesthetic as a "cover" that she uses to disguise an aesthetic of female difference.[16]

At first, it may seem that this critical discord amongst critics of *A Room of One's Own* has little to do with reading *A Room of One's Own* alongside *The Golden Notebook* or reading "Virginia Woolf"—the speaker whom the writer Virginia Woolf creates to articulate her theories about writing in *A Room of One's Own*—alongside "Anna Wulf"—the speaker through whom Doris Lessing articulates another set of theories about writing in *The Golden Notebook*. Yet it is noteworthy that the conflicts between these critical perspectives on Woolf's polemic mirror similar conflicts that typify critical responses to Lessing's *The Golden Notebook*. Whether critics resist or embrace Woolf's androgynous aesthetic reflects whether critics resist the idea of achieving a kind of aesthetic unity through androgyny or whether they embrace the ideal of unity as one with aesthetic potential. Similarly, as critics approach Lessing's *The Golden Notebook,* their readings reflect whether they resist the novel's movement toward unity as a totalizing fiction or whether they see that movement toward unity as one that allows the protagonist Anna to move past the "block" against writing for publication that necessitates that she divide herself and write in the private notebooks. Ultimately, critics of *The Golden Notebook* divide themselves into critical camps that mirror the three camps of criticism of Woolf's androgynous aesthetic in *A Room of One's Own*.[17]

Reading *The Golden Notebook* as a direct response to *A Room of One's Own* allows us to imagine a critical perspective that does not demand that we choose to locate our critiques within one of these dominant critical camps. In fact, by looking at these two texts alongside one another, examining their points of convergence and divergence, we can move through the critical impasse that requires us to choose to celebrate, to denigrate, or to excavate some "real motivation" beneath the textual mask. Such a project requires us, however, to accept three premises at the outset: 1) Woolf's androgynous aesthetic has utility as a theory for women's writing, and it does not necessarily require that women's writing mimic styles, structures, and values conventionally deemed "masculine" or associated with writing by men; 2) Lessing's protagonist values the effacement of her authorial self as a prerequisite to being a "good" writer, which indicates that her values for good writing are compatible with those articulated in *A Room of One's Own;* and 3) "Anna Wulf," in Lessing's *The Golden Notebook,* constitutes a direct engagement with "Virginia Woolf," the feminist and modernist icon, the character who narrates *A Room of One's Own* and the dominant figure for the "woman writer" in twentieth-century literature.[18] In accepting these premises, it becomes possible to begin to make sense of Anna's insistence on self-effacement in her texts, as well as to begin to see Woolf's androgynous aesthetic as compatible with the aesthetic vision that drives *The Golden Notebook*.

An androgynous aesthetic depends on authorial self-effacement, and I contend that Anna's aesthetic vision does so as well. In spite of the obsessive record that Anna attempts to make of her body, her emotions, and her thoughts, what Anna values in writing is the antithesis of that record. As she writes near the close of the Blue Notebook, which serves as the most conventional "diary" of Anna's four notebooks, "Something strange happens when one writes about oneself. That is, one's self direct, not one's self projected. The result is cold, pitiless, judging. Or if not judging, then there's no life in it—yes, that's it, it's lifeless. I realise, in writing this, I'm back at the point in the black notebook where I wrote about Willi."[19] As Anna comes full circle in this passage, she discounts the ability for writing about herself to be "alive" in the way that she believes the best writing should be. Writing one's self, Anna might argue, compromises one's liberty as a writer. Therefore, Anna's repeated, though intermittent, insistence on self-effacement—whether through effacing her own personality when she associates with people who have more dominant personalities, through "lapsing out" into love or sex, or through projecting herself onto another persona—denotes the main point of compatibility between her aesthetic vision and Woolf's androgynous aesthetic.[20] As a character, Anna is not entirely without ordinary, social, and gendered identity; rather, readers observe repeated erasures of that ordinary identity in writing. Each of these erasures takes place in language: in Anna's texts, from the notebooks to her second novel, "Free Women," readers witness repeated scenes of self-effacement, in which Anna's identity is wiped out and then returns, only to be wiped out again.

Nevertheless, it is important not to confuse this impulse toward the wiping out of social and gendered identity in writing with an impulse toward anonymity or annihilation of the self. Instead, the self-effacement that I describe cuts a space between a female aesthetic that depends on self-expression and a masculinist aesthetic that doesn't acknowledge social and gendered identity. As Trinh T. Minh-ha notes, "[b]etween the twin chasms of navel-gazing and navel-erasing, the ground is narrow and slippery."[21] Lessing attempts to navigate between these two chasms, and in her characterization of Anna, she makes a distinction between the female subjectivity of the person-who-is-Anna and the business of writing in which Anna engages. Minh-ha argues that "[a] distinction needs to be made between 'Write yourself. Write your body' and write about yourself, your body, your inner life, your fears, inhibitions, desires, and pleasures. The first refers to a scriptive act—the emergence of a writing-self—the second, to a consolidation of writing from the self."[22] It is this consolidation of writing from the self that Anna resists and that Anna's intermittent effacements of her self in the notebooks oppose. Thus, while this aesthetic of self-effacement to some extent participates in a conservative tradition of attempting to locate intrinsic value in art and to distinguish it from the personal, it also revises that conservative tradition and interrogates it, suggesting a *personal* impersonality that is firmly rooted in female subjectivity.

In this way, Anna's conception of the relationship between writing and the self illustrates values that Patricia Waugh discerns in the work of "many twentieth-century women writers (whether consciously feminists or not)." According to Waugh, these writers explore "a definition of self in relationship which does not make identity dependent axiomatically upon the maintenance of boundaries and distance, nor upon the subjugation of the other."[23] When Anna effaces her self in the notebooks, she does not do so in a project of self-annihilation, but rather in a project of resistance, for she believes, as Waugh explains in her discussion of *The Golden Notebook,* that "any attempt to *represent* feminine subjectivity will result in parody: of the 'coy' woman's style of the magazines, of the sentimental fulfillment of romantic desire in the Hollywood movie."[24] Thus, Anna's project of self-effacement fails to preserve the binary opposition between the personal and the impersonal. Rather, Anna writes from her self, but "she writes, finally not to express, nor so much to materialize an idea or a feeling, as *to possess and dispossess herself of the power of writing.* Bliss."[25] *A Room of One's Own* endorses this same operation.

Thus, neither text aims to make "woman" anonymous, or to annihilate woman-who-writes through writerly self-erasure. Both texts dispute the potential for "Anon" to erase the subjectivity of the author in a fashion that would let the author produce literature of the highest quality. "Anon" may constitute an important figure for authoriality for both, as "Anon" has allowed those to speak who ordinarily would fear to do so, but neither text suggests that anonymity begets aesthetic virtuosity. "Anon" fails to guarantee the writerly wiping out of the self that both texts advocate. In fact, it paradoxically draws attention to that self.

For example, in *A Room of One's Own,* Woolf's narrator famously suggests "that Anon, who wrote so many poems without signing them, was often a woman."[26] The text uses Anon as the foundation for a woman's literary tradition in England. In this way, Anon performs a necessary rhetorical function within the narrative, but the purpose that it serves—to put a woman's face on the name "Anon"—subverts its potential to signify an author whose writing exceeds the constraints of sex. Indeed, using Anon as a literary foremother binds Anon to sex; it genders the texts that Anon produces as feminine. Anon is not androgynous: Anon is synonymous with woman. By gendering Anon in this way, the narrator uses Anon as a generic name for the female author; it acquires what Michel Foucault would call an author-function, which the narrator then uses to support her claims about women and writing.[27]

In other words, deploying Anon at this point in the text serves the narrator's rhetorical purpose, but the narrator does not associate Anon with a freeing effacement of sex; moreover, using Anon in this way renders the-name-of-the-author and the-sex-of-the-author radically unstable and unreliable categories through which to evaluate literature: the figure of Anon does not signal an effacement of identity but rather allows for readers and critics to supply a name for Anon that suits their own ideological demands. As Sydney Janet Kaplan explains, "With Virginia Woolf, feminine consciousness is explored as part of reality, but ultimate reality can only be perceived by going beyond it. Only in the highest form of creativity, in which there is a moment of vision caught and eternalized in *form,* is universal consciousness achieved. And there distinctions between sexes must disappear."[28] Thus, Woolf's use of Anon constitutes a necessary component of her broader rhetorical agenda, but it ultimately does not constitute a strategy through which women might produce great writing. Woolf uses the figure of Anon to start tracing a history of women's literature, which is a necessary first step in her larger theoretical project, but this move paradoxically underscores the impossibility of arriving at such a factual account. Indeed, it challenges the usefulness of such accounts in broader discussions of aesthetic merit.

Implicit in Woolf's deployment of Anon is the message that this figure will not serve an androgynous aesthetic. *The Golden Notebook* corroborates this implicit message with its own explicit critique of Anon. When Anna reads the "dead, banal writing" of fellow Communists, she recognizes this writing as the inverse of the personal writing of her first novel, which she regards as an artistic failure.[29] This fact notwithstanding, she regards attempts at literature from the Communist perspective as "dead stuff." She writes: "The point is that this writing is essentially impersonal. Its banality is that of impersonality. It is as if there were a new Twentieth Century Anon at work."[30] Anna thus rejects the personality of her first novel *along with* the impersonality of writing that leaves no room for emotion and originality. She does not *replace* a "personal" aesthetic with an "impersonal" one.

Critics often overlook this aspect of Anna's theory of writing, focusing instead on her rejection of the personal in her first novel. For example, Jeannette King reads Anna's rejection of the aesthetic potential of "personal" writing to reflect a larger argument implicit in the text—that one cannot liberate oneself through art: "Does art represent freedom, or is it simply another discourse? Since every discourse is inscribed within the values of a particular ideology, there appears to be nowhere for the individual voice to be heard. The notion of 'free speech,' like freedom itself, is an illusion, as is the Romantic concept of the artist as the voice of the free individual speaking out against society's conventions and values."[31] King's analysis of the role of art and the artist implies that Anna's rejection of the personal writing that characterized her first novel constitutes a response to the futility of individual expression in the face of the structures of oppression that inscribe the individual in modern life. By extension, this analysis implies that Anna's turn toward self-effacement indicates her subjection within those structures of oppression. This dark view, however, ignores Anna's statements about the fact that an entirely impersonal aesthetic, too, produces bad writing. Anna wants to forge a form for writing that is both personal and impersonal—and neither. She imagines a form of "impersonal" writing that emerges from "deep, suddenly stark, undisguisable private emotion."[32]

But if anonymity does not signal erasure of sex or the self, an "impersonal" approach that allows for a "curious sexual quality" to come through, then what does? Interestingly, both *A Room of One's Own* and *The Golden Notebook* align the effacement of the writing body that lays the ground for great writing with a diffuse sexual pleasure that permeates the text. As Roxanne J. Fand notes, "[a]lthough Woolf's narration lacks explicit bodily content, her poetic style is driven by the semiotics of the body, whereas Lessing often speaks *about* the body in the *dis*embodied voice of an omniscient narrator."[33] Both texts conjoin the personal and impersonal: both the personal and the impersonal are necessary in each.

Additionally, both texts do define pleasure separately from penetration and/or ejaculation, which may at first seem to indicate a specifically "female" aesthetic, but both texts still seem to insist that the woman writer must "free" herself from her specifically female subjectivity. Thus, both texts display a tension between an aesthetic that is appropriate to individual female creativity but that simultaneously demands the effacement of individual identity and radically undermines the integrity of individual subjects as artists. Both texts interrogate the conventional ways in which Western culture genders and divides the categories of "personal" and "impersonal," "individual" and "collective," and they do so through the theories about writing that they present.

As Fand explains, the "very designations of 'impersonal,' for transcending or integrating subjectivities, and 'personal' for limited subjectivities, are deeply implicated in gendered discourses."[34] For Fand, one of Woolf's great achievements is the way that she attempts to "achieve liberation from the personal—constructed as narrowly feminine—both in her writing and in her life."[35] Still, this move on Woolf's part, as Fand notes, can challenge readers who come to Woolf seeking a model for feminist creativity whereby the truth of female identity might be revealed. "The female reader who comes to Woolf's work seeking some model whereby to affirm a female self will not be given a simple answer to an identity crisis," writes Fand. "Instead, she will be treated to a way of seeing multiple possibilities within the given conditions of her culturally constructed experience."[36] Thus, if readers take Woolf's narrative in *A Room of One's Own* on its own terms, they see that the figures that the narrator engages, from Anon to Judith Shakespeare, serve not to provide ultimate models for female creativity but rather to demonstrate the ways in which creativity is inflected by culturally constructed experience. For Woolf, the terms of that culturally constructed experience must be challenged—and not necessarily celebrated—in order for women and men to make great art.

For example, using the figure of Anon alongside Judith Shakespeare, Woolf's narrator links the prohibition against writing women to the prohibition against sexually free women in patriarchal culture, and in this move, the narrative explicitly connects cultural norms for women's access to pleasure to cultural norms that deny women writers access to entering the canon of great literature. According to Woolf, "Chastity had then, it has even now, a religious importance in a woman's life, and has so wrapped itself round with nerves and instincts that to cut it free and bring it to the light of day demands a courage of the rarest. To have lived a free life in London in the sixteenth century would have meant for a woman who was a poet and playwright a nervous stress and dilemma which might well have killed her."[37] Making this connection, Woolf demonstrates how a social endorsement of sexual chastity for women can lead to a literary chastity for women writers. Readers may at first suppose that this claim enforces a one-to-one relation between the person who creates a literary text and the text that is created: "woman's writing" is defined by the body of the woman who writes. Ellen Carol Jones explains it this way: Woolf believes that "art comes out of and reflects the artist. The artifact itself originates from the body of the artificer. The male's insistence on female chastity, then, prevents the woman artist from creating because it denies her the freedom to write fully and honestly about her passions and her body, and, more important, it ultimately denies her the very right to create, to 'give birth' to a work of art."[38] For Woolf, norms for femininity come to produce norms for feminine writing: "feminine" writing can never attain the "freedom," the promiscuity, that great art demands. Moreover, ever conscious of maintaining her chastity, the woman writer is also ever conscious of her sex, and this precludes the effacement of sex that an androgynous aesthetic promotes. Because the woman writer has chastity on her mind, she cannot move beyond her femaleness into an artistic space that is both masculine and feminine, both male and female. If this is the case, however, the question then becomes, how can a woman writer hope to create great art?

Woolf does not provide a clear answer. After the brief meditation on the relationship between chastity and creativity, the narrative leaves the subject, seeming to skip a step that would offer women writers a map for how to proceed. The narrator does not suggest alternatives through which women writers could escape the double bind between social norms for femininity and aesthetic ideals, but instead the narrative changes course and asserts that "the mind of an artist, in order to achieve the prodigious effort of freeing whole and entire the work that is in him, must be incandescent, like Shakespeare's mind [. . .]. There must be no obstacle in it, no foreign matter unconsumed."[39] Woolf quickly leaves the idea that the body determines creativity, abstracting the body of the artist, characterizing that body, whether male or female, as an obstacle to art. Perhaps Woolf's own historical gender position informs this rhetorical skip, enforcing the gap between a discussion of the relationship between sexuality and creativity for women who write and an analysis of what constitutes literary merit in texts once they have left the control of the author.

In contrast, *The Golden Notebook* fills this gap in a more direct fashion. As Fand explains, "Doris Lessing, like Virginia Woolf, cycles and recycles the impersonal through her personal experience as a woman. Her work takes up where Woolf's leaves off around mid-twentieth century, and continues to demonstrate that the subjectivities of women are not confined to narrow domesticity and immediate personal relations, but may encompass larger social collectives in the material historical world and in the imaginative ahistorical world of the collective unconscious, which extends to visions of the cosmos."[40] Nevertheless, Anna's personal experiences as a woman and particularly her experiences of sexual pleasure prove crucial to her articulation of an aesthetic vision that depends on the effacement of the self rather than the expression of it. Anna's experience of sexual pleasure within her "texts," whether as "Anna" or as "Ella," whether in terms of its physical experience or the intellectual experience of recounting it, depends on an effacement made possible by Anna's lived rejection of a double standard in which women must be chaste while men might be promiscuous. Rejecting this double standard in her life, even though her socialization in Western culture makes this difficult for her, allows Anna to try to reject it in her art.

2: "Anon," "Free Women," and the Pleasures of Impersonality

And yet, living as a "free woman" in her personal life doesn't necessarily facilitate the easy translation of that freedom into her work as a writer. In the Yellow Notebook, Anna writes: "Sex. The difficulty of writing about sex, for women, is that sex is best when not thought about, not analysed. Women deliberately choose not to think about technical sex. [. . .] [T]hey want to preserve the spontaneous emotion that is essential for their satisfaction."[41] Anna makes two related claims: first, that women have difficulty writing about sex because language forces them into an analytical model, and, for women, this model is antithetical to pleasure; second, that women resist thinking technically about sex because to do so forecloses their potential for physical satisfaction. In other words, women resist not only writing about sex but also thinking about sex analytically. At the root of this resistance is a desire to preserve pleasure.

For Anna, a viable aesthetic would honor pleasure, as well as produce aesthetic pleasure. Anna hopes to create freely, promiscuously. Anna seeks integrity in her writing that her first novel, which emerged solely from her personal, individual experience, did not have. Significantly, Anna explicitly connects her definition of integrity to female orgasm. In the Yellow Notebook, Ella, Anna's alter ego, thinks: "for women like me, integrity isn't chastity, it isn't fidelity, it isn't any of the old words. Integrity is the orgasm."[42] For Ella, "real" orgasm "is a dissolving in a vague, dark, generalised sensation like being swirled in a warm whirlpool,"[43] an erasure of her individual subjectivity. According to Kaplan, "Much of the concern with sexuality expressed throughout the notebooks is based on very conventional notions of women's supposed sexual passivity,"[44] but the fact that these representations are conventional does not empty them of their significance as markers of Anna's aesthetic vision. Anna's erasure or effacement through sexual pleasure has value precisely because it suggests that individual subjects can move within a collective, universal sensation. Sexual pleasure depends, for Ella and for Anna, on the momentary dissolution of individual subjectivity, and this definition of pleasure directly influences Anna's aesthetic vision. Anna may not be a "free woman"—indeed, the text's use of this terminology is deeply ironic—but by disputing the possibility of becoming a free woman through writing, Anna's texts allow for greater potential freedom for the writing subject within discourse, within power. Moreover, when Anna distinguishes between integrity and chastity, readers remember *A Room of One's Own*'s critique of chastity, and they suspect that Anna Wulf picks up where Virginia Woolf leaves off.

The question for current readers of *A Room of One's Own* and *The Golden Notebook* becomes, then, how to put the aesthetic claims of these texts, which indicate a movement through pleasure toward an effacement of gendered subjectivity in the service of great art, into a workable theoretical context in the twenty-first century. This proves crucial to any conclusions we might reach about the relationship between these two texts and the significance of that relationship. Moreover, it proves central to coming to terms with these two texts as foundational to a feminist canon of literature, for the choices that we make in situating these texts within theory threaten to limit the ways in which we can negotiate the convergences and divergences between them.

It seems clear that both *A Room of One's Own* and *The Golden Notebook* advance a vision for great writing that does not necessarily demand that great writing empower disenfranchised or marginalized subjects, even though such a move may seem contrary to much contemporary feminist theory and perhaps to our own personal feminisms. Woolf famously dismisses Charlotte Brontë's *Jane Eyre* because "it is clear that anger was tampering with the integrity of Charlotte Brontë the novelist. She left her story, to which her entire devotion was due, to attend to some personal grievance."[45] Similarly, Anna dismisses her first novel, *Frontiers of War:* "I said nothing in it that wasn't true. But the emotion it came out of was something frightening, the unhealthy, feverish illicit excitement of wartime, a lying nostalgia, a longing for licence, for freedom, for the jungle, for formlessness. It is so clear to me that I can't read that novel now without feeling ashamed, as if I were in a street naked."[46] In both cases, the narratives distinguish between the author-as-real-person and the writing subject; in both cases, the narratives regard the expression of the emotions of the author-as-real-person within the text of a novel as contrary to the aims of great art. Neither sees the writing of the self as a valuable aesthetic aim. In fact, such writing in both is constituted as failure. Instead, each promotes writing *from* the self, in which the writer "*must* learn to forget" her personal identity.[47]

This learned forgetting of the self has the potential to enable freer movement of writing subjects within discourse. Significantly, however, this freer movement does not constitute liberation from patriarchal power structures in a simple way, but rather it suggests that writing subjects have the power to navigate within these structures in the service of the text. Ultimately, both Woolf and Lessing position the liberty of the text within dominant discourses as above the liberation of real women from patriarchy. Indeed, the "freeing" of real women from patriarchy constitutes only an inversion of ideologies in which women are subjected within patriarchy, a reification of the binary oppositions that we inherit from Cartesian philosophy. This accordingly offers no "real" escape. Thus, I would like to propose an alternate approach to these texts that privileges a writerly erasure of the body, an erasure that opposes constructing the body as the center of meaning, which in the case of female bodies constitutes a reinscription of patriarchal modes of controlling the feminine.

Nevertheless, to propose such an alternate model does not, as critics of androgyny might have it, do away with the centrality of bodies to texts, nor does it privilege the mind over the body or oppose the mind to the body. Indeed, it proposes a way of thinking of the relationship between bodies and texts as one that is not expressive—in which the body comes before the text and causes the text but one that is simultaneous and symbiotic. Instead of thinking of texts as "feminine" and equating the feminine with subversion,[48] it proposes that we think of texts in the way that Roland Barthes proposes: in terms of pleasure and of bliss. Barthes defines the text of pleasure as "the text that contents, fills, grants euphoria; the text that comes from culture and does not break with it, is linked to a comfortable practice of reading."[49] The impulse toward aesthetic unity in both *A Room of One's Own* and *The Golden Notebook* corresponds to Barthes's ideas about what a text of pleasure includes, while at the same time this impulse does not eliminate or undercut representational modes inscribed within patriarchal discourses.

It is for this reason that feminist critics can have difficulty placing these texts, which *feel* so grounded in feminism, within specifically feminine theories of creativity. If, as Barthes contends, "a writer is not someone who expresses his thoughts, his passion, or his imagination in sentences, but *someone who thinks sentences:* A Sentence-Thinker (i.e., not altogether a thinker and not altogether a sentence-parser),"[50] then that leaves little room for a theory of writing that presupposes that the woman writer of merit will *by nature* aim to express her individual female subject position in a literary text against the patriarchal culture that inscribes her, to speak feminist truth to power. Barthes's theory may seem to indicate that this androgynous aesthetic aims to absent real women from agency in writing. Minh-ha suggests, however, that the woman writer as sentence-thinker "radically questions the world through the questioning of how-to-write,"[51] and this constitutes a useful formulation through which to consider what both Woolf and Lessing achieve. Indeed, both Woolf and Lessing value the craft of writing, and the craftsmanship that each emphasizes is "a self-confessed, sometimes self-reflexive, form of art for art's sake that holds pragmatic bourgeois activity up to ridicule and, at best, invalidates it. By laying bare the codes of literary labor, it unequivocally acknowledges the writer's contradictory stand—her being condemned to do 'good work' in choosing to 'write well' and to produce Literature."[52] While it is true that Barthes's theory disputes the possibility that one can get outside the structures of power, and thus nullifies feminist theoretical approaches that insist that feminist writing enables liberation, if we read Barthes through Minh-ha, it becomes possible to see room for feminist writing that does not depend on writing the woman writer's experiences into the text. Instead, feminist writing might include what Barthes would call "texts of pleasure," texts that come from culture and do not break with it.

Still, readers should not assume that the idea of the text of pleasure is the only guiding idea within Woolf's and Lessing's texts. Indeed, both texts seem to engage not only a model of the text of pleasure but also a model of what Barthes calls the text of bliss. In fact, only by considering Woolf's and Lessing's texts in terms of both pleasure and bliss can one account for the effacements, displacements, and disruptions of subjectivity that seem to guide the aesthetic theories of both. For Barthes, the text of bliss is "the text that imposes a state of loss, the text that discomforts (perhaps to the point of a certain boredom), unsettles the reader's historical, cultural, psychological assumptions, the consistency of his tastes, values, memories, brings to a crisis his relation with language."[53] It is this crisis in the writing subject's relation with language that Woolf's androgynous aesthetic anticipates and that Anna's various self-effacements, and particularly those self-effacements in relation to physical pleasure, indicate. The personal-impersonal aesthetic that both Woolf and Wulf imagine, which on the one hand articulates emotion but on the other depends on an objective correlative, might ultimately be positively filtered by readers through Barthes's notion of the text of bliss.[54]

Emotion, for Barthes, is not "antipathetic to bliss," but rather constitutes "a disturbance, a bordering on collapse: something perverse, under respectable appearances; emotion is even, perhaps, the slyest of losses, for it contradicts the general rule that would assign bliss a fixed form: strong, violent, crude: something inevitably muscular, strained, phallic."[55] Thus, when Woolf imagines the mind of the writer, through Coleridge's theory of androgyny, as "resonant and porous; that it transmits emotion without impediment; that it is naturally creative, incandescent, and undivided,"[56] and when Anna Wulf is "forced to acknowledge that the flashes of genuine art are all out of a deep, suddenly stark, undisguisable private emotion" and that "even in translation there is no mistaking these lightning flashes of genuine personal feeling,"[57] both imagine and acknowledge that the text of true literary merit is the text of both pleasure and bliss. As Barthes writes, "the text of pleasure is not necessarily the text that recounts pleasures; the text of bliss is never the text that recounts the kind of bliss afforded literally by an ejaculation."[58] Nevertheless, Barthes affiliates the text of pleasure with intellectual experience and the text of bliss with embodied experience. In imagining a text of literary merit as encompassing both pleasure and bliss, both intellectual and

2: "Anon," "Free Women," and the Pleasures of Impersonality

embodied emotional responses, Woolf and Lessing envision the possibility for literature to break apart the opposition between mind and body, and they offer that this might be achieved through the abjection and effacement of the subject, whether male or female.

In fact, both *A Room of One's Own* and *The Golden Notebook* constitute the relationship of the subject—the "I"—to the text as one that is by turns arbitrary and problematic. In *A Room of One's Own,* Woolf considers the effect of the "I" on the text. First, in the opening pages of the polemic, the narrator "Virginia Woolf" asserts: "'I' is only a convenient term for somebody who has no real being."[59] She continues: "Here then was I (call me Mary Beton, Mary Seton, Mary Carmichel or by any name you please—it is not a matter of any importance)."[60] In this introduction, by disputing the utility of the "I" to confer authority on a text, Woolf radically undermines the relationship between author and text. Instead, ideally, the text would take on a life of its own: the subject is critiqued, split, and effaced, and, in the words of Barthes, "then perhaps the subject returns, not as illusion, but as *fiction.* A certain pleasure is derived from a way of imagining oneself as individual, of inventing a final, rarest fiction: the fictive identity. This fiction is no longer the illusion of a unity; on the contrary, it is the theater of society in which we stage our plural: our pleasure is *individual*—but not personal."[61] Thus, for Woolf, the point is not to realize some truth of individual subjectivity through writing, but rather to imagine a writing subjectivity through which the individual subject is dispersed. The ideal subjective position for the writer—if not for the woman—is one in which she loses consciousness of her self. Instead of imagining the potential for a woman writer to speak her truth, her anger, her pleasure, Woolf instead imagines the perfect image of a writing subject as a man and a woman getting into a taxicab:[62] a plural image in which the writing subject appears as both male and female and—significantly—as mobile.

In contrast, when the writing subject is construed through the idea of an individual "I," aesthetic virtuosity becomes unattainable. This becomes most clear in the famous passage near the end of *A Room of One's Own* in which Woolf's narrator discusses Mr. A's novel. She describes her thoughts as she reads, and initially she reacts positively. As she gets further into the novel, however, she becomes frustrated: "a shadow seemed to lie across the page. It was a straight dark bar, a shadow shaped something like the letter I."[63] This shadow, the reader infers, blocks Mr. A's novel from attaining the androgynous aesthetic that the narrator earlier ascribes to all great literature. Mr. A's intrusive "I" impedes a full transmission of emotion. Mr. A's mind is not, we infer, "incandescent and undivided"; indeed, the shape of the "I" divides Mr. A's text from its reader. In spite of the direct quality of the writing to which the narrator responds positively, the "I" interrupts that pleasure, and she must begin "dodging this way and that to catch a glimpse of the landscape behind it."[64] As the narrator accuses Mr. A's "I" of blocking her view of the story at hand, readers often perceive an indictment of masculine subjectivity for obscuring truths that the androgynous aesthetic would make available. According to this interpretation, phallic "I" becomes not only the enemy of women but also the enemy of great literature. This implicit claim for many readers signals *A Room of One's Own*'s significance as a foundational feminist text. Nevertheless, if we take the reading of Mr. A's novel alongside the earlier considerations of the "I" in the text—the relationship of individual subjectivity to great writing—it becomes clear that the charge against Mr. A's novel is more expansive than just a charge against his masculine subjectivity. The point, as we look more deeply into *A Room of One's Own*'s consideration of subjectivity, seems to be that writing subjects—whether male or female—must absent their egos from the text in order to achieve great writing.

The Golden Notebook performs a similar operation, in which at first the narrative seems to critique specifically masculine subjectivity as antithetical to great art, but, when that critique is put into broader context, it becomes clear that the limitations of gendered subjectivity for both male and female writers are of greater concern than just the critique of the deleterious effects of an aggressive masculine subjectivity. This becomes clear as Anna describes an interchange between herself and Saul in the Blue Notebook: "He went on shouting, and I recognised the feeling I'd had the day before, of descending another step into will-lessness. I, I, I, I, he shouted, but everything disconnected, a vague, spattering boastfulness, and I felt as if I were being spattered by machine-gun bullets. It went on and on, I, I, I, I, and I stopped listening and then I realised he had become silent, and was looking at me with anxiety. 'What's wrong with you?' he said."[65] Such passages often signal for feminist critics the ways in which Saul's masculine subjectivity oppresses Anna, or they signal, as Gayle Greene argues, "that both male and female behaviors represent crippling adjustments to a destructive society, but that men are more crippled because they lock themselves into postures that prohibit change."[66] However, such readings of these interactions between Anna and Saul fail to acknowledge the ways in which Anna's ability to lapse out of consciousness, to emotionally and psychologically remove herself while interacting with Saul, ultimately facilitates her return to writing for publication. One might argue that by stepping "into will-lessness" and by refusing to engage with Saul on his terms, Anna can, as Sprague argues, achieve "some measure of freedom from repetition" and achieve "some release from the stereotype of woman as victim."[67] In fact, by refusing to engage with Saul as the female other that confirms and reinforces his masculine subjectivity, by refusing as she does in this moment to serve as a mirror to him and, to borrow Woolf's language, to reflect "the figure of man at twice its natural size," she opens up a new possibility for how she will enter into discourse, as a woman and as a writer.

This new possibility is confirmed when, in the inner Golden Notebook, Saul provides Anna with the opening of her second novel, "Free Women."[68] As Magali Cornier Michael writes, "the ambiguity of voice and the overlapping of various fragments of *The Golden Notebook* problematize authorship and undermine any notion of original or ultimate meaning, so that Anna can only be approximated but never pinned down."[69] By the novel's end, Anna finds a way to move within discourse as a writer that does not demand that she express herself as a female subject. She gains mobility, much as a man and a woman getting into a taxi, Woolf's image for her androgynous aesthetic, are defined by their mobility. As a woman in patriarchal culture, the narrative seems to indicate, Anna might not achieve liberation. Nevertheless, as a writer, Anna has the potential to free herself from the demands of her female subjectivity, if only intermittently, thus allowing her to break free from the solipsism of the notebooks and to break through the block that stops her from writing her second novel for publication.

Thus, as we place *A Room of One's Own* and *The Golden Notebook* alongside one another, each puts forward a theory that disrupts writing subjectivity from the individual gendered subjectivity of the author-who-writes. In so doing, both texts disrupt the attempts that readers might make to locate them through gynocriticism. The narratives of both the "Virginia Woolf" who narrates *A Room of One's Own* and the "Anna Wulf" who narrates the various texts that make up *The Golden Notebook* refute the potential for literature that does not go beyond the female body of the female author to do anything but reify the opposition between masculine and feminine upon which patriarchal discourses have conventionally relied. Instead, each proposes an aesthetic vision that locates both pleasure and bliss not in the female body of the author but rather in the text itself. By positioning pleasure and bliss thus, such an aesthetic figures the literary text as a space in which binaries not only between masculine and feminine but also between mind and body might be disrupted. In contrast to Barthes, who argues that "the pleasure of the text is that moment when my body pursues its own ideas—for my body does not have the same ideas that I do,"[70] both Virginia Woolf's and Anna Wulf's texts imagine a pleasure-bliss of the text in which a writerly body-mind pursues ideas without reference to the personality or identity of the author.

The idea here is not to imagine an aesthetic that depends on real female bodies or minds and their articulation but rather an aesthetic that does away with the idea of either the body or the mind as the source of meaning, truth, or existence. This would then give the writing subject greater mobility within those structures of discourse from which there is no potential for escape. In the case of both the "Virginia Woolf" of *A Room of One's Own* and the "Anna Wulf" of *The Golden Notebook*, this is exactly the aesthetic vision that is privileged: one that allows the writer, if not the woman, to move freely within discourse, to impregnate and to contaminate, with malleable particles that nonetheless are "irreducible, indomitable."

Throughout most of the twentieth century, this aesthetic might have seemed to directly undermine a feminist political agenda in part because of its challenge to both philosophical and scientific accounts of human subjectivity, which continued to rely on the binary opposition of mind and body as did feminists' models for women's empowerment. For Antonio Damasio, these tendencies in both philosophy and science can be traced directly to Descartes' *cogito ergo sum*, which "suggests that thinking, and awareness of thinking, are the real substrates of being. And since we know that Descartes imagined thinking as an activity quite separate from the body, it does celebrate the separation of mind [. . .] from the nonthinking body."[71] For Damasio, this is "Descartes' error," and that error remains pervasive in its influence, with many continuing to see Descartes' views "as self-evident and in no need of reexamination."[72] It is for this precise reason, argues Damasio, that such a reexamination must take place: "Versions of Descartes' error obscure the roots of the human mind in a biologically complex but fragile, finite, and unique organism; they obscure the tragedy implicit in the knowledge of that fragility, finiteness, and uniqueness. And where humans fail to see the inherent tragedy of conscious existence, they feel far less called upon to do something about minimizing it, and may have less respect for the value of life."[73] This more recent reading of the danger in relying on the binary opposition between mind and body corresponds neatly with some reasons that may underlie the aesthetic offered by Woolf and Lessing: most notably, the antagonism of each to war and the proliferation of the technologies of war throughout the course of the twentieth century.

Writing from a feminist perspective, Donna Haraway takes an activist stance similar to Damasio's and similarly insists on the necessity to demonstrate the constructedness of the binary oppositions through which theories of humanity have conventionally been organized. She contends, "The dichotomies between mind and body, animal and human, organism and machine, public and private, nature and culture, men and women, primitive and civilized are all in question ideologically. The actual situation of women is their integration/exploitation into a world system of production/reproduction and communication called the informatics of domination. [. . .] The cyborg is a kind of disassembled and reassembled, postmodern collective and personal self. This is the self feminists must code."[74] The aesthetic that I have traced here, while it does not directly engage in contemporary scientific and technological debates about the nature of the self, does manage, nevertheless, to offer a medium through which Descartes' error might be challenged and through which the "disassembled and reassembled, postmodern collective and personal self" might be coded. Moreover, just as Haraway construes her project as one that argues "for *pleasure* in the confusion of boundaries and for *responsibility* in their construction,"[75] so too is the aesthetic for literary achievement that both Woolf and Lessing advocate.

As Ellen G. Friedman and Miriam Fuchs note, "the iconization of Woolf as a quintessential *female* author, together with her reputation as a secondary experimentalist, has clouded a sense of her total achievement."[76] Perhaps this is one reason why it has been a matter of some difficulty for scholars interested in making connections between Virginia Woolf's and Doris Lessing's texts to do so: Lessing has tended to distance herself from a tradition of *women's* literature, much as Woolf herself did in positing her theory of androgyny. Nevertheless, Friedman and Fuchs continue: "although the *legend* of Virginia Woolf may represent a suffocating ideal, the real Woolf provided instruction and strategies for feminine narrative."[77] Perhaps the key to evaluating "Virginia Woolf" alongside "Anna Wulf" is understanding that the legend of Virginia Woolf constitutes a modern version of the "angel in the house," which Woolf argues in her "Professions for Women" the woman writer must kill, "for, as I found, directly I put pen to paper, you cannot review even a novel without having a mind of your own, without expressing what you think to be the truth about human relations, morality, sex. And all these questions, according to the Angel of the House, cannot be dealt with freely and openly by women; they must charm, they must conciliate, they must—to put it bluntly—tell lies if they are to succeed."[78] One might argue that the legend or icon of Virginia Woolf operates similarly for the "women writers" who succeed her: they are stopped from telling "the truth about human relations, morality, sex" because the shadow of Virginia Woolf, lady novelist, novelist of interiority, stands over them.

Lessing's author-protagonist Anna Wulf, as she attempts to write her way through her block and as she negotiates the treacherous terrain of relations between the sexes at mid-twentieth century, does not overtly cite Virginia Woolf as a literary foremother. She does not seem to see herself as a "woman writer." Her texts do not seem consciously to allude to Virginia Woolf's texts. Nevertheless, she, like Woolf, writes, struggles with madness, and takes her authorial name from a husband, and so perhaps it makes sense for readers to examine how Anna's texts might covertly engage the very theory—the androgynous aesthetic—that is at the heart of Woolf's *A Room of One's Own*. In the end, Anna finds a way out of the room of her own, which ultimately imprisons her, and she finds it by embracing an androgynous aesthetic.

NOTES

1. Doris Lessing, Introduction [to *The Golden Notebook*] (1971; London: Michael Joseph, 1972; repr., New York: HarperPerennial, 1990), xii. This 1971 introduction [to *The Golden Notebook*] is also titled Preface [to *The Golden Notebook*] and is listed under that title in the bibliography to this volume [editors' note].

2. For example, see the 1993 introduction to *The Golden Notebook*, Introduction 1993 (1994; repr., London: HarperPerennial Classics, 1999). See also Lessing's comments at the Edinburgh International Book Festival in 2001. Fiachra Gibbons, "Lay off Men, Lessing Tells Feminists": Special Report: Edinburgh Festival 2001, guardian.co.uk, August 14, 2001, http://www.guardian.co.uk/uk/2001/aug/14/edinburghfestival2001.edinburghbookfestival2001 (accessed May 26, 2008).

3. Virginia Woolf, *A Room of One's Own* (New York: Harcourt, Brace, Jovanovich, 1929), 76. See also Robin Visel's historicized thematic comparison of Woolf and Lessing: "House/Mother: Lessing's Reproduction of Realism in *The Sweetest Dream*," in Part One in this volume [editors' note].

4. Lessing, Introduction [to *The Golden Notebook*], xv.

5. Lessing, *The Golden Notebook*.

6. Patricia Waugh, *Feminine Fictions: Revisiting the Postmodern* (New York: Routledge, 1989), 20.

7. Woolf, *A Room of One's Own*, 4.

8. As I discuss further on in the essay, Woolf's more abstract theories in *A Room of One's Own*, to which we might refer as her "androgynous aesthetic," have been interpreted in a variety of ways—both positive and negative—by critics. This fact does not negate the utility of Woolf's comments related to androgyny as a way into Lessing's novel. See also Nancy Topping Bazin's important discussion of androgyny in *Virginia Woolf and the Androgynous Vision* (New Brunswick, NJ: Rutgers University Press, 1973).

9. In fact, both writers' ambivalence about being categorized as feminist becomes clear in the examination of the texts under consideration here. See especially *A Room of One's Own* (37, 99) and Doris Lessing's 1971 introduction to *The Golden Notebook*.

10. Claire Sprague, "Multipersonal and Dialogic Modes in *Mrs. Dalloway* and *The Golden Notebook*," in *Woolf and Lessing: Breaking the Mold*, ed. Ruth Saxton and Jean Tobin (New York: St. Martin's Press, 1994), 3–14, 3.

11. Woolf, *A Room of One's Own*, 104.

12. The term "great writing" is problematic because of the exclusionary, masculinist aesthetic tradition and practices of canonization that it evokes. I use it here consciously, however, to demonstrate that Woolf and Lessing both situate themselves in relation to this tradition as they attempt to theorize the relationship between female writing subjects and the texts that they produce. Moreover, Longinus's *On Great Writing (On the Sublime)*, trans. and intro. G. M. A. Grube (Indianapolis, IN: Hackett Publishing Company, 1991), which serves as a foundational text to discourses about aesthetics, offers a discussion of "great writing" that seems compatible with, if not identical to, Woolf's and Lessing's ideas. Longinus writes: "Great writing does not persuade; it takes the reader out of himself. The startling and amazing is more powerful than the charming and persuasive, if it is indeed true that to be convinced is usually within our control whereas amazement is the result of an irresistible force beyond the control of any audience. We become aware of a writer's inventive skill, the structure and arrangement of his subject matter, not from one or two passages, but as these qualities slowly emerge in the whole work. But greatness appears suddenly; like a thunderbolt it carries all before it and reveals the writer's full power in a flash" (4).

13. Lessing herself, however, seems to espouse similar ideals, according to her comments in a 1983 interview with Stephen Gray in "Breaking Down These Forms," in *Putting the Questions Differently: Interviews with Doris Lessing, 1964–1994*, ed. Earl Ingersoll (London: Flamingo, 1994). [In the United States this collection is titled *Doris Lessing: Conversations* and is listed under that title in the bibliography at the end of this volume (editors' note). "I don't feel at all when I'm writing that I am a woman writing. I don't think it's a good thing to do that," says Lessing. "It's another prison to think I am a woman writing this. It means that you deliberately narrow all your sensibilities" (119).

14. Woolf, *A Room of One's Own*, 93.

15. Karen Kaivola, "Revisiting Woolf's Representations of Androgyny: Gender, Race, Sexuality, and Nation," *Tulsa Studies in Women's Literature* 18.2 (1999): 235–61, 237. Kaivola surveys the shifting critical approaches to androgyny in Woolf from the 1970s to the 1990s.

16. For examples of these different critical approaches, see Marilyn R. Farwell, "Virginia Woolf and Androgyny," *Contemporary Literature* 16.4 (1975): 433–51, which sees the androgynous aesthetic as a retreat from *A Room*'s more radical claims about women's writing; Ellen Carol Jones, "Androgynous Vision and Artistic Process in Virginia Woolf's *A Room of One's Own*," in *Critical Essays on Virginia Woolf*, ed. Morris Beja (Boston: G. K. Hall and Company, 1985), 227–39, which sees the androgynous aesthetic as enabling female creativity; Karen Kaivola, "Revisiting Woolf's Representations of Androgyny"; and Frances L. Restuccia, "'Untying the Mother Tongue': Female Differences in Virginia Woolf's *A Room of One's Own*," *Tulsa Studies in Women's Literature* 4.2 (1985): 253–64, which see the androgynous aesthetic as a cover for an aesthetic of female difference.

17. For examples of these three kinds of critical approaches to *The Golden Notebook*, see Roberta Rubenstein, *The Novelistic Vision of Doris Lessing: Breaking the Forms of Consciousness* (Urbana: University of Illinois Press, 1979); Elayne Antler Rapping, "Unfree Women: Feminism in Doris Lessing's Novels," *Women's Studies* 3 (1975): 29–44; Molly Hite, "Doris Lessing's *The Golden Notebook* and *The Four-Gated City*:

Ideology, Coherence, and Possibility," *Twentieth Century Literature* 34.1 (1988): 16–29; and Katherine Fishburn, "Wor(l)ds within Words: Doris Lessing as Meta-Fictionist and Meta-Physician," *Studies in the Novel* 20.2 (1988): 186–205.

18. See Brenda Silver, *Virginia Woolf Icon* (Chicago: University of Chicago Press, 1999). Silver addresses the slipperiness of interpreting Woolf as an icon—how the "multiple" and "contradictory sites" Woolf "occupies in our cultural discourses" work to complicate the image (11).

19. Lessing, *The Golden Notebook*, 545.

20. For examples of Anna effacing her own personality when she associates with people who have more dominant personalities, pay special attention to her interactions with Molly and Mother Sugar/Mrs. Marks. For examples of Anna effacing her own personality through sex, pay special attention to Anna/Ella's interactions with George, Paul, and Saul.

21. Trinh T. Minh-ha, *Woman, Native, Other: Writing Postcoloniality and Feminism* (Bloomington: Indiana University Press, 1989), 28.

22. Ibid.

23. Waugh, *Feminine Fictions*, 22.

24. Ibid., 202.

25. Minh-ha, *Woman, Native, Other*, 18.

26. Woolf, *A Room of One's Own*, 49.

27. See Michel Foucault, "What Is an Author?" in *The Foucault Reader*, ed. Paul Rabinow (New York: Pantheon Books, 1984), 101–20.

28. Sydney Janet Kaplan, *Feminine Consciousness in the Modern British Novel* (Urbana: University of Illinois Press, 1975), 77.

29. Lessing, *The Golden Notebook*, 333.

30. Ibid., 334.

31. Jeannette King, *Doris Lessing* (London: Edward Arnold, 1989), 44.

32. Lessing, *The Golden Notebook*, 334.

33. Roxanne J. Fand, *The Dialogic Self: Reconstructing Subjectivity in Woolf, Lessing, and Atwood* (Selinsgrove, PA: Susquehanna University Press, 1999), 98.

34. Ibid., 44.

35. Ibid.

36. Ibid., 51.

37. Woolf, *A Room of One's Own*, 49–50.

38. Jones, "Androgynous Vision and Artistic Process in Virginia Woolf's *A Room of One's Own*," 235.

39. Woolf, *A Room of One's Own*, 56.

40. Fand, *The Dialogic Self*, 96.

41. Lessing, *The Golden Notebook*, 203.

42. Ibid., 311.

43. Ibid., 204. See Suzette Henke's discussion of this same passage in Part Four of this volume in "The Challenge of Teaching Doris Lessing's *The Golden Notebook* in the Twenty-First Century" [editors' note].

44. Kaplan, *Feminine Consciousness in the Modern British Novel*, 158.

45. Woolf, *A Room of One's Own*, 73.

46. Lessing, *The Golden Notebook*, 61.

47. Minh-ha, *Woman, Native, Other*, 27.
48. Ibid., 269.
49. Roland Barthes, *The Pleasure of the Text*, trans. Richard Miller (New York: Hill and Wang, 1975), 14.
50. Ibid., 50–51.
51. Minh-ha, *Woman, Native, Other*, 17.
52. Ibid., 18.
53. Barthes, *The Pleasure of the Text*, 14.
54. T. S. Eliot's notion of an "objective correlative" through which one articulates emotional content in literature seems like a useful term through which to trace Woolf's and Lessing's attempts to imagine a personal-impersonal writing. Woolf, of course, was a contemporary and friend of Eliot's; Claire Sprague makes a strong case for Eliot's influence on Lessing in "Lessing's *The Grass is Singing, Retreat to Innocence, The Golden Notebook* and Eliot's *The Waste Land*," *Explicator* 50.3 (1992): 177–80.
55. Barthes, *The Pleasure of the Text*, 25. When Barthes uses the term "phallic" to describe bliss, I do not believe that he equates bliss with male versions of desire/pleasure or subordinates female versions of desire/pleasure to male ones. I believe that Barthes's resistance against equating bliss with ejaculation (Barthes, 55) supports this reading. Rather, "phallic" seems to refer to the economy of experiences that are valued and authorized in heteronormative, patriarchal culture, which would mean that both male and female experiences of desire/pleasure are subordinated to a phallic cultural economy.
56. Woolf, *A Room of One's Own*, 98.
57. Lessing, *The Golden Notebook*, 334.
58. Barthes, *The Pleasure of the Text*, 55.
59. Woolf, *A Room of One's Own*, 4.
60. Ibid., 5.
61. Barthes, *The Pleasure of the Text*, 62.
62. Woolf, *A Room of One's Own*, 96.
63. Ibid., 99.
64. Ibid.
65. Lessing, *The Golden Notebook*, 554.
66. Gayle Greene, *Changing the Story: Feminist Fiction and the Tradition* (Bloomington: Indiana University Press, 1991), 113.
67. Claire Sprague, "Doubletalk and Doubles Talk in *The Golden Notebook*," *Papers on Language and Literature: A Journal for Scholars and Critics of Language and Literature* 18.2 (1982): 181–97, 192.
68. The publication of the "journals" that Anna writes with James Shafter, another American writer, an event that Anna records in the Black Notebook (415–17), foreshadows the vision of authorship that is promoted when Saul gives Anna the opening of her novel and she gives him the opening of his story, a vision in which the personal identity of the author seems to be displaced by the text, which has a life of its own.
69. Magali Cornier Michael, *Feminism and the Postmodern Impulse: Post–World War II Fiction* (Albany: State University of New York Press, 1996), 214.
70. Barthes, *The Pleasure of the Text*, 17.
71. Antonio Damasio, *Descartes' Error: Emotion, Reason, and the Human Brain*

(New York: G. P. Putnam's Sons, 1994), 248.

72. Ibid., 250.

73. Ibid., 251. See also Debrah Raschke, who argues that Woolf subverts binary oppositions in *A Room of One's Own* in order to discover a new sexual imaginary, in *Modernism, Metaphysics, and Sexuality* (Selinsgrove, PA: Susquehanna University Press, 2006).

74. Donna J. Haraway, *Simians, Cyborgs, and Women: The Reinvention of Nature* (New York: Routledge, 1991), 163.

75. Ibid., 150.

76. Ellen G. Friedman and Miriam Fuchs, *Breaking the Sequence: Women's Experimental Fiction* (Princeton, NJ: Princeton University Press, 1989), 12.

77. Ibid., 15.

78. Virginia Woolf, "Professions for Women," in *Virginia Woolf on Women and Writing: Her Essays, Assessments and Arguments,* selected and introduced by Michelle Barrett (London: Women's Press Limited, 1979), 57–63, 59–60.

House/Mother

Lessing's Reproduction of Realism in *The Sweetest Dream*

ROBIN VISEL

A 1960s London household is anchored by a wise, empathetic maternal figure, inhabited by an intergenerational affinitive family of intellectuals and misfits, artists and politicos, washed by the successive tides of the *Zeitgeist*, rocked by revolutions in Africa and Europe. The great house is more than a microcosm; rather it is a laboratory for the utopian hypotheses of the mid-twentieth century: Communism, psychoanalysis, decolonization, feminism. Through the great house blow the winds of change; to the great house flock youth from every continent, whose creative energies might save humanity, but whose inherited neuroses will doom them to repeat the mistakes of their elders. In her 2001 novel, *The Sweetest Dream*,[1] Lessing uses their experiences, interwoven with the stories of the preceding generations, to challenge the abstract isms and dogmas of her time. In the twenty-first century, she resituates the London house of Anna Wulf and Martha Quest as the home of a new kind of mothering with the potential to resolve some of the ideological binaries and colonialist hierarchies that bedevil her earlier characters.

The promise of youth and the tragedy of generational repetition is a constant motif in Lessing's work, as is the dynamic interplay between colony and metropole, Africa and Europe. As its predominantly warm reviews in the British press acknowledged,[2] *The Sweetest Dream* is a reprise of the themes, settings, and characters of her major novels of the 1960s: *The Golden Notebook* (1962)[3] and *The Four-Gated City* (1969).[4] *The Sweetest Dream* is a revisionary memory of these earlier novels and a reaffirmation of the genre of social-psychological realism as central to Lessing's oeuvre. The attributes and preoccupations of the millennial novel's central female character, Frances Lennox, are remarkably consistent with *The Golden Notebook*'s Anna Wulf and *The Four-Gated City*'s Martha Quest. Like Martha Quest, whose story culminates in the fifth, London novel, of the autobiographical *Children of Violence* series, which began with *Martha Quest* (1952),[5] Frances Lennox mothers a surrogate family, balancing responsibility and freedom, love and work, traditional femininity and countercultural feminism, the political and personal, the individual and the collective. Unlike Anna, through whom Lessing explored the creative territory of madness, or Martha, who led her author's forays into postapocalyptic fiction, Frances is firmly anchored in social realism, a tradition that Lessing fully exploits in *The Sweetest Dream*.

The house-mother is Lessing's fulcrum, the ordering figure around whom swirl the chaotic visions and contradictory emotions of the young, in particular the surrogate daughters who might carry on her work of nurturing and protecting the human good, of saving the world on their home ground. This essay focuses on the millennial mutations of the house-mother who has long been Lessing's trope for the woman writer of her generation, class, and colonial provenance; Martha Quest in her various fictional permutations is a daughter of Virginia Woolf's Mary Beton with a room of her own and 500 pounds a year.[6] However, like Woolf's alter ego in "Professions for Women,"[7] Lessing's authorial alter egos are also haunted by the demonic Angel in the House, the specter of self-effacement and self-censorship, idealized in Coventry Patmore's Victorian poem.[8] Thus the unresolved tension between the homemaker and the woman-who-writes-at-home is a continuing theme for Lessing as well as for Woolf. Whereas the writer-character Anna Wulf follows her namesake in breaking free of the specter of the Angel, inventing a literary form to embody her creative struggle, Frances Lennox fails to become an independent artist, remaining enmeshed in the needs of others but also finding her vocation in expressing their concerns. Like the Rhodesian-bred Martha Quest, who also has internalized the ideology of second-class status among the London elites, Frances is disempowered by class as well as gender. Taken together, the three blocked-artist house-mother characters depict the range of choices that their author saw for women such as herself in midcentury Britain. Through Frances and her surrogate daughter Sylvia, whose stories—unlike Martha's—remain anchored in the here and now, Lessing seems to celebrate the creative potential of traditional feminine values of self-sacrifice and collaboration to build community and to repair the ravages wrought by the totalitarian systems she has come to deplore.

Whereas Woolf was a lifelong Englishwoman *at home* in upper-class bohemian London, Lessing was a déclassé white African in exile; in her work, mother (country) and home (land) are complicated markers of identity for a woman writer *making* a home in postwar, postcolonial London at mid-century, then revisioned at the turn of the millennium. Frances Lennox is a class outsider, who, like Martha Quest, the colonial outsider, renovates, domesticates, and reorders the lives of London insiders, taking on an upper-middle-class house and family in need of her care, as she is in need of a home to repair and children to re-mother. The cost is the sacrifice of their individual creative identities for the collective good, to live—like Woolf's Mrs. Ramsay in *To the Lighthouse*[9]—for and through the children and the children's children. Martha and Frances are, finally, heroic maternal figures who create for and through their beloved others. As Mrs. Ramsay's heirs repair her house and paint her vision, so Martha's survivors reinvent human society after nuclear catastrophe, and Frances's children repair and reinvent the bond between metropolitan London and postcolonial Africa. The substantial section of *The Sweetest Dream* that narrates the story of Frances's surrogate daughter Sylvia as a mission doctor in Zimlia is analogous to the Black or African Notebook in *The Golden Notebook* and can be read as a bookend to the Zambesia novels that precede *The Four-Gated City*. The AIDS orphans Sylvia brings home to the Lennox house might be the descendents of Martha's surrogate child Joseph, the mutant black boy born of nuclear survivors in the Faroe Islands, who carries his gifts to Nairobi, where the remnants of world civilization are resettled. Thus Lessing's lifelong transformation of her own white-settler heritage in her novels circles through *The Sweetest Dream,* in which postcolonial idealism and apocalyptic vision continue the dance that fuels her fictional imagination.

Doris Lessing, as she has recorded in both her fiction and her autobiography,[10] arrived in postwar London from British colonial Southern Rhodesia, the manuscript of her first novel in one hand, her young son in the other. The two children from her first marriage, left with her ex-husband in Africa, haunt her narratives, creating a void that her autobiographical protagonists fill with surrogate children and youths whom they shelter, feed, and counsel. The beloved farmhouse of her childhood, described memorably in *Martha Quest* and appearing throughout her writing, also haunts her narratives, creating a void that is filled in the London novels by houses modeled on those the author has inhabited. The London house—solid, Victorian, multistoried and multilayered with social and literary history, windows open to urban gardens and great trees—replaces, but doesn't quite supplant, the pole-and-thatch farmhouse—a blend of European and African construction, hybrid and makeshift (like white-settlerdom itself), open to the elements, with a magnificent vista of high veldt and distant mountains. As critics such as Victoria Rosner have demonstrated,[11] this house in Rhodesia comes to symbolize the white woman writer's ambivalent relationship to colonial motherhood and her complicated nostalgia for Africa. Its counterpart, the iconic London house, comes to symbolize the exile's artistic self-invention and her experiments with new kinds of maternal relationships that offer models for resolving the feminine dilemma of the woman who must balance the needs of self and others, private and public. It is in this postcolonial urban setting that Lessing's female heroes confront and work through the great public issues of the midcentury, translating and testing the great abstract isms in the realm of the real, of everyday experience. Martha, Anna, and Frances reinvent not only conventional wife-and-motherhood and the feminine artistic tradition, but also the masculinist conventions of politics, including the supposedly progressive, oppositional politics of the Left. They model in the private, domestic sphere a workable version of the Socialist-Communist ideals—"the sweetest dreams" of a new social order—that have been largely discredited in the public, political sphere. In Frances's household, for example, the adults pool their resources to pay the school fees of whichever kids are in need, following Marx's dictum "from each according to his abilities, to each according to his needs." And her evening meals, a cross between soup kitchen and political salon, literally nourish the progressive counterculture.

Lessing follows Woolf in challenging the dichotomy between the domestic novel on the one hand and the discourse of history and politics on the other. As Nancy Armstrong argues, "[t]o consider the rise of the domestic woman as a major event in political history is not, as it may seem, to present a contradiction in terms, but to identify the paradox that shapes modern culture."[12] Woolf uses modernism and feminism to recouple the language of private life with the language of politics in *A Room of One's Own* and *Three Guineas*,[13] as well as in her novels which, as recent Woolf criticism has demonstrated, engage profoundly with the great issues of her day: from war and imperialism to scientific discoveries and new systems of knowledge.[14] Whereas Lessing absorbed Woolf's modernist critique of received wisdom and conventional ways of knowing—her fiction, like Woolf's, depicts consciousness as fluid, character as multiple, and closure as suspect—she does not reject, but rather reconceives, the tradition against which Woolf positioned herself, that of nineteenth-century social realism. Lessing travels back to realism through modernism and postmodernism, having assimilated Woolf's attack on the superficiality of realism in favor of exploring the interiority of consciousness: "this varying, this unknown and uncircumscribed spirit" as Woolf describes in "Modern Fiction."[15] As critics who have compared the two authors demonstrate, they employ similar multipersonal and dialogic modes (argues Claire Sprague),[16] share nostalgia for the lost mother (suggests Roberta Rubenstein),[17] and write from the perspective of the outsider within (according to Christine Sizemore).[18]

Lessing's recasting of themes and techniques of Woolf's feminist modernism in her predominantly realist fiction is part of a wider movement in British fiction. Literary historians of the contemporary British novel have argued that the genre of social realism has been remarkably adaptable and vibrant. Dominic Head describes the second half of the twentieth century as a creative renaissance for the novel of society, whose "key developments . . . have been made in the spirit of supplementing, rather than rejecting, given forms."[19] Head suggests that even the genre he identifies as "British Postmodernism" is "a hybrid form of expression that renegotiates tradition" and involves "the reader's willing acceptance that the text provides a bridge to reality."[20] Andrzej Gąsiorek finds realism and experimentalism to be a false dichotomy in contemporary British fiction, arguing in particular that Doris Lessing "produces texts in which realism splinters into a wide range of alternative narrative modes" without abandoning the traditional narrative contract between text and context, artifice and reality.[21] He maintains that the work of Lessing and other contemporary realists "seeks in distinctive ways to retain realism's strengths, particularly its attention to the social and intersubjective nature of human life, while at the same time confronting the problem of representation. . . . [T]hese novels avow realism's referential impulse but reject any simple reflectionist aesthetic."[22]

Lessing's reaffirmation of the realist tradition has also been noted by the reviewers of *The Sweetest Dream* in the British press. Lisa Appignanesi writes that it is like "coming upon a long lost novel by George Eliot or Balzac. . . . *The Sweetest Dream* belongs with *The Golden Notebook* and the *Children of Violence* sequence: the great novels of Doris Lessing's period of social and psychological realism. It's not only a matter of style or authorial voice, but of history."[23] Jane Shilling opines that her "moral engagement with her material, like her pungent characterization and flaying of hypocrisy, together with the confidence with which she sets a scene and her unexpected moments of sentimentality, mark out Lessing as a 21st-century virtuoso in the great 19th-century fictional manner."[24] And Lisa Allardice proclaims that Lessing is "the grande dame of big ideas. . . . The current vogue is for literary self-absorption and slim historical anecdote; this unfashionably worthy behemoth belongs to a more idealistic age. . . . despite her disenchantment with past obsessions, it seems she still believes in the power of literature to change the world."[25]

The Sweetest Dream embodies Lessing's reengagement with the nineteenth-century realist novel and, more contentiously, her reengagement with the nineteenth-century feminine ideal of the Angel in the House—albeit critically—at the expense of the Free Women, celebrated—albeit ironically—in *The Golden Notebook*. For example, Anna Wulf's long writing table with the color-coded notebooks wherein she creatively orders her experiences becomes in *The Sweetest Dream* Frances's kitchen table whereat she feeds the talk and fuels the activism of others—from her charismatically delusional ex-husband Comrade Johnny, to the variously troubled and talented youth whose myriad causes replace the spectrum of colors in Anna's notebooks. A domestication of the notebooks might also be read in the structure of the great house in Hampstead, whose floors echo the literary divisions created by Anna Wulf. Although Frances, like Anna, is a writer, a respected journalist, her writing pays the school fees and feeds the hungers of her ever-extending family. Her "real" work is the theater, but she turns down several exciting creative opportunities in favor of the steady income from her earnest, socially responsible books and articles. Virginia Tiger argues that this "Condition of England novel" replaces "*The Golden Notebook*'s competing narrative frames" with "competing narrative focalizations . . . that emerge from the constantly shifting points of view."[26] The divided selves of the creative individual, as represented by the fragmented narratives of Anna's notebooks, are replaced in *The Sweetest Dream* by the collective of narratives in which the creative individual's voice is submerged. In place of the earlier novel's Golden Notebook of (at least provisional) creative unity and transcendence, the later novel offers the vicarious achievement of the passing on of the maternal role from grandmother to grandchildren, symbolized by the spinning dance in which little Celia weaves her extended family.

Frances, like Martha Quest in *The Four-Gated City,* is a nurturer of and collaborator in the work of others. But in contrast to Martha's discovery that the creative insights of madness will enable the clairvoyant few to survive nuclear holocaust, Frances's aspirations are realistically modest: to pay everyone's school fees and get a hot meal on the dinner table. The narrative of Doctor Sylvia in Zimlia, which might seem to expand the ambitions of the Lennox family story, is similarly constrained by the realistic details of local poverty and state corruption: when Sylvia comes home to London to die, she leaves the mission with a shelf of books and a cupboard of basic medicines. In place of Martha's postnuclear child, Joseph, who is the harbinger of a new human race, Sylvia's wards, Clever and Zebedee, are bright survivors of a real-life plague without magical cure. However, Sylvia's emigration to Zimlia and the return of the African children to London completes the symbolic pattern that began with Martha's emigration from Zambesia and Joseph's return to Africa in her stead. Thus *The Sweetest Dream* does more than replay or recast the earlier novels: its realistic satire and relatively modest aspirations critique the ambitious vision and grand scale of the *Children of Violence* series; its depiction of Zimlia moves Lessing's critique of British colonialism in Southern Africa into the era of HIV/AIDS and neocolonial corruption, in the process reaffirming the historical responsibility that "London" has for "Zambesia."

Whereas Frances's self-sacrifice may be read on the autobiographical level as atonement for Lessing's own ambivalence toward her biological children, on the larger cultural level, Frances's re-mothering is a compensatory revision of the emotional cost of authorship for the woman writer-artist in the mid-twentieth century. In *The Sweetest Dream,* Lessing has not killed the Victorian specter of the self-sacrificing Angel in the House, but rather rehoused her in a domestic space that is large enough to contain the public sphere, to make and be made by history. Like the earlier novels, this novel engages deeply and knowingly with the clichéd but essential adage that the personal is political and vice versa. And in this novel most markedly and unambiguously the door of the great house in London opens upon the world. Politics and history are not so much domesticated as embodied and housed in the Lennox residence. At Frances's capacious kitchen table, Lessing skewers the dangerous naïveté of some of the big ideas of the twentieth century—Communist revolution, anticolonial nationalism, youth counterculture, and feminism—then reimagines them in more realistic, small-scale, familial terms.

When *The Sweetest Dream* begins in the mid-1960s, Frances is a journalist for *The Defender* (i.e., the venerable, left-of-center *Guardian*): "She had a name for solid balanced articles that often shone an unexpected and original light on a current scene."[27] She critiques the mystique of "Carnaby Street" and "Swinging London," as "some sort of collective hallucination."[28] She targets the conformity of sixties fashion—unisex clothes, Vidal Sassoon haircuts, Biba dresses—and "the fad for [the] alien excitements" of Eastern mysticism—from the I Ching to the Maharishi.[29] Many of Frances's stories are inspired by the trends and common concerns she notes in the letters to the newspaper's advice columnist, Aunt Vera. These distraught missives from confused housewives and mothers are echoed in the problems of Frances's own unruly household, in which her wards, too, shoplift, have unprotected sex, smoke marijuana, drop out of school, and run away from home. As in the case of Anna Wulf's prolific literary productivity in *The Golden Notebook,* it is unclear when Frances actually finds the time to write her long, well-researched articles for *The Defender;* whereas much of *The Golden Notebook* is taken up with Anna's busy and dramatic erotic life, so *The Sweetest Dream* focuses more on Frances's absorbing maternal duties than on her creative work. In both cases, however, the characters' personal concerns and responsibilities deeply color but do not seem to impede their intellectual productivity. The Angel in these houses does not stop the woman writer from writing, but rather reminds her of her connections to the others for whom she writes. In Anna's case, the pull of the individual's responsibility to the community—from her daughter, lovers, and friends to the Communist Party and then the Labour movement—*becomes* the story, as Anna's fragmented notebooks *become* the novel. In Frances's case, the pull of responsibility to others channels her creative aspirations away from the medium of the theater (her longed-for career, always snatched from her reach by practical considerations) into the more reliable, better-paid medium of journalism (a choice that she initially sees as pedestrian and second-rate). Frances's articles are anchored in, even weighed down by, the domestic concerns she shares with her female readers, yet these concerns, and her balanced, nuanced treatment of them, epitomize the conflicts of the times, which revolve around the all-important relationship between the generations: between the past and the future.

At the end of the sixties, a hardening of feminist orthodoxy complicates Frances's relationship with the other women journalists on *The Defender,* whose self-righteous adherence to the politically correct party line conflicts with her more nuanced and questioning stance. She also opposes (as Lessing did) the paper's support for unilateral nuclear disarmament, leading Frances "to conclude that working for *The Defender* was not unlike being Johnny's wife: she had to shut up and think her own thoughts. This was why she had always taken so much work home."[30] Within this house, Frances maintains a complicated relationship with her mother-in-law, Julia, a Clarissa Dalloway figure whose old money maintains the new family configuration. In descending order of generations, Julia keeps her elegant, old-fashioned aerie at the top of the house while Frances and her changing cast of "kids" occupy the space below. The downstairs kitchen with its huge table is "the life of the house," where Frances serves such iconic meals as "a large, filling, winter stew of beef and chestnuts, from a recipe of Elizabeth David's."[31] Frances's recipes from *French Country Cooking,* the narrator notes, are also informed by the *Zeitgeist*: the "culinary revolution" in British cooking serves as a kind of domestic preview of the French student revolt of 1968. Frances herself is rarely described as eating. Like Woolf's Angel, who, when there is chicken, takes the leg (and when there is a draft, sits in it), Frances feeds her delicacies to the kids (whom she also tries to protect from life's cold drafts). Unlike the mythical Angel, however, she is realistically resentful of, if unsurprised by, the heedlessness and greed of the young.

Frances receives letters from other women like herself:

> Thus did the house-mothers, the earth-mothers, who proliferated everywhere in the Sixties slowly become aware of each other's presence out there, and understand that they were part of a phenomenon: the *geist* was at it again. . . . They were a network of . . . *neurotic* nurturers. As "the kids" had explained, Frances was working out some guilt or other . . . working on her karma, damaged in a previous life.[32]

As are Lessing's other autobiographical protagonists Anna and Martha, Frances is depicted as a representative social type, emblematic of her gender, class, and historical moment. The novel traces the trajectory of about twenty years, during which the children leave the nest, Julia (like Mrs. Ramsay) passes from the narrative, and Frances, at sixty, finds love "of the quotidian, daily-bread sort, not at all a teenagers' romp" with a younger colleague,[33] whom she marries and whose children she then takes on, ever the house-mother.

The novel's critical retrospection on its period is conveyed through Frances's sardonic point of view of "the spirit of universal liberal idealism . . . that spirit of *everything is for the best in the best of all possible worlds,* which would one day be shorthand for 'the Sixties.'"[34] The crises of the house are enacted against the backdrop of world crises: when Comrade Johnny drops by to cadge a meal, he brings to the table the Cuban missile crisis, the assassination of John F. Kennedy, the burgeoning independence movements of Southern Africa, the popular uprisings in Eastern Europe, and the war in Vietnam. Among those who eat at Frances's midcentury table are future members of the anticolonial national liberation movements of Zimlia, such as Franklin, a scholarship boy at her son's progressive school, whose puzzled, lonely perspective on the excesses of groovy London parallels Frances's jaundiced middle-aged critique. As the kitchen empties and Frances's life narrative is becalmed, the setting shifts to Zimlia, where Franklin achieves power in the government of another of Frances's dinner guests, Comrade, now President, Matthew Mungozi (a fictionalized depiction of Robert Mugabe).

The African narrative centers on Sylvia's ascetic life as a doctor at a Catholic mission hospital in rural Zimlia, where the scarcity of resources and stoic suffering of the people provide another critical angle on the hedonism of sixties London—as well as another incarnation of its idealism. The mission is beset by governmental corruption and anticolonial paranoia, as through the narrative of Doctor Sylvia's quest, Lessing chronicles the postindependence history of Zimbabwe under Mugabe. Whereas Sylvia's medical intervention might be read as a more practical and useful version of Martha Quest's ineffectual Communist meetings in the *Children of Violence* series, Lessing's mercilessly realistic narrative condemns her too to failure. Sylvia is doomed in part by the dynamic of relationships that began at Frances's table. Whereas Frances's son Andrew has become an international aid guru, resentful hanger-on Rose is a sensation-seeking journalist who writes paeans of praise for President Mungozi and diatribes against her childhood rival Sylvia. Lessing, ever attuned to journalistic bias, parodies Rose's exposé: *"Granddaughter of a notorious Nazi, daughter of a career communist, Sylvia Lennox has found a hideyhole in Zimlia, where she owns a private hospital, supplied by equipment stolen from the local government hospital."*[35] Smeared by Rose, defeated by a hostile government, laid low by malaria, the dying Sylvia returns home to London with her two AIDS orphans. Clever and Zebedee, the survivors of the catastrophic epidemic, are the millennial version of the mutant children who survive nuclear catastrophe in *The Four-Gated City*. In Martha Quest's narrative, the children's story emerges from the fragments of documents in the appendix to the realistic novel. In *The Sweetest Dream,* the story of the African boys is integrated into the realistic narrative, under the aegis of the house-mother and her daughters. In Lessing's millennial reworking of the Africa-Europe, colony-metropole dichotomy, the African narrative is not bracketed into a Black Notebook or displaced into a dystopic future, but rather becomes the central story. The orphaned Zimlians are adopted into the London family whose power and influence, like that of Britain itself, has become muted and diffuse. The future of the Lennoxes, Lessing signals, is in the hands of the eager, precocious black children of empire.

"Once a Sixties household, then always a Sixties household," declares Frances's son Colin,[36] as in the final scene of the novel, Frances and Johnny and their new configuration of English and African children, stepchildren, and grandchildren gather round the kitchen table again. In this last scene, Frances's small granddaughter, Celia, runs from one family member to another, claiming them, binding them, spinning them together. In the novel's closing sentence, Celia is not "gathered and held" by her family, but rather "sing[s] for herself and to herself."[37] Unlike the house-mothers in this and other Lessing novels, Celia is not (yet) bound by responsibility and guilt. Thus she represents the sweetest dream of all in Lessing's work: the girl who will *not* become her mother. Yet although Celia spins and sings for and to herself, full of possibilities, her song names the family: "Yes, my Colin, yes, my Sophie, yes, and there's my poor little Johnny. . . ."[38] Her affectionate diminutive for her grandfather signals that she is a protomother, an incipient Angel in the House, spinning the web of care, singing the lullaby of reassurance. As Virginia Tiger puts it, "For all its derisive debunking of feminism, *The Sweetest Dream* is really about women who simply get on with it. Julia, Frances, Sylvia: these are the women who engage in small, but sustaining, acts of philanthropy."[39] Lessing's depiction of these characters seems to argue that although mothering is freed from its biological bonds (as house-mother Frances and Doctor Sylvia exemplify), and each of the female characters reinterprets the mother role with different emphases, they cannot evade this *sine qua non* of the feminine. What they can do is to reinterpret the maternal by translating its ethos into the public sphere: from Frances's domestic journalism to Sylvia's missionary medicine.

In this late Lessing novel, then, the social-psychological realism of *The Golden Notebook* and the *Children of Violence* series is reaffirmed: the "small personal voice" that the author has defended since the beginning of her career continues to provide trenchant political commentary; the domestic space is contiguous with the public sphere, the individual feminine life woven into the continuing life of the collective.[40] The character of Frances benefits from her author's hindsight as she looks back with the ironic detachment and common sense of old age on the chaotic and painful decades she chronicles. Frances is shrewder and wiser than her often tortured, introspective fictional foremothers Anna and Martha. Whereas Lessing warns in the author's note to the novel, "I am not writing volume three of my autobiography because of possible hurt to vulnerable people," she also has long proclaimed her faith in the historical accuracy and emotional truth of fiction.[41] Through Frances, Lessing seems to make peace with her own ex-husbands and lovers, biological and surrogate children. Even the horrific mother figure of Mrs. Quest (based on the author's sense of her own mother as smothering and controlling) is replaced with Julia, the distant but kindly mother-in-law who graciously cedes control of the house that she in fact owns. Although the ideological rhetoric of the sixties is satirized, the characters and settings are depicted with nostalgia; the dizzy round of demos and parties and meetings is vividly recalled; the Christmas feasts are lingered over; and the Biba dresses and Sassoon hairstyles are lovingly detailed.

In terms of the African material, which balances and contextualizes the London setting in *The Sweetest Dream* as in *The Golden Notebook* and *The Four-Gated City,* the exploitation of Rhodesia by British colonialists is downplayed in comparison with the exploitation of the citizens of independent Zimlia by the postcolonial regime (Robert Mugabe's Zimbabwe)—in partnership with the neocolonialism of the international donor community. The white farmers and missionaries in Zimlia heroically resist the destructive corruption of the black-ruled state and its international allies. Thus Lessing might be accused of nostalgia for more than Biba dresses and Elizabeth David food: Is the novel nostalgic for the colonial order, the retrospectively sweet dream of an African continent tinted British pink, traversed by the ghost vision of Cecil Rhodes' Cape-to-Cairo railroad? Or does it reflect the author's contemporary disillusionment with the autocratic and exploitative Mugabe regime, which has betrayed the dreams of African nationalism and the anti-colonial movements that she has supported throughout her career? Lessing has long examined the "lying nostalgia" of colonial memory (as Anna Wulf names it in the notebooks). Roberta Rubenstein argues that Lessing's writing, like Woolf's, reflects the tension between "nostalgia as a comforting recollection and nostalgia as a deception of memory; between profound emotional loss and imaginative reparation and healing."[42]

This ambivalent nostalgia for the mother (country) is embodied in Lessing's depictions of her childhood home in Southern Rhodesia. The white-settler house is a site of ambivalence, resented as a boundary-marker of colonial femininity, a maternal skin, but valued for its permeable walls, its construction out of native materials, its impurity and impermanence. Writes Victoria Rosner, "domestic space in the colonies was inexorably linked to the maternal body, creating the grounds for the psychological and territorial contest of a daughter's separation from her mother."[43] She notes Lessing's desire to "*break down* the house/bush division" enforced by the mother, and so to "reject the racist logic upon which settler culture rests."[44] The settler house was built to impose European domestic order on the African land, but in Lessing's account it failed. Martha Quest and the similarly rebellious young female protagonists of many of the African stories rejoice in the Africanization of their mothers' houses: the invasion by tree roots and termites, dust and humidity. They sleep with their doors open and welcome the noisy African night. Yet these daughters of British farm owners cannot bridge the racial, linguistic, economic, and legal gulf between their romantic good intentions and the brutal realities of colonial apartheid in the 1930s and 1940s. Martha Quest moves to town and becomes a Communist with the aim of turning this social order upside down. The *Children of Violence* novels and *The Golden Notebook* analyze the failure of the white revolutionaries to establish links with indigenous political movements and to translate the Party line into practical action. The novels depict as inevitable Martha's and Anna's flight into exile in London, their idealism tarnished but their ambitious sense of mission intact. Sylvia's mission hospital in the bush, where she works for change with a cast of African characters more nuanced and developed than the cardboard figures in the early novels, is a more solid and promising version of Europe-in-Africa than Martha's imaginary city in the veld. The story of its failure is, in Lessing's view, the story of the failure of the postcolonial project, of the dream of African liberation.

As the ideal of postcolonial Africa dims in Lessing's late novel, the lights of the house in London burn more brightly. The cosmopolitan house in which the rebellious colonial daughter reinvents the middle-class British family on her own antipatriarchal, postcolonial terms is modeled on the ideal architecture of the lost African home as a potential site of the coexistence of culture and nature, Europe and Africa. Like the pole-and-thatch house in *Martha Quest* and Sylvia's bush hospital, the house in Hampstead also defies the border between inside and outside, private and public. It too is a site of "the border-defying body of the mother" (as Rosner paraphrases Julia Kristeva's theory of the maternal in her analysis of settler architecture).[45] The London house is home, in the fictional logic of *The Sweetest Dream,* to a new kind of mothering, and potentially reproduces progressive ideologies that counter the logic of settler colonialism, with its either/or binaries and white/black hierarchies. The return of Sylvia and the Zimlian boys reinforces this hopeful argument. The impoverished African orphans Clever and Zebedee will be integrated into the elite British Lennox family, promising that the "colour-bar" of Southern African apartheid, long a preoccupation in Lessing's work, will finally become obsolete.

Certainly, each of Lessing's novels bears the marks of its own time, its particular moment in political and social history: as she writes in *The Sweetest Dream,* "When the *geist* speaks, the *zeit* must obey."[46] At the turn of the twenty-first century the *geist* speaks with different emphases than it did in the midst of the 1960s: it is a reminiscent and revisionist spirit that animates this novel, alternately generous and critical, rosy and jaundiced. As the reviewers noted in their comparisons to Balzac and George Eliot, this big old-fashioned novel remembers the postmodern mid-twentieth century through nineteenth-century realism as well as Woolfian modernism. To follow the trajectory of Lessing's autobiographical characters, from Martha Quest and Anna Wulf to Frances and Sylvia Lennox, is to see that the old archetypes of feminine self-sacrifice have not been laid to rest by the feminist ideals of self-actualization and authority. The Angel in the House has proved remarkably resilient and potent. However, Lessing's mordantly realistic depiction of women characters embedded in history, absorbing and (re)producing ideology, suggests that she isn't simply rewriting Eliot, that she has in fact rethought the nineteenth-century realist novel from the perspective of a mid-twentieth-century British colonial outsider—a "reverse immigrant" to London, as she has called herself. Lessing's house-mothers are descended from the outsider heroines, the rebellious daughters of Victorian fiction, from Charlotte Brontë's Jane Eyre to Olive Schreiner's Lyndall: protagonists who use their class or colonial differences to critique dominant ideologies and so to renovate the house of fiction.[47] Lessing's domestic women follow Woolf's Clarissa Dalloway and the Marys of *A Room of One's Own* in breaking down the distinctions between private and public spheres, between the personal and political, between self and other, insider and outsider, house and world. Frances's homebound story, like Martha's house-centered quest, like Clarissa's domestic odyssey, refigures and reorients the depiction of the domestic sphere in the novel of social realism. To be a mother in Lessing's fiction is to be inescapably a vehicle for the reproduction of the social order of patriarchy, capitalism, and colonialism; but the mother is also a nurturer of potentially revolutionary social change: from French cooking to French protest movements. It is especially the non-biological house-mother who can break the psychological bonds of inherited ideology.

The Annas and Marthas, the Franceses and Sylvias in Lessing's fiction have the power to remake the past and salvage lives. The endings of the three novels seem very different in genre and tone. The ironic ending of *The Golden Notebook* stresses the realistic compromises of "free women"; in the visionary science-fiction ending of *The Four-Gated City*, Martha's quest is passed on to other survivors of planetary cataclysm; in the sentimental ending of *The Sweetest Dream*, the maternal figure is reunited with her "kids" and the next generation's Angel sings her song. In each version of closure, however, the protagonist's historical memory and intellectual vision evolve into new forms; her creative lifeblood is transfused to the representatives of the next generation in the (forlorn but persistent) hope that they might learn from the mistakes of their elders. In the novel of the new millennium, satire shades into romance, Africa comes "home" to London, and Lessing reaffirms her faith in mothering as a profoundly creative endeavor grounded in the realistic experience of ordinary women.

NOTES

1. Doris Lessing, *The Sweetest Dream* (2001; repr., New York: HarperCollins, 2002).

2. For example, Jerome Boyd Maunsell writes, "Scathingly dry, yet somehow optimistic; calm, yet still emotional, Lessing is on untouchable form," review of *The Sweetest*

Dream, by Doris Lessing, *The Times* (London), July 27, 2002: 19, Custom Newspapers (InfoTrac-Gale) http://find.galegroup.com (accessed September 14, 2006). See also Appignanesi, Shilling, and Allardice, notes 23, 24, and 25 below.

3. Lessing, *The Golden Notebook* (1962; repr., New York: HarperPerennial, 1999).

4. Lessing, *The Four-Gated City*, vol. 5 of *Children of Violence* (1969; repr., New York: Penguin, 1976).

5. Lessing, *Martha Quest*, vol. 1 of *Children of Violence* (1952; repr., New York: Penguin, 1970).

6. Virginia Woolf, *A Room of One's Own* (1929; repr., *The Norton Anthology of English Literature*, 7th ed., vol. 2, ed. M. H. Abrams and Stephen Greenblatt [New York: Norton, 2000]), 2153–214.

7. Woolf, "Professions for Women" (1942; repr., *The Norton Anthology*, ed. Abrams and Greenblatt), 2214–18.

8. Coventry Patmore, "The Angel in the House" (1854–62; excerpted in *The Norton Anthology*, ed. Abrams and Greenblatt), 1723–24.

9. Woolf, *To the Lighthouse* (New York: Modern Library, 1937). See also Ruth Saxton's discussion of the ways that Frances Lennox comes to terms with her own needs and those of others and, especially, with her sexuality in her chapter, "Sex After Sixty: *love, again* and *The Sweetest Dream*," in Part Four of this collection [editors' note].

10. For example, Lessing, *Walking in the Shade: Volume Two of My Autobiography, 1949–1962* (New York: HarperCollins, 1997).

11. Victoria Rosner, "Home Fires: Doris Lessing, Colonial Architecture, and the Reproduction of Mothering," *Tulsa Studies in Women's Literature* 18.1 (1999): 59–89, http://www.jstor.org/ (accessed July 17, 2006). See also Pat Louw's chapter, "Domestic Spaces: Huts and Houses in Doris Lessing's *African Stories*," in Part Four of this collection [editors' note].

12. Nancy Armstrong, *Desire and Domestic Fiction: A Political History of the Novel* (New York: Oxford University Press, 1987), 3.

13. Woolf, *Three Guineas* (1938; repr., New York: Penguin, 1977).

14. For example, Melba Cuddy-Keane, *Virginia Woolf, the Intellectual, and the Public Sphere* (New York: Cambridge University Press, 2003); Mark Hussey, ed., *Virginia Woolf and War: Fiction, Reality, and Myth* (Syracuse, NY: Syracuse University Press, 1991); Holly Henry, *Virginia Woolf and the Discourse of Science: The Aesthetics of Astronomy* (New York: Cambridge University Press, 2003).

15. Virginia Woolf, "Modern Fiction" (1925; repr., *The Norton Anthology*, ed. Abrams and Greenblatt), 2150.

16. Claire Sprague, "Multipersonal and Dialogic Modes in *Mrs. Dalloway* and *The Golden Notebook*," in *Woolf and Lessing: Breaking the Mold*, ed. Ruth Saxton and Jean Tobin (New York: St. Martin's Press, 1994), 3–14.

17. Roberta Rubenstein, "Fixing the Past: Yearning and Nostalgia in Woolf and Lessing," in Saxton and Tobin, 15–38.

18. Christine Sizemore, "The 'Outsider-Within': Virginia Woolf and Doris Lessing as Urban Novelists in *Mrs. Dalloway* and *The Four-Gated City*," in Saxton and Tobin, 59–72.

19. Dominic Head, *The Cambridge Companion to Modern British Fiction, 1950–2000* (Cambridge, UK: Cambridge University Press, 2002), 224.

20. Ibid., 229.

21. Andrzej Gąsiorek, *Post-War British Fiction: Realism and After* (London: Edward Arnold, 1995), 181.

22. Ibid., 181–82.

23. Lisa Appignanesi, "Idealists at Home and Away," review of *The Sweetest Dream*, by Doris Lessing, *The Independent* (London), September 8, 2001: 11, Custom Newspapers (InfoTrac-Gale) http://find.galegroup.com (accessed September 14, 2006).

24. Jane Shilling, "Human Engagement," review of *The Sweetest Dream*, by Doris Lessing, *The Times* (London), October 6, 2001: 20, Custom Newspapers (InfoTrac-Gale) http://find.galegroup.com (accessed September 14, 2006).

25. Lisa Allardice, "Sniping at Sisters," review of *The Sweetest Dream*, by Doris Lessing, *Daily Telegraph* (London), September 8, 2001: 6, Custom Newspapers (InfoTrac-Gale) http://find.galegroup.com (accessed September 14, 2006).

26. Virginia Tiger, "Made from Memories," *Doris Lessing Studies* 22.2 (2002): 1, 8–10, 24.

27. Lessing, *The Sweetest Dream*, 2.

28. Ibid., 40.

29. Ibid., 126.

30. Ibid., 228.

31. Ibid., 14.

32. Ibid., 143.

33. Ibid., 230.

34. Ibid., 21.

35. Ibid., 421.

36. Ibid., 472.

37. Ibid., 479.

38. Ibid.

39. Tiger, "Made from Memories," 10.

40. Cf. Lessing, "The Small Personal Voice," her 1957 writer's manifesto, in which she declared her commitment to a Marxist-humanist worldview and the realistic fiction that springs from it, using the *Children of Violence* series as an example of fiction whose primary theme is the relation between the individual and the collective. Repr., *A Small Personal Voice: Essays, Reviews, Interviews*, ed. Paul Schlueter (New York: Vintage, 1975), 3–21. See Alice Ridout's comparison of "The Small Personal Voice" and Lessing's later essays in *Prisons We Choose to Live Inside* in her chapter, "'What is the Function of the Storyteller?': The Relationship between *Why* and *How* Lessing Writes," in Part Two of this collection [editors' note].

41. This is a claim she affirms in the 1993 introduction to *The Golden Notebook*, in which she says, regarding the writing of her autobiography, "I have to conclude that fiction is better at 'the truth' than a factual record." Introduction 1993 [to *The Golden Notebook*] (1994; repr., New York: HarperPerennial, 1999), ix.

42. Rubenstein, *Home Matters: Longing and Belonging, Nostalgia and Mourning in Women's Fiction* (New York: Palgrave/St. Martin's Press, 2001), 7.

43. Rosner, "Home Fires," 60.

44. Ibid., 84.

45. Ibid., 83. Rosner refers to Julia Kristeva, *Powers of Horror: An Essay on Abjec-*

tion, trans. Leon S. Roudiez (New York: Columbia University Press, 1982).

46. Lessing, *The Sweetest Dream,* 96.

47. Cf. Lessing's 1968 afterword to *The Story of an African Farm,* by Olive Schreiner, in which she describes her early identification with the autobiographical protagonists of that novel (New York: Fawcett World Library, 1968), 273–90; repr., *A Small Personal Voice,* 97–120).

✥ Part Two

ENGAGING THE POSTMODERN DEATH OF HISTORY

Redefining Context and Historical Narrative

"What Is the Function of the Storyteller?"

The Relationship between *Why* and *How* Lessing Writes

ALICE RIDOUT

In an interview with Christopher Bigsby in 1980, Doris Lessing raises a crucial question: "why do we tell stories? What is the function of the storyteller?"[1] She admits that it "is a thought that [she] can't come to terms with."[2] It is a thought that Lessing has, however, tried to come to terms with on several occasions throughout her career in her interviews and essays and, of course, in her own stories. Her most famous attempt to answer this question is her 1957 essay "The Small Personal Voice."[3] Although I do not dispute the importance of this essay as an *early* declaration of Lessing's beliefs, it has received excessive critical attention in relation to other statements she has made regarding the function of the storyteller. Furthermore, it continues to be cited without adequate acknowledgment of how much Lessing's vision of the storyteller has changed. Most particularly I want to contrast the popularity of "The Small Personal Voice" with the relative neglect of Lessing's Massey Lectures, sponsored by the Canadian Broadcasting Corporation, which were published under the title *Prisons We Choose to Live Inside*[4] in 1986. This text offers a different notion of the function of the storyteller from that offered in "The Small Personal Voice," one that leads us to consider the influence of the failure of Communism on Lessing's sense of *why* she writes. This exploration of the changes in why Lessing writes provides an illuminating context for the more controversial and widely discussed change in *how* she writes—her rejection of realism in favor of "space fiction."

This narrative of Lessing's development from a realist to a speculative writer was one Lorna Sage traced in her short monograph on Doris Lessing for the Methuen "Contemporary Writers" series. Sage's book exemplifies how "The Small Personal Voice" has been used to understand Lessing's sense of the function of the storyteller.[5] Following her reading of that essay as an expression of Lessing's commitment to realism, Sage goes on to trace Lessing's "exemplary transformation from a socialist realism that recalls her nineteenth-century predecessors, to the speculative forms she borrows from 'mystical' writing and space fiction."[6] This shift in *how* Lessing writes is widely accepted by critics. It appears again as a central thesis of Jeannette King's 1989 book on Lessing, in which she traces the "significant stages" in the development of Lessing's fiction and the "variety of formal experiments" Lessing "has undertaken." King further argues "that those experiments were a necessary and inevitable consequence of her search for literary forms which would allow for a more radical critique of Western culture."[7] Again, "The Small Personal Voice" is used to explicate Lessing's attitude toward realism and to demonstrate her understanding of the function of the storyteller.[8] However, despite her interest in the relationship between Lessing's literary choices and her cultural critiques, King fails even to include Lessing's publication of *Prisons We Choose to Live Inside* in 1986 in her chronological table of Lessing's life and publication. Nor does she use those lectures in the body of her work to provide a context for understanding the changes in *how* Lessing writes. Much more recently, Nick Bentley's essay "Doris Lessing's *The Golden Notebook*: An Experiment in Critical Fiction" in *Doris Lessing: Border Crossings* again uses "The Small Personal Voice" to assist in understanding not just Lessing's attitude toward realism but also, to borrow Bentley's phrase, "the nature of fiction itself and the relationship between literary forms and politics"[9] but makes no mention of *Prisons We Choose to Live Inside*. Perhaps critics have neglected Lessing's later nonfictional work because *The Golden Notebook* is itself so self-conscious and theoretically aware that, as Bentley argues, it functions as critical theory.[10] Lessing's cultural and theoretical critiques are so clearly apparent in her later fictional work that critics have felt less need to turn to her later nonfiction to understand her changing sense of the function of the storyteller. I hope this chapter will function as a corrective to that neglect by demonstrating how helpful *Prisons We Choose to Live Inside* is for giving us insight into what Lessing perceived her role as a writer to be in her post-Communist world.

Playing the storyteller myself, I will describe the highly significant contexts in which I first discovered *Prisons We Choose to Live Inside* a decade ago. I was completing a master's thesis on Lessing while posted as a visiting exchange lecturer at Palacky University in the Czech Republic. Inevitably, I became fascinated by the ways in which Lessing had been and was being interpreted and presented in that political context. For example, the tiny English department library, which had not yet received enough funds to update its old Communist collection of books, had multiple copies of Lessing's *Children of Violence* series only up to *A Ripple from the Storm*,[11] the novel *before* Martha Quest becomes disaffected with Communism. Instead of updating its libraries, Palacky University was focusing its spending on new staff. Once the university had "purged" itself of Party members, it was faced with an extreme shortage of lecturers. The English department's post-Communist head of department, for example, had spent the Communist years doing manual labor in a boiler room because he had been considered too critical of the regime to remain in the academy. In an attempt to update methodology and fill the many vacancies, Palacky University employed a high number of mainly American and British lecturers, often with international funding that I frequently heard being described rather cynically as "guilt money." (My post, for example, was funded by the British Council.) Ironically, or perhaps appropriately, many of these lecturers were themselves disaffected Western Communists like Lessing, who were trying to work through the failures of the ideology they had once believed in passionately. They created an interesting community of ex-Communist English speakers in the Czech Republic. Therefore, perhaps I should not have been surprised to discover in an English-language bookstore in Prague multiple copies of a Lessing text I had never seen in any British bookstore. That text was *Prisons We Choose to Live Inside*.

I returned to Durham University in England during the Christmas break to submit my master's thesis. Through a great coincidence, my supervisor was cohosting a lecture series that included Lessing as one of the speakers. As a graduate student working on Lessing in the department, I was honored to be invited to join Lessing and a small group of lecturers for dinner. I discussed my thesis with her and told her the anecdote about her *Children of Violence* novels in the English department library at Palacky University. She immediately said to me, "There is a book I wrote that you would find helpful but very few critics ever talk about it. It's called *Prisons We Choose to Live Inside*." These were the rather peculiar contexts in which I first discovered *Prisons,* and they certainly informed my reading of the text. The post-Communist context in which I first purchased a copy of *Prisons* and Lessing's own personal assertion of both its usefulness and its relative neglect by critics are very important starting points for this essay.

4: "What Is the Function of the Storyteller?"

During debates in the 1980s and '90s over the definition of "postmodernism," many critics drew attention to the contradictory ways in which the term implies the continuation of modernism by repeating the term within itself, as well as the rejection or completion of modernism and the start of something new through the prefix "Post." Similar debates are now swirling around the term "postfeminism." Likewise, in describing *Prisons* as a "post-Communist" text I mean to imply exactly this kind of contradictory relationship of continuity and rejection between Lessing's text and Communism. *Prisons* itself teaches us the importance of these contradictory patterns. In the lecture "You Are Damned, We Are Saved," Lessing discusses the "structures" or "patterns"[12] of belief that enable groups in society to confidently assert the title of the lecture: "you are damned, we are saved." Even when the ideas are new, Lessing argues, the pattern of believing yourself and your group to be right while everyone else is wrong is the oft-repeated "heritage of the structure of Christian thought."[13] It is, of course, this "heritage" that George W. Bush drew on to legitimate his "War on Terror." *Prisons* can be read as Lessing's own attempted jailbreak out of this heritage and these patterns of thought—a kind of rethinking that is particularly engaging given our current political climate.

Drawn to *Prisons* by Lessing's own insistence on its importance and to a new awareness of the relevance of Communist and post-Communist contexts to Lessing's work, I started to compare *Prisons* with Lessing's more famous manifesto, "The Small Personal Voice," and I was struck by how Lessing's sense of the function of the storyteller had changed. The first main difference is in how Lessing describes the relation of the individual, who is usually the storyteller, to the group. In "The Small Personal Voice," Lessing makes her famous statement that the *Children of Violence* series "is a study of the individual conscience in its relations with the collective."[14] This is also a theme of "The Small Personal Voice" itself. She rejects both "man as the isolated individual unable to communicate, helpless and solitary" and "collective man with a collective conscience" in favor of a compromise between the two, what she describes as "a resting point, a place of decision, hard to reach and precariously balanced."[15]

She concludes "The Small Personal Voice" with two contradictory visions of how the storyteller can achieve this balance. First, Lessing suggests that "the minimum act of humility for a writer" is "to know that one is a writer at all because one represents, makes articulate, is continuously and invisibly fed by, numbers of people who are inarticulate, to whom one belongs, to whom one is responsible."[16] This vision of the writer representing, being fed by, belonging to, and being responsible for the inarticulate mass is a utopian one that Lessing repeats elsewhere during this period of her career and clearly demonstrates the influence of Communist models of the artist and the collective on Lessing. For example, in a 1969 radio interview with Studs Terkel, Lessing states: "Our function as writers, I maintain, is to express what other people feel. If we're any good, it's because we're like other people and can express it."[17] In her 1971 preface to *The Golden Notebook* she describes "making the personal general" and suggests that "growing up is after all only the understanding that one's unique and incredible experience is what everyone shares."[18] Ironically though, one of the functions of the preface she added to *The Golden Notebook* was to correct what she perceived to be the *mis*reading of the novel by exactly these "numbers of people who are inarticulate, to whom one belongs." Here Lessing also famously refutes that the novel represents its feminist readers. Although the novel clearly represented and made articulate (to borrow from Lessing's quotation above) a hitherto inarticulate mass of proto-second-wave feminists, Lessing refused to belong to or be responsible for those readers. This contradiction echoes the tension that Lessing's character Anna feels in *The Golden Notebook* when she is delivering her lectures celebrating collective art. She starts to stammer, cannot finish the lecture, and then stops giving the lectures altogether, because she cannot help but realize that the Communist art she has been reading in her job at the Communist Party is "dead literature."[19] The "flashes of genuine art" are all born from "undisguisable private emotion."[20] This valuing of art because it expresses the private and personal is the basis of the second formulation of the storyteller's relation to the collective that Lessing offers in "The Small Personal Voice."

Lessing concludes "The Small Personal Voice" by emphasizing the individual as opposed to the collective:

> The novelist talks, as an individual to individuals, in a small personal voice. In an age of committee art, public art, people may begin to feel again a need for the small personal voice; and this will feed confidence into the writers and, with confidence because of the knowledge of being needed, the warmth and humanity and love of people which is essential for a great age of literature.[21]

Lessing clearly contradicts herself in "The Small Personal Voice" in her attempt to find that balance between the "isolated individual" and "collective man." She argues first that it is only by initially recognizing that the individual is already part of and responsible for the collective that the writer can succeed, but then suggests that the small personal voice of the individual storyteller connects individuals in order to form the collective.[22] However, the models share an assumption that a balance between the individual and collective can be achieved even if it is difficult. Also, in both models Lessing expresses a positive attitude toward the collective, which is another example of the influence of Communism on her thinking at this time.

In *Prisons,* Lessing is much more skeptical and negative about how the collective operates. "What we live through," she says, "in any age, is the effect on us of mass emotions and of social conditions from which it is almost impossible to detach ourselves."[23] Given this more negative notion of the collective, the individual, and particularly the individual storyteller, becomes even more important. At the end of *Prisons,* Lessing states that "[e]verything that has ever happened to me has taught me to value the individual, the person who cultivates and preserves her or his own ways of thinking, who stands out against group thinking, group pressures."[24] Although this echoes her notion of the novelist talking "as an individual to individuals, in a small personal voice" that I have quoted above, it is a very different understanding of the individual's relation to the collective from that described in both "The Small Personal Voice" and the preface to *The Golden Notebook.* Instead of "making the personal general"[25] as a means of solving the problem of the subjective, isolated individual as she proposes in "The Small Personal Voice," the collective constantly threatens to annihilate the individual in *Prisons.* Her statement in *Prisons* that "the detached, curious, patient, investigative attitude" is "the most valuable thing we have in the fight against our own savagery, our long history as group animals,"[26] contrasts with her claim in "The Small Personal Voice" that "literature should be committed."[27] This contrast is one example of the rejection of Communism that is apparent in *Prisons* and marks it as a post-Communist text. Lessing's negative model of the group in *Prisons* results in the storyteller taking on a very different function in *Prisons* from the one assigned in "The Small Personal Voice."

In "The Small Personal Voice" Lessing argues that once a writer accepts responsibility for the effects made on readers, "he must see himself, to use the socialist phrase, as an architect of the soul." She goes on to argue that "if one is going to be an architect, one must have a vision to build towards." Furthermore, "[it] is not merely a question of preventing an evil, but of strengthening a vision of good which may defeat the evil."[28] The moral certainty of Lessing here has been echoed by those who argued for military intervention in Iraq and by those who continue to argue for intervention in other states on the grounds of rightness of cause. This sense of the moral function of the novel is intimately related to realism in "The Small Personal Voice." She states with great certainty that the "highest point of literature" was the nineteenth-century realist novel and goes on to "define realism as art which springs so vigorously and naturally from a strongly held, though not necessarily intellectually defined, view of life that it absorbs symbolism."29

In *Prisons,* Lessing is keen to celebrate writers of science fiction and utopia rather than realism. She suggests that the writer's function is not to build up a vision of the good but to criticize. In an interesting and not entirely convincing move, she positions utopias as "criticisms of current societies." She ignores and erases their possible social function as "visions to build towards" and instead insists that utopias and science fiction create critical distance and detachment from the real world.30 In *Prisons* she identifies novelists' most useful function "for their fellow citizens" to be that of "enabl[ing] us to see ourselves as others see us."31 The vision of good and the moral certainty that she calls for in "The Small Personal Voice" is replaced with self-conscious doubt in *Prisons*. In her interview with Bill Moyers for PBS in 2003, Lessing makes this change very clear when she answers Moyers's question as to whether it is the "mission of writers to give us a vision" by flatly stating that "I don't think writers should have missions."32 Earlier in the same interview, Lessing dismisses her young Communist dreams as "rubbish." When Moyers asserts that "dreams are not rubbish," Lessing retorts that "[they're] rubbish if they lead you to very unrealistic actions. That's what's bad about them. If you're dreaming about wonderful Utopias, and great horizons, and great dawns and all that, you're not really seeing what's there, and what could be done."33

Admittedly, this critique of Communism as being blind to "what's there" and as unprepared to engage with real problems is evident much earlier in Lessing's work. For example, in *The Golden Notebook,* Richard (Molly's capitalist ex-husband) tells his son that if he were chief of police trying to hunt down the Communists he would ask them one question: "Would you go to an undeveloped country and run a country clinic for fifty people?" He believes that all Communists would refuse because of their belief that the whole system needs to be changed.34 Anna, listening to Tommy describing his father's strategy, has to admit the validity of its critique. *The Golden Notebook* is in many ways Lessing's own notebook in which she started to work through the philosophical and formal consequences of her rejection of Communism and of what she perceived to be the moral certainties of realism. Therefore, there are several moments, such as this one, that already point toward *Prisons*. In notes she added to a reissue of *The Golden Notebook* in 1994, Lessing acknowledges this herself: "I was writing my way out of one set of ideas, even out of a way of life, but that is not what I thought while I was doing it."35 Thus the change in Lessing's vision of the storyteller from

4: "What Is the Function of the Storyteller?"

one who provides moral certainty to one who encourages critical doubt does seem to be intimately related to her rejection of both Communism and realism. Furthermore, it is a vision that seems particularly helpful to explore in our current political climate of clashing moral certainties.

A further change in Lessing's model of the storyteller is in her attitude toward the novel's function as a source of knowledge about places and people that the reader and the general public are ignorant of. In *The Golden Notebook,* Anna expresses a strongly negative view of the changing function of the novel:

> I find that I read with the *same kind of curiosity* most novels, and a book of reportage.... Yet I am incapable of writing the only kind of novel which interests me: a book powered with an intellectual or moral passion strong enough to create order, to create a new way of looking at life.... I have only one, and the least important, of the qualities necessary to write at all, and that is curiosity. It is the curiosity of the journalist.[36]

Clearly, it is important to recognize the difference between Lessing's fiction and her nonfictional essays and interviews, as well as to realize (as I mentioned above) that in *The Golden Notebook* (1962) Lessing is already rethinking the vision of the storyteller's function that she presented in "The Small Personal Voice" (1957).[37] This is her character Anna Wulf thinking, not Lessing herself. However, this section from *The Golden Notebook* echoes "The Small Personal Voice" closely enough that it is reasonable to assume that these were ideas that Lessing herself grappled with as an author between 1957 and 1962. This section clarifies some of the ideas present in "The Small Personal Voice" by describing the contemporary novel as a "function of the fragmented society" and by clarifying the "moral passion" of the realist novel as being "the quality of philosophy."[38] The example she uses in *The Golden Notebook* is Thomas Mann, whom she describes as "the last of the writers in the old sense, who used the novel for philosophical statements about life."[39]

It is noticeable that all of Lessing's examples of "great realists" are white males despite there being prominent women in that tradition. Similarly for Lessing, the "great" Communists were all male, although again there were also women in that tradition. Thus, despite her early commitment to progressive socialist politics there seems to be no awareness of gender equality in her representation of the tradition of "great realists." Perhaps it is no coincidence that the novel in which Lessing writes herself out of both realism and Communism—*The Golden Notebook*—was read as a "trumpet for Women's Liberation."[40] A more detailed examination of Lessing's resistance to feminism is beyond the scope of this chapter, but it is important to acknowledge that her rejection of both realism and Communism could well be more closely related to her gender than Lessing likes to admit. Lessing's later novels *The Good Terrorist* (1985) and *The Sweetest Dream* (2001)[41] demonstrate a much more nuanced understanding of the gender politics within the Communist movement than Lessing demonstrated earlier in her career. It is pertinent that Lessing suggested that she wrote *The Sweetest Dream* instead of the next volume of her autobiography, implying that its contradictions were ones she herself had faced.[42]

In direct contrast to her apparent despair at the new function of the novel as an "outpost of journalism" expressed in *The Golden Notebook,* Lessing seems keen to celebrate this function of the novel in her 2003 interview with Bill Moyers. Following her confident statement that writers should not have missions, Lessing draws attention to the way in which novels function to introduce "areas of life which we haven't thought of before, that haven't really been in public consciousness until that novel." She goes on to give the examples of the "great Southern novelists" who have brought our attention to America's Deep South and to the Russian novelists who have taught us of Russia, concluding with the thought that "that is a function of the novel we forget."[43] Anna's rejection in *The Golden Notebook* of novels that teach of unknown areas of life, and of the curiosity that motivates the writers and readers of those novels, is reversed in this 2003 interview and in Lessing's celebration of curiosity and investigation in *Prisons*. This represents a very significant shift in Lessing's sense of the role of the storyteller and function of the novel.

In the 1980 interview from which I have taken the title of this paper, Christopher Bigsby asks Lessing why she moved away from the nineteenth-century realism she aligned herself with in "The Small Personal Voice." Her answer helps to explain her movement from commitment and moral certainty to doubt and critical distance that I have outlined, and it illustrates that why and how Lessing writes are connected. In her reply to Bigsby, Lessing explains her move away from realism as a reaction to changes in the real world: "you cannot any more get comfort from old moral certainties because something new is happening. All our standards of values have been turned upside down, I think."[44] This sense of uncertainty is present in "The Small Personal Voice," but what seems to have changed by the time of *Prisons* (1986) is Lessing's willingness to explore and celebrate the possibilities of the new uncertainties.

This change in Lessing's attitude toward uncertainty seems to be related to her loss of conviction in Communism. I want to refer at this point to the speech "The Need for Transcendence in the Postmodern World," which

4: "What Is the Function of the Storyteller?"

Václav Havel delivered when he was president of the Czech Republic, in Independence Hall, Philadelphia, on July 4, 1994, because its similarities with Lessing's *Prisons* illustrate the ways in which *Prisons* particularly speaks to and out of a post-Communist context. Lessing's belief that we are living in a changing world is echoed by Havel: "Today, many things indicate that we are going through a transitional period."[45] Havel expresses exactly the same type of frustration with the inadequacy and ineffectiveness of our scientific knowledge of ourselves as Lessing does in *Prisons*. He juxtaposes technological advancements, such as being able to see Earth from space as "another star in the sky," with the sense that "we do not know exactly what to do with ourselves, where to turn."[46] This echoes Lessing's repeated opinion throughout *Prisons* that "we *do* know more about ourselves now than people did in the past, but . . . very little of this knowledge has been put into effect."[47] Admittedly, Havel's and Lessing's diagnoses of why all this knowledge is failing are very different. Havel claims that it is because modern scientific knowledge is fundamentally inadequate. It "fails," he says, "to connect with the most intrinsic nature of reality and with natural human experience."[48] In contrast, Lessing believes that the knowledge we have of ourselves is extensive, but that we fail to apply it in our everyday lives and institutions because of fear and because of the ways in which governments maintain control over the information.[49]

Despite this difference between Lessing's and Havel's understandings of the contemporary world, the similarity in their thought is more significant. Speaking in 1985[50] and 1994, respectively, Lessing and Havel agreed that the world was undergoing a paradigm shift. Even more significantly, both authors call for a similar solution: a reimagining of the individual's relationship to the collective, to the cosmos even, that is self-conscious or self-transcendent. Havel calls for a return to an "awareness that we are not here alone nor for ourselves alone, but that we are an integral part of higher, mysterious entities against whom it is not advisable to blaspheme." This type of awareness, Havel argues, "endows us with the capacity for self-transcendence."[51] This vision of the self offers a critique of selfish egotism similar to Lessing's vision in which she argues that we can achieve moments when we realize that the "I am right, you are wrong" attitude we so often live by is, in her words, "quite simply, nonsense." She explains: "All history, development goes on through interaction and mutual influence, and even the most violent extremes of thought, of behaviour, become woven into the general texture of human life, as one strand of it."[52] This is a temporal model of humanity's relation to the universe that closely parallels Havel's spatial model of the individual as being part of something much larger than him- or herself. For Lessing, time eventually weaves every idea into the "general texture of human life," and for Havel we are always "an integral part of higher, mysterious entities." Both writers stress the interrelatedness of human beings. Lessing's wish that we "learn how to look at ourselves and at the society we live in, in that calm, cool, critical, sceptical way which is the only possible stance for a civilized human being,"[53] is closely aligned with Havel's conclusion: "Transcendence as the only real alternative to extinction."[54] The solution to this problem of the individual's relation to the collective is for the individual to escape the limitations of his or her own perspective through purposeful self-conscious questioning or through self-transcendence.

I have explored these parallels between Lessing's and Havel's political visions for two main reasons. The first is that the parallels between Lessing's *Prisons* and Havel's "The Need for Transcendence in the Postmodern World" are a further indication of the fact that *Prisons* is helpfully understood in a post-Communist context.[55] It is a text marked by Lessing's concern for Communist states and by her loss of belief in Communism. "The Small Personal Voice" presents, in contrast, a Communist view of the function of the artist as a committed "architect of the soul."[56] Whereas "The Small Personal Voice" attempts to find a model for the artist's function that borrows from the socialist model and, therefore, privileges realism, *Prisons* expresses the need for a new paradigm altogether. This difference points to the fact that *why* Lessing writes affects *how* she writes. Throughout her career, Lessing has insisted that form and content are inseparable in her work. Her description of the structure of *The Golden Notebook* as making a "wordless statement"[57] is one of many examples of her asserting that her form has content and is inseparable from it. Clearly, her narrative forms are as intimately related to *why* she writes. Her conception of the function of the storyteller has moved away from one in which the writer is the confident defender of ethical goodness with a clear realist vision to impart to one in which the artist's function is to criticize and question. This new artist whom Lessing envisions should try to alienate the reader from him- or herself and the world so that he or she may view it with self-conscious doubt. It is because of this goal that Lessing has been drawn toward parody (as in "Free Women" in *The Golden Notebook*) and "space fiction" (as in her *Canopus in Argos* series). Lessing's use of the analogy of wanting to see the world "as, perhaps, a visitor from another planet might see us"[58] implies that creating imagined galaxies as she does in *Canopus in Argos* offers her critical distance from the real world. In *Prisons,* Lessing relates utopias to science fiction and, in turn, sees them both as expressions of the detachment she is calling for.⁵⁹ This problematic reading of utopias positions them as detached criticisms of society, not as visions of moral certainty. This allows Lessing to position science fiction in a long and illustrious tradition that is juxtaposed with the long realist tradition she celebrates in "The Small Personal Voice." It is clear from this that in Lessing's own mind her move from commitment to detachment is directly related to her rejection of realism in favor of space fiction. The pattern of the changes in Lessing's writing as it emerges in these later stages of her career tends to get told in two separate stories—one about her rejection of realism and one concerned with her rejection of Communism. In her preface Lessing insisted that the main lesson of *The Golden Notebook* was supposed to be "that we must not divide things off, must not compartmentalize."⁶⁰ *Prisons* makes it clear that these two stories about *why* and *how* Lessing writes must not be divided off from each other.

The second reason for my having positioned *Prisons* in a post-Communist context is that this may offer an explanation for why Western critics have largely failed to acknowledge the importance of this text in Lessing's oeuvre. As Lessing herself explains in *Prisons,* societies west of the iron curtain have not experienced what it is like to have the artist's function curtailed as it was in Communist countries:

> We live in an open society.... One only has to meet people from behind the Iron Curtain, particularly from the Soviet Union, where ideas are not allowed to circulate, where information is suppressed, where there is a close, claustrophobic, oppressive atmosphere, to be reminded how very fortunate we are, even with all the defects our societies do have. We are fortunate in that we are able to teach ourselves what we will ...
>
> I think we should make more use of these freedoms than we do.⁶¹

Indeed, it was exactly the experience of meeting people from behind what was the iron curtain that enabled me to more fully engage with and understand the importance of *Prisons*. As I have attempted to suggest throughout this essay, the rhetoric of "I am right, you are wrong" that Lessing is so keenly critical of in *Prisons* has been creeping back into the media and into our political vocabularies and visions—if, indeed, it ever left. This is a particularly important and relevant time to engage in more appreciative readings of *Prisons We Choose to Live Inside* and to take up Lessing's call to "make more use of these freedoms than we do."⁶²

NOTES

1. Doris Lessing, "The Need to Tell Stories," interview by Christopher Bigsby, in *Putting the Questions Differently: Interviews with Doris Lessing, 1964–1994*, ed. Earl G. Ingersoll (London: HarperFlamingo, 1994), 84. This collection is also titled *Doris Lessing: Conversations* and is cited that way in the bibliography to this volume [editors' note]. Hereafter cited as *Conversations*.
2. Ibid.
3. Lessing, "The Small Personal Voice," in *A Small Personal Voice: Essays, Reviews, Interviews*, ed. Paul Schlueter (London: Harper Flamingo, 1974).
4. Lessing, *Prisons We Choose to Live Inside* (1986; repr., New York: Harper Row, 1987).
5. Lorna Sage, *Doris Lessing* (London: Methuen, 1983). See pages 43–49 for her reading of "The Small Personal Voice."
6. Ibid., 10–11.
7. Jeannette King, *Doris Lessing* (London: Edward Arnold, 1989), ix.
8. Ibid., 2–3.
9. Nick Bentley, "Doris Lessing's *The Golden Notebook*: An Experiment in Critical Fiction," in *Doris Lessing: Border Crossings*, ed. Alice Ridout and Susan Watkins (London: Continuum, 2009), 44.
10. Ibid.
11. Lessing, *A Ripple from the Storm*, vol. 3 of *Children of Violence* (London: Michael Joseph, 1958). See Sandra Singer's "London and Kabul: Assessing the Politics of Terrorist Violence" in Part Two of this collection for discussion of Lessing's engagement, then disillusionment, with Communism in relationship to her views on urban Western and Afghan terrorism [editors' note].
12. Lessing, *Prisons*, 23, 26.
13. Ibid., 26.
14. Lessing, "The Small Personal Voice," 8.
15. Ibid., 15.
16. Ibid., 24.
17. Lessing, "Learning to Put the Questions Differently," interview by Studs Terkel, in *Conversations*, 20.
18. Lessing, Preface, *The Golden Notebook* (London: Harper Flamingo, 2002), 13. This 1971 preface is also titled Introduction 1971 [to *The Golden Notebook*] [editors' note].
19. Lessing, *The Golden Notebook*, 312.
20. Ibid., 311.
21. Lessing, "The Small Personal Voice," 25.
22. This is reminiscent of T. S. Eliot's famous formulation in "Tradition and the Individual Talent." There is a similar contraction between Eliot's desire to erase the individual personality of the poet and his assertion that only poets with personality and emotions know the significance of erasing those things. As he says: "Poetry is not a turning loose of emotion, but an escape from emotion; it is not the expression of personality, but

an escape from personality. But, of course, only those who have personality and emotions know what it means to want to escape from these things." T. S. Eliot, *Selected Prose*, ed. John Hayward (Harmondsworth, England: Penguin, 1963), 29.

23. Lessing, *Prisons*, 6.

24. Ibid., 73–74. I think Lessing's shift in vocabulary from the word "collective" that she uses in "The Small Personal Voice" and the preface to "group" here is significant because the word "collective" had positive connotations in Communist thought. The word "group" does not have the same Communist implications.

25. Quoted above. Lessing, *The Golden Notebook*, 13.

26. Lessing, *Prisons*, 20.

27. Lessing, "The Small Personal Voice," 10.

28. Ibid., 11.

29. Ibid., 8.

30. Lessing, *Prisons*, 7.

31. Ibid.

32. Lessing, "Bill Moyers Talks with Doris Lessing," interview by Bill Moyers, *Now* (2003), http://www.pbs.org/now (accessed May 28, 2005), 6 (page number taken from printable version).

33. Ibid., 3. This comment highlights how problematic Lessing's reading of utopias is in *Prisons*. In *Prisons* she insists that utopias function as criticisms of society not as visions of a better future. She positions them as the forefathers of science fiction rather than of Communism. However, utopias can be read as *both*. They can be criticisms of current society that encourage intelligent doubt and critical distance, as well as being committed visions of a better society that encourage socialist politics.

34. Lessing, *The Golden Notebook*, 237.

35. Lessing, "A Reissue of *The Golden Notebook*," in *Time Bites: Views and Reviews* (London: HarperCollins, 2004), 140. This essay is also titled Introduction 1993 [to *The Golden Notebook*] and is cited that way in the bibliography to this volume [editors' note].

36. Lessing, *The Golden Notebook*, 75–76. Lessing's italics.

37. Nick Bentley's designation of *The Golden Notebook* as "critical fiction" is pertinent here. See "Doris Lessing's *The Golden Notebook*: An Experiment in Critical Fiction," 44–60.

38. Lessing, *The Golden Notebook*, 75.

39. Ibid.

40. Lessing, Preface, *The Golden Notebook*, 8.

41. Lessing, *The Good Terrorist* (London: Jonathan Cape, 1985); Lessing, *The Sweetest Dream* (2001; repr., New York: HarperCollins, 2002).

42. See the author's note that prefaces *The Sweetest Dream*.

43. Lessing, "Bill Moyers Talks with Doris Lessing," 6. (Page number taken from printable version.)

44. Lessing, "The Need to Tell Stories," interview by Christopher Bigsby, 72.

45. Václav Havel, "The Need for Transcendence in the Postmodern World," Czech Embassy (July 4, 1994), http://dieoff.org/page38.htm (accessed May 30, 2006). (This Web site does not have pagination.)

46. Ibid.

47. Lessing, *Prisons*, 5. Lessing's italics.
48. Havel, "The Need for Transcendence in the Postmodern World."
49. Lessing, *Prisons*, 60.
50. *Prisons We Chose to Live Inside* was first delivered as the five-part 1985 Massey Lectures, which were broadcast in October 1985 on CBC Radio's "Ideas" series.
51. Havel, "The Need for Transcendence in the Postmodern World."
52. Lessing, *Prisons*, 16.
53. Ibid., 71.
54. Havel, "The Need for Transcendence in the Postmodern World."
55. Please refer to my comments above concerning the phrase "post-Communist."
56. Quoted above. Lessing, "The Small Personal Voice," 11.
57. Lessing, Preface, *The Golden Notebook*, 13.
58. Lessing, *Prisons*, 44.
59. Ibid., 7.
60. Lessing, Preface, *The Golden Notebook*, 10.
61. Lessing, *Prisons*, 76.
62. On this note, I would like to dedicate this essay to my students and colleagues at Palacky University, who still did not take an open society for granted when I met them in 1996; and to all those who dare to "make more use of these freedoms" than we usually do.

London and Kabul

Assessing the Politics of Terrorist Violence

SANDRA SINGER

INTRODUCTION

With the destruction of the Twin Towers, discussions related to terrorism have reverberated on global mass media outlets and moved to the forefront of academic discourse. It is in the context of this debate about contemporary (new-millennial) political violence that it is timely to reread and question Doris Lessing's earlier explorations and evaluations of the terrorist enterprise and of political violence in general. Of particular relevance in today's debates on terrorism is her reading of the Afghan muhjahidin with whom she sympathized fervently in the 1980s in her nonfictional work *The Wind Blows Away Our Words and Other Documents Relating to the Afghan Resistance*. Later—after the falling of the Twin Towers—many of these very same muhjahidin were labeled as Taliban terrorists and members of the "axis of evil"; then, they were consequently crushed by American military might.

Lessing's close affinity to issues affecting the Middle East springs from both her childhood roots and her adult dialogue with her teacher, the Sufi writer Idries Shah. Her reverence for the Afghan people's struggle against the Soviet occupation of Afghanistan from 1979 to 1989 can be explained in relationship to her immersion in Sufism in the late 1960s. Lessing's Sufi mentor, Idries Shah, was originally from Afghanistan. Presumably it is that relationship that led Lessing to be so interested in the situation of the muhjahidin in Afghanistan.[1] Lessing herself attributes her engagement with Afghanistan to memories of growing up in what are now Iran and Zimbabwe, and refers to these memories on her journey to Pakistan: "I was born in Persia and lived there until I was five. Yes, all kinds of scents and sounds came back."[2] She also compares Afghanistan to Southern Rhodesia as a conduit of trade leading to warfare and to desolation.[3]

Both Lessing's fictional *The Good Terrorist* (1985; cited hereafter as *GT*) and journalistic *The Wind Blows Away Our Words and Other Documents Relating to the Afghan Resistance* (1987) are in need of postcolonial interpretation. By postcolonial, I am referring to both a collection of writings and a history of group struggle against exploitation and oppression that considers the overthrow of colonial regimes as the first of many necessary steps toward a desired place of equality and freedom. The origins of postcolonialism as a field of study often cite the pioneering writings of Frantz Fanon and Che Guevara.[4] The Tricontinental Conference of 1966 in Havana has been described as the flashpoint where race, religion, and gender were considered as revolutionary potential in transnational, but localized, liberation struggles.[5] Alice Mellings (*GT*) and Tajwar Kakar (*Our Words*) are prototypical postcolonial protagonists in Doris Lessing's writings; both main characters are female freedom fighters in armed struggle against what they view as colonial oppressors.

While "one person's terrorist is another's freedom fighter" is a common sound byte heard in the media, the presumed logical equivalence of these terms is blatantly false.[6] There are many different types or subsets of freedom fighters. One subset of freedom fighter uses nonviolent techniques, perhaps following the teachings of Mohandas Gandhi. Another type of freedom fighter is the armed guerilla (rural and urban), who uses violent methods to strike and combat the armed forces of a perceived oppressor. Terrorists can also be viewed as a further subset of freedom fighters. Terrorists are a subset of freedom fighters, but not all freedom fighters are terrorists.

Although Noam Chomsky's *9-11* and *The Culture of Terrorism,* along with Edward Said's "The Essential Terrorist," distinguish clearly between the roles of terrorist and armed guerilla, it can be hard to separate these two subsets of freedom fighters because they often work closely in conjunction with each other.[7] As well, sometimes it is difficult to separate out financiers, spies, or arms dealers in order to know who is a combatant and who is a noncombatant, and accordingly what and who is a legitimate guerilla target.[8] Nonetheless, I argue that the distinction between a terrorist and an armed guerilla remains crucial to understanding Lessing's appraisal of these two very different postcolonial protagonists.

Terrorist "actions" are violent, but terrorists—unlike armed guerillas—do not engage and combat an army or police force directly. Rather, terrorists use indiscriminate violence to inflict maximum psychological (shock) effect on the public in order to destabilize the smooth functioning of a targeted political system and for messaging purposes. When successful at the street level, terrorist warfare is analogous to capturing and shaping the course of the ship of state. Both Alice Mellings and Tajwar Kakar, the protagonists of Lessing's 1980s fictional and journalistic texts, *The Good Terrorist* and *The Wind Blows Away Our Words,* respectively, use violent means to achieve political objectives; but fictional Londoner Alice Mellings, from the novel, should best be considered strictly as a terrorist, while Afghan Tajwar Kakar, an actual person discussed in a nonfiction work, should primarily be understood as a member of a nationalist armed guerilla unit.

THE LONDON TERRORISTS

Speaking of the Algerian resistance to French colonial rule, Sartre's preface to Fanon's *The Wretched of the Earth* justifies political violence: "perhaps, when your back is to the wall, you will let loose at last that new violence which is raised up in you by old, oft-repeated crimes."[9] Acts of resistance, including violence against oppression, are debated throughout Lessing's plots. Are such acts defensible? Do lofty ends legitimate compromising other lofty values as violent means including terrorism alter and transform the desired political ends?

Lessing's novel ironically called *The Good Terrorist* asks the reader to consider what constitutes a "good" or "not good" terrorist: as if to question why certain terrorist campaigns are perceived, at least by some, as viable, while others are not. The notion of a good terrorist (resistance fighter) can be located in the historical archive of anarchism. At the end of the nineteenth century, anarchists sought to undermine feudal power relations, for example in Czarist Russia, by way of tyrannicide. Noncivilian targets such as kings were selected with consideration and care. The anarchist wanted the masses to evaluate his actions as that of a heroic, valorous, larger-than-life individual, whom others would contrast with their own poverty-stricken, highly regulated, and powerless lives. The historical account of Ivan Kaliayev, who refrained from throwing a bomb into Grand Duke Sergei's carriage while he was accompanied by his family, represents this moral stance of the "good" terrorist. (Later without the Grand Duke's family at risk, the suicidal murder mission was accomplished.)[10]

The Good Terrorist describes two London bombings carried out by politicized squat members who constitute a loose terrorist cell. Alice Mellings's group plans to activate the initial bomb at night, thereby testing the power of the explosives being put together in the squat, without causing civilian casualties. Housemate and amateur bomb maker Jocelin "stud[ies] handbooks on how to be a good terrorist" (259–60). She produces her explosive devices from goods including those taken from arms "matérial" passing through the house adjacent to the squat, from which individuals set out for Russian paramilitary training camps, presumably to further other "heroic" revolutionary causes. The novel ironically minimizes the possible harm of terrorist violence by referring to Jocelin's bombs as "a variety of devices which she was concocting out of the books she referred to as 'recipe books'" (286–87). At the end of the tale, the "recipe" is "cooked," but the London terrorists fail. The bombings are not successfully carried out: the first does much more damage than expected, and the second detonates at the wrong time, killing the bomb carrier and innocent civilians, while not destroying any strongly recognizable, symbolic target.

The tale of *The Good Terrorist* seems to be modeled historically after the brief terrorist action of the Angry Brigade in England from 1970 to 1972. During the 1960s and 1970s there were a number of similar terrorist groups of young radicals throughout the Western world, including the Weathermen in the United States and the FLQ in Canada. This form of Western terrorism has been coined "groupuscular terrorism," a term that refers to the small, discrete activist groups, with a tendency to break up into parts, that spread across the Western world in the 1970s.[11] The British anarchist Angry Brigade was responsible for dozens of bombings and a series of bank robberies, but fell apart when some of its leading members were convicted in highly publicized criminal trials. Their subversive efforts did not succeed in garnering them a following of members, or in having their libertarian Communist message widely disseminated. The other historical source material for Doris Lessing's account of terrorism in England was that of the ever-present IRA, which targeted England in general and London in particular during the 1980s, the time of her writing *The Good Terrorist*.

At the outset of the novel, the reader initially sympathizes with Alice Mellings, the protagonist in *The Good Terrorist*. Alice is part of a group of unemployed, disenfranchised, younger adults in Thatcher's England. They form through a series of connected squats an entity called the CCU—Communist Centre Union. Alice's individual squat claims allegiance to established political subversive entities, even after two group emissaries are made unwelcome when they go to make petitions to the IRA in Ireland and the Communist Party in the Soviet Union. Alice initially engages the reader's sympathy through her resolute resourcefulness. She maintains the squat—cooks, cleans, and keeps the bill collectors at bay. The reader may consider Alice a "good" terrorist because her homemaking capacity and middle-class know-how make the squat livable. Without Alice's organization and communication skills, the poor and disenfranchised members of the squat would not have a working, camouflaged base or the monetary means to plan and carry out their political aims.

However, *The Good Terrorist* investigates in detail Alice's brand of terrorism and in the process dissects and rejects her revolutionary aspirations as infantile, misguided, and dangerous. Alice and her tiny group of "vanguard," mostly middle-class malcontents, are socially isolated. Their motives are fed by the need for personal recognition, more than any political desire for social change. These malcontents are driven by their belief that the world owes them more—more recognition, more happiness, more freedom. Alice's actions, Lessing seems to say, are symptomatic of her rearing. The best gloss on *The Good Terrorist* may be Lessing's comments at the end of chapter 2 of her autobiography, *Under My Skin*. There she talks of an almost instinctive assumption shared by many—particularly those on the Left who oppose "authority" and "the Establishment"—that happiness is their right and can be gauged in personal terms of measurable increase. "Millions of people in our time behave as if they have been made a promise—by whom? when?—that life must get freer, more honest, more comfortable, always better. . . . I feel I have been part of some mass illusion or delusion."[12] Lessing enacts her fictional assessment and dismissal of Alice's CCU groupuscular cell in a number of ways: through the use of vulgar and banal language, jokes, and familial domestic politics reproduced in the squat; through the use of Dorothy Mellings as her authorial voice; and through implied psychoanalytic diagnosis of Alice and her group.

The Good Terrorist examines the terrorist's morality, behavior, and language as influenced by the ordinary poor and disenfranchised. The novel's language is not heroic, but rather banal, partly because it is excessively descriptive concerning details of the flat life, such as people getting along, performing household chores, cooking, and repairing the electricity or plumbing. A method of understatement asks readers to make their own judgments as to the metaphorical applications of fecal matter, for instance. Referred to as such, "shit" is a motif in the text, introduced when, in order to make the squat habitable, a young black man, Jim, and Alice empty buckets of waste that occupy two rooms on the top floor of the house.[13] The toilets had been cemented in by the City Council. In burying the excrement, Alice is trying to deceive the authorities about the transient occupants and the deteriorated physical condition of the building. On a visit to the squat, police officers throw a bag of excrement toward Alice: "'This is what you like, isn't it?'

[one] guffawed, and flung, in a strong underarm action, a filled plastic bag into the hall. 'Shit to shit,' said the other" (315). In the end, rather than a positive valuation of Alice's character as resourceful or resolute, the reader is left with the police officer's comparison of Alice to a bag of shit.

The devaluation of language is explored further through mimicry, which all the characters participate in, even though they may not be consciously aware of it.[14] Faye and Roberta mimic British working-class roots. "As good as a music-hall turn: Faye the cockney lass and her feed. Roberta was not speaking cockney, but had a comfortable, accommodating homely voice with the sound of the North in it. Her own voice? No, it was a made-up one. Modelled on Coronation Street, probably" (27). In this meeting, which includes Faye, Roberta, Bert, Jasper, Pat, Jim, and Alice, "[t]he only other person in this room, apart from Alice, with his own voice, unmodified, was Jim, the genuine cockney" (29). Throughout the text, Alice is picking up on clues to disingenuousness or misrepresentation. Squat speech, then, is often banal or designed for effect like the latest fashion statement. Meanwhile, in order to "fit in" to a role within the squat, Alice struggles against her middle-class roots (including what Lessing would call Alice's own "small personal voice"). Alice must learn to participate in the bravado of her comrades. She also analyzes squat speech so as not to be trapped within a group political discourse of indoctrination.

The text of *The Good Terrorist*, I would argue, is modeled on the structural mechanics of popular jokes. Jokes structurally function on the fulcrum of a punchline where, as in the tipping movement of a teeter-totter, the expectations of the listener shift toward a second, usually unexpected and possibly disturbing, meaning. At first, through free indirect discourse, the authoritative, third-person narrative is aligned with Alice's consciousness. The reader relates sympathetically to an idealistic, Alice-in-Wonderland figure. Using the metaphor of the tipping point of the teeter-totter, the reader's sympathy for Alice teeters into disgust or detached indifference at the end of *The Good Terrorist*. The misfired or peccant bomb functions as the punchline, which firmly undermines the reader's sympathy for Alice, the thirty-six-year-old lost cause, and the other CCU members and their terrorist practice.[15]

Thematic concerns that the reader recalls from Lessing's earlier work are again set out in *The Good Terrorist*. In her early career, Doris Lessing, like many other Western leftist- and progressively minded people, looked to the Soviet Union for a model of human liberation. Most leftists, including Lessing, reevaluated their positions as information about Stalin's repressive regime was revealed by the 1956 Hungarian Revolution, by Nikita Khrushchev during the Twentieth Congress meetings, and by Russian writers, such as

5: London and Kabul

Alexander Solzhenitsyn in *The Gulag Archipelago*. Soviet power vis-à-vis the powerlessness of democratic Communist parties was similarly documented, for example, in *The Golden Notebook* (1962), which used a fictional newspaper account of Stalin's death to show its effect on protagonist Anna Wulf and her left-wing friends. The powerlessness of individual Western Communists is made light of through amusing or poignant descriptions of fantasized and "real" trips by characters in the novel to the Soviet Union on personal missions to tell Stalin and other Soviet officials how their Communist vision has lost credence. The Soviet Union also intimidates and attracts Alice's partner Jasper and housemate Bert in *The Good Terrorist* (115, 240–41). Their fantasy, of carrying out a personal journey to the Soviet Union, is mocked by another housemate, Pat: "They had it all worked out. They will say to the Intourist Guide: 'Comrades, we want to speak to someone in authority.' . . . The Intourist guide will of course say at once, 'Whom would you like to see, comrades? Comrade Andropov [General Secretary of the Soviet Communist Party, 1982–84]?'" (240).

The narrative from the above lines takes the form of a joke. The punchline regarding visiting Comrade Andropov occurs at the end of the fantasy sequence. The unexpected absurdity of Jasper and Bert's answer creates the reader's humorous response. While at first we can sympathize with Jasper and Bert as young idealists of high purpose, the reader on second thought can but wonder whether these two comrades might actually believe in the possibility of just such a high-level meeting (perhaps reported by the BBC). How inflated are their egos and how misguided are they to visualize their leadership role at the forefront of the proletariat? Would Jasper and Bert even comprehend the joke, which Pat construes? The double meaning contained in the joke relates to our heroes' fantasies and egos, as the young men's aspirations (supported by the author, then the reader) are let go of; and, as in the teeter-totter example, they and their ideals are dropped. The authority of Pat's view is upheld in the novel when she leaves the squat and undertakes Russian paramilitary training. Neither Jasper nor Bert is deemed adequate for such training by the IRA, the Soviets, or the leadership figures in No. 45, the paramilitary squat.

Alice also has strong personal aspirations. She wants to forgo both her middle-class society's and her family's frames of reference. Even so, her dependency is shown by her constantly stealing property and money from her divorced parents' homes and business. As her mother wryly observes, "it turned out that you spend your life exactly as I did. Cooking and nannying for other people" (329). While Alice wants to rid herself of her (divorced) family, she eventually comes to fear that she has—ironically—set her own "trap" in the squat, which is modeled on her family past: "This house, for which she had fought, she now felt as a trap, ready to deliver her back to Jasper, from whom she must escape" (268–69). Her ambivalence toward her father is mirrored in her nonsexual relationship over many years with homosexual partner Jasper. Jasper sleeps apart from her, and constantly seeks money from middle-class Alice for "cottaging, cruising" purposes (152). Jasper is physically hurtful toward her, yet she defers to him. From the first page, Jasper's "hand [repeatedly] shot out, and her wrist was encircled by hard bone. It hurt" (5), but Alice awaits a kind word or affirmation from Jasper. Jasper is a replacement father figure especially after her father has told Alice to go away, consequent on her stealing money from his firm and on her throwing a rock through his front window, narrowly missing his young daughter from his new marriage.

Decidedly, Alice's participation in bombing a public place involves a constitutive break from civil society and from Lessing's ideal—responsible human agency. Alice had felt guilty already for not satisfying her parents' expectations of her, especially her mother's ambitions. The bombings, particularly the one in which a fellow comrade, Faye, is killed, signify Alice's final separation from "all the poor silly ordinary people in the world . . . her father . . . [who] was too awful to waste time on . . . [h]er mother . . . she might have said a final goodbye to her, instead of just having had one of their silly quarrels!" (366).[16] Furthermore, with the bombing, the fracturing of her actual family is repeated within the terror cell "commune," her created "family" (232).

Years before, social issues, notably over power disparities, had propelled both Dorothy and her daughter to political action. Dorothy describes herself and Alice as "peasants" in comparison to leaders, who resemble efficient bureaucrats: "This world is run by people who know how to do things. They know how things work. They are *equipped* [educated]. Up there, there's a layer of people who run everything. But we—we're just peasants" (330). The reference to being peasants reminds the reader of Mao's leadership of the peasant revolution (the Cultural Revolution), Western Marxist-Leninist (Maoist) youth, or perhaps a line from John Lennon's song "Working Class Hero," in which he belts out, "you're still fucking peasants as far as I can see." And Dorothy had once agreed with the expected youthful response, to not being able to "do anything," to just "Do It" (which was the rallying call of Jerry Rubin and the Yippies of the '70s). Now, she cynically finishes the above thought: "We don't understand what's going on, and we can't do anything" (330).

Dorothy knows from experience that Alice will not "pull it [capitalist imperialism] all *down*" (330) by attending pickets. Referring to their decades of political activism, Dorothy says to her longtime friend Zoë Devlin: "It's for kicks. It's for *fun*. . . . people picketing, or marching or demonstrating. They are having a marvellous time. And if they are beaten up by the police so much the better" (335). By her comments, Dorothy dismisses her own previous activism and likewise Alice's group for demonstrating and picketing (even before events escalate to the bombings). Dorothy Mellings most clearly embodies Lessing's critique of 1960s politics; through the mother's dismissal of Alice, Lessing directs derisive humor at this "grown-up," postwar, baby boomer. In Lessing's view, Alice's revolutionary ideals invite a self-destructive outcome in the same manner fated for 1960s-style radicalism.[17]

The Good Terrorist reveals the lingering drive for personal recognition through political action, from picketing to planning urban terrorist attacks. Activism is the group's way of gaining recognition in the media, whose recording of their attacks the group scrutinizes as a process of group identity formation. When the first bombing is reported in "a little paragraph in the *Guardian*" as the antics of "hooligans," the group's ridiculous reaction is "We'll show them" (312). A paragraph in the local *Advertiser* is taken by the group as "a snub . . . another in a long series of belittlings of what they really were. . . . They were murderous with the need to impose themselves, prove their power" (314).

Reacting against the lack of media attention, Jocelin explains the proposed use of in-house-assembled electronic controls in the second explosive device: "it's a question of how to make the greatest impact . . . this way, it'll be front page in all the papers tomorrow and on the News tonight" (346).[18] Jocelin's second peccant bomb indiscriminately kills and maims citizens in the London street. The timer for the device is deliberately set by squat member Faye to kill herself and others not at the site chosen by the group. This is Faye's third suicide attempt, which her lesbian lover Roberta attributes to Faye having been "a battered baby" (121), to which Alice quips mockingly in return: "Well, I suppose Faye will die of it one of these days. She has tried to commit suicide, hasn't she?" (122). The squat's lofty ideals of proletarian revolution are subverted by Faye's personal desire for freedom from the complex pain of her life. Faye's fanatical death wish is evident in her three suicide attempts and her final plan, to indiscriminately murder other civilians.

But chaos in the group is highlighted also by Alice's warning to the authorities—a farcical subplot—that a bomb blast is imminent, a bomb she attributes falsely to the IRA, which dismisses the amateurish effort, threatening to "knee-cap those who committed such acts in their name" (364). Alice conveniently forgets her call made to authorities from the bomb site, just as she conveniently forgets the fact of her involvement with selling her family's home. When the media attributes the second bombing to the IRA, as Alice had told them, Jocelin responds, "'What a fucking nerve.' 'Absolutely,' said Alice, not connecting her telephone call with this development. Then, after a few minutes, listening to the indignation, the frustration of the others, she did connect it, and she realised that she could never tell them what she had done. Never. She never would be trusted again" (360).

Faye—who committed suicide in the bomb blast—earlier appreciated Alice's perceptual confusion as akin to that of the dreamy namesake story figure. "A wonder, she is . . . Alice the Wonder, the wondrous Alice . . ." (82, ellipsis in original). Not only does Alice Mellings play with the meaning of words, as does Carroll's Alice, but also, like Alice in *Through the Looking-Glass,* Alice Mellings inhabits her own fantasy world: "When her mind started to dazzle and to puzzle, frantically trying to lay hold of something stable," then Alice "allowed herself . . . to slide back into her childhood where she dwelt pleasurably on some scene or other that she had smoothed and polished and painted over and over again with fresh colour until it was like walking into a story that began, 'Once upon a time there was a little girl called Alice, with her mother Dorothy'" (368). After she has taken experiences and misrepresented them to herself and others, she slips into states of imagined security and storybook solipsism.

Alice does not succeed in maturing beyond childish interactions and understanding. For instance, near the end of the novel Alice reveals to a British spy—Peter Cecil—the existence of a Russian spy—Gordon O'Leary—and evidence of arms passing through No. 45, the adjacent squat. By divulging the identity of the Russian agent in this spy and counterspy sequence, Alice has put herself, the Russian agent, and her terrorist cell at risk of prison or worse. Severing its close association with Alice's maneuverings, speculating on Alice's conduct, the story leaves her: "Smiling gently, a mug of very strong sweet tea in her hand, looking this morning like a nine-year-old girl who has had, perhaps, a bad dream, the poor baby sat waiting for it to be time to go out and meet the professionals [the spies]" (370). The reader retreats from the work, into which she or he has been led, in order to consider the story from a greater distance. Any sympathy with the main, focalized character (a form of revolutionary hero worship or heroine identification perhaps, encoded in the novel form) seems unwarranted, as Alice is revealed finally as a disturbed neurotic criminal, in need of "professional" psychiatric assistance.

Meanwhile, Jocelin the bomb maker remains at large, capable of deploying further terrorist explosives. Previously Alice had held onto Jocelin as her heroine or "touchstone," but an innocent reading of their accord does not hold: "And herself, Alice? Did Jocelin despise her too? It occurred to her that she was using Jocelin as a touchstone, a judgment-point. As though Jocelin were the key to everything? Well, it was she who was at work on the bombs, or whatever" (291). Jocelin is, in Kleinian psychoanalysis, a good-mother replacement for the one who is perceived as bad, for Dorothy, whom Alice is attempting to exorcize.[19] Melanie Klein explains the psychological mechanism whereby we construct by projection good-mother figures, who theoretically compensate us for the repressive wrongs committed by perceived bad-mother figures, whose attributes we also assemble. The third-person narrator admonishes Alice's need of support and self-understanding: "Oh yes, Alice did know that she forgot things, but not how badly, or how often" (368). Forgetful and scattered, Alice is easily manipulated, outplayed, and in need of mothering.

This coy narrative requires readers to slightly distance their vantage point from the third-person narrator in order to diagnose patterns in the group's or Alice's behavior, such as Alice's need of mothering by strong female squatmates. Lessing explains that she was more detached than usual in writing *The Good Terrorist*.[20] This analytic detachment is a necessary part of the assessment process for the reader's grasp of Alice as a "good"—now recast as a childlike—terrorist. In the end, the narrative voice passes disparaging judgment on Alice Mellings as a Western malcontent, who desperately desires personal gratification and reward through terrorist enterprise.

SEARCHING OUT AFGHAN FEMALE GUERILLAS

At issue in *The Good Terrorist* is Lessing's consideration of terrorism within Western political struggle. Should one conclude that a slave's violent reaction is sometimes necessary to defeat an oppressor, but that Alice's problem is that she imagines an oppressor where one does not exist in order to do battle and, thereby, satisfy emotional needs? The theme of examining women and terror during the course of Thatcher's England continues in *The Wind Blows Away Our Words,* but, in contrast, Lessing's journalistic work admires the heroism of Moslem women and men against occupation. The cause of the muhjahidin rebels against the Soviet occupying army, Lessing seems to say, is arguably reasonable.

Lessing tailors two distinct narrative forms for her appraisal of Alice Mellings and Tajwar Kakar as very different postcolonial subjects. Through detached realism, in *The Good Terrorist,* she is examining the cultural and psychological factors that make disaffected Western middle-class youth become terrorists. Her careful analysis of misguided youthful militant activity in the novel contrasts with the journalistic intentions in *The Wind Blows Away Our Words,* which are to make an emotional appeal to Western readers, in order to draw them into a sympathetic appreciation of the 1980s guerilla struggle within Afghanistan and the situation of Afghan women and child refugees in Pakistan.

The persuasive argument regarding violence for political ends in *The Wind Blows Away Our Words* is different from the novelistic dismissal of terrorist activity in *The Good Terrorist*. Lessing seems to qualify her conclusions in *The Good Terrorist* in her written recollections of a charity-sponsored journey to Pakistan in 1986 where she sought out freedom fighters whom she depicts as resistance figures, rather than terrorists. Published two years after *The Good Terrorist, The Wind Blows Away Our Words* commends the muhjahidin rebels (subsequently part of the Taliban) in their struggle against the Soviet occupation. In the text (dedicated "[t]o the gallant people of Afghanistan"), Lessing records her visits to the Afghan refugee camps in Pakistan during September 1986 on behalf of Afghan Relief. "[A]ssociated with the Afghan struggle for some years, through Afghan relief" (34–35), she was invited "to come and see . . . so as to write articles about the conditions of the refugees and about the muhjahidin, among whom, rumours said, were women fighting in all-female groups" (39). Lessing notes with particular concern the hospitals of Pakistan full of children with hands and feet blown off by "most horrifying" Russian antipersonnel bombs disguised as toys or fruit (33–34). Her text "[d]ocuments" the refugee plight that began in 1979 when the people began to "flow out" of Afghanistan into Iran and Pakistan, and the "Resistance" to the Afghan Communists, followed by the Russian occupation, began.

Lessing describes the muhjahidin struggles in "The Resistance—called 'the Jihad' by the Afghans, the Holy War" (33): for seven years since the Russian occupation,

> the muhjahidin have fought without aid from outside, though very recently more arms have been reaching them; never enough, however, and never as much as the western powers, particularly America, have claimed. Some of the most extraordinary battles of our time have been fought between armies of modern tanks, and ragged men, women and children armed with homemade grenades, catapults, stones, ancient rifles—and the Afghans have won, again and again. The Afghans have even brought down helicopters with hand grenades tied to kites. (34)

5: London and Kabul

In an entry from December 1986 she notes that Stingers (American ground-to-air missiles) reaching the muhjahidin "must be doing everything for their morale" (139).

She records favorably her meeting with a female member of the muhjahidin. Through the entire text her small group (composed of three women—Lessing, a Texan, and an Afghan born in Britain—and also a male Swedish filmmaker) makes unsatisfactory attempts to film alone female fighters. Islamic laws of Purdah limit access to these women. "At last we found a woman [Tajwar Kakar] we could interview and film without supervision by some self-appointed monitor. What had previously seemed so hard to do [in refugee camps policed by mullahs] became simple as these things do when they happen after long difficulties" (136).[21]

A monthly bulletin published by the London "Afghan Information Centre," which is included as part of Lessing's text, admires "Tajwar Sultan, A Resistance Fighter." As a teacher, Kakar reportedly provided schoolchildren with rubber balloons and toy explosives in order to disrupt the first-anniversary-observance ceremony of the Communist regime in April 1979: "It was panic. The parading party members ran for cover. The official tribune was in confusion. Many people were hurt in the rush. Even the wife of the provincial governor was injured and admitted to a hospital. The ceremony was cancelled" (146). This description stands in contrast to the repulsion felt against carnage and death caused by bombs going off in London in *The Good Terrorist* or the antipersonnel bombs maiming children and civilians in *The Wind Blows Away Our Words*.

Usually Lessing's fiction champions the individual who opposes group pressure or coercion. Lessing's comment, applauding "all Afghanistan rising against the Russians" (33) as a measure of Afghan communal spirit and determination against centuries of imperial war and occupation, does not agree with her lifelong value for individual thinking against the pressures of group consensus. Such individualism is promoted in her 1985 Massey Lectures, *Prisons We Choose to Live Inside*, where she credits those rare individuals who can withstand social pressures, whether ordinary or coercive.

The Afghan resistance "intensified what was only an aspect of their character"—fanaticism within the group personality (135)—but the group she holds responsible for (its incapacity to hear and inflexibility to act upon) Afghan suffering is a "largely indifferent" Western media and their consumers, to whom her text is addressed (34). Lessing links Western media consumption and spectacle: "What has happened is that we have been conditioned to see Hitler's Germany, which lasted for thirteen years, a very short time, as the archetype of evil for our time; have accepted this continual hammering on one nerve" (169). Accordingly, absolute evil is construed as the truth, which causes the media to favor horror and spectacle—for example, the December 2003 dramatic arrest of a disheveled Saddam Hussein from a tiny farmhouse cellar in Iraq, or the subsequent release of a film of his December 2006 hanging—thereby pushing aside other important social justice issues from public view.

Explaining our incapacity to solve deep-seated differences except through war, Elaine Scarry has examined the conundrum of human apathy toward destruction. Indifference and difficulty comprehending the complex issues about war that Scarry raises in *The Body in Pain* may prevent our critical engagement with Lessing's (fictional) London situation and the (actual) Afghan struggle.[22] The contrast between Lessing's texts can be seen in the focus of each: *The Good Terrorist* succeeds in interrogating Alice's psychological motivations, while showing the threat of such drives as real and devastating. *The Wind Blows Away Our Words,* a documentary, attempts to draw sympathy from the West toward the long-suffering Afghan people, then under repressive Soviet occupation. This journalistic description is sociological and historical, although, in searching out Kakar, it shares with *The Good Terrorist* an interest in women's involvement in political violence.

Here one should note that Lessing's search for Kakar has historical relevance; until recently, the Western press described Islamic women as imprisoned in the bhurka, not as disguised bomb carriers.[23] Meanwhile, she argues against seeing difference only in terms of conflict and provides other relevant information that the Western media were not conveying.[24] Lessing warned that our "ignorance" concerning Islam could foster the extremism she recognized as frightening to the West:

> We are full of ignorance and prejudice and so are they [Moslem countries]. It is unfortunate that the West, particularly America, associates the words "Islam," "Moslem" with "Terrorist," or with Fundamentalist Islam, such as we read about in connection with Khomeini and Ghadafi. This is only one strand of Islam and not, in my view, the most important one, though it may, alas, become the most important. (46)

Lessing's prescience in examining ideological political differences being played out in war is shown in this work. She foregrounds the benefits to the Afghan refugees should the international community become involved as a result of her journalistic intervention and has the foresight to warn of the importance of international monitors if the refugees are sent home, in order to prevent slaughter (139–41).

5: London and Kabul

Unrelenting analysis through fiction and documentary is Lessing's typical style. In *The Good Terrorist* and *The Wind Blows Away Our Words,* violence is understood as a political option. The often-quoted political philosopher Hannah Arendt dismisses the notion of necessary aggression and violence in human relations as errant biologism.[25] In her book-length study, Arendt queries violence as a means to solving human problems: "The practice of violence, like all action, changes the world, but the most probable change is to a more violent world."[26] While Lessing concurs with Arendt's view about the unreasonableness and the futility of political violence in the long term, Lessing explores a notion of primal aggression in the form of reaction against oppression in her account of Afghanistan.

Acting against known destructiveness, especially oppression in her life, Tajwar Kakar in her biography admits both violence and dialogue as viable in the political process. In June 2002—sixteen years after Lessing met Kakar in Pakistan, and after the end of the Russian occupation and subsequent to the War on Terror and the Western-led attacks against Afghanistan—when the Loya Jirga, the Afghan grand tribal council, convened in order to decide Afghanistan's government, Tajwar Kakar, as Deputy Minister of Women's Affairs, opposed the "powerful warlords" during the assembly. She called for their removal from the council, arguing: "Many of the warlords in control of the provinces are the Mujahideen, freedom fighters who fought against the Soviets. Now some of them are fighting hard to subjugate women."[27] Advocating on behalf of children in her role within Women's Affairs, from May 8–10, 2002, Kakar was one of five Afghan delegates to the United Nations for the General Assembly Special Session on Children.[28]

Lessing's account of Tajwar Kakar looks favorably at her early efforts to release Afghans from Russian control. Since Kakar has always fought alongside Western interests—"the good guys"—she might not be considered a terrorist by definition, as some countries following the United States' lead define terrorism as any military action by a subgroup against a liberal democracy or Western-leaning government. However, most academics and Lessing's texts add further complexity to the American definition of terrorist. The '80s Tajwar Kakar could be construed as a "state-sponsored terrorist," since the muhjahidin were primarily armed by the United States and financed largely by its OPEC allies.[29] However, I suggest that Tajwar Kakar and the muhjahidin do not fit neatly into any terrorist category—including state-sponsored terrorists—as most of their subversive activities were those of a combatant or armed guerilla of the resistance.

Today's terrorist attacks target civilians in their normal (often consumerist) routines and perceived political somnolence. Unlike Alice Mellings, who is, strictly speaking, a terrorist (of the Western groupuscular strain) whose role is that of a bomb carrier, Tajwar Kakar does not seek to blow up civilian targets. The muhjahidin fought only the Russian army. Even when creating havoc in the Soviet Anniversary Parade for maximum psychological effect, the explosives Kakar's students detonated were mostly harmless, and the street scene could be imagined as guerilla street theater. Doris Lessing calls Tajwar Kakar a resistance fighter, which seems a latter-day reworking of the term guerilla fighter. Perhaps resistance fighter captures better the essence of an exemplary postcolonial subject who first resists colonial oppression as a nationalist and then resists sexual oppression by the very same nationalist liberators. As a protean being, Tajwar Kakar employs tactics that vary according to the circumstances and include a variety of nonviolent and violent means.

Although based on different historical times, both *The Good Terrorist* and *The Wind Blows Away Our Words* are worthy of reflection in the post-9-11 millennium. In comparison to *The Good Terrorist,* the present composition of Western groupuscular terrorist cells has changed, as they consist mostly of angry male Islamic youth. Another difference is that the (tapped) Internet has come to replace the (tapped) telephone as the communication device of choice. Nonetheless, the terrorist's aspirations of using bombs to shock the unaware general public into political action and into facilitating change has not radically altered since the writing of *The Good Terrorist.* Just as Lessing scrutinizes the CCU cell in *The Good Terrorist,* the reader of "Current Events" should be skeptical of the efficacy of Western Islamic terrorists arguably attempting to further the cause of decolonization in the Middle East by targeting Western sites. It is likely that the reaction of the public to the terrorist cell within its midst is to cower and kowtow to increasingly militarized, popularly elected governments.

In the developing-world national liberation struggles, the guerrilla fighter such as Tajwar Kakar is a familiar, repeated role, a role often cast in heroic tales. The trajectory of this historical timeline of armed resistance to colonial oppression goes back at least to the American and French Revolutions, and in more recent times includes the liberation of South Africa from apartheid (with the assistance of Cuban troops and weapons). Even so, times change, and in our postmodern world of simulation and game-playing scenarios, this reader cannot but wonder about the future role of armed guerilla fighters in national liberation struggles. It is ambiguous whose interests are served by these games of conflict: whether guerrilla resistance benefits more the arms dealers, the competing global and regional powers (fighting proxy wars), or the truly impoverished peoples of the world.

5: London and Kabul

NOTES

1. There is a suggestion that some of her intense emotional identification with Afghanistan's plight also came out in her writing of *The Fifth Child*. See Sedge Thomson's interview with Lessing where Lessing talks of fuel for *The Fifth Child*: "Drawn to a Type of Landscape," *Doris Lessing: Conversations,* edited by Earl G. Ingersoll (Princeton, NJ: Ontario Review Press, 1994), 190. Hereafter cited as *Conversations.*

2. Doris Lessing, *The Wind Blows Away Our Words and Other Documents Relating to the Afghan Resistance* (New York: Vintage, 1987), 49. She refers to Sufism in an interview with Amir Mohamedi, leader of the (liberal) Hiriquat Party: "I have read enough about Islam to know some of its basic ideas, history, and great historical figures, and was not surprised that he [Mohamedi] looked like pictures of [the Sufis'] Rumi or El-Ghazali, the very image of a medieval saint" (*Our Words,* 65).

3. *Our Words,* 70–72, 74, 97, 100–101, 123. Further, Lessing has stated her attraction to a "*type* of landscape. When I went to Granada in Spain, I suddenly remembered the mountains around Kermanshah, where I was born, a town which is now, I'm told, battered flat by war, a very ancient trading town, which is now in ruins. It is a landscape which is high, dry, and dusty. That is, in fact, the landscape I had in Zimbabwe—sorry, in the old Southern Rhodesia" (Sedge Thomson, "Drawn to a Type of Landscape," in *Conversations,* 189). My thanks to Phyllis Sternberg Perrakis for reminding me of the salient interviews in Ingersoll's collection; and to both her and Debrah Raschke for searching commentary on my terrorist discussion.

4. Guevara is identified as a revolutionary "type" in *The Good Terrorist* (London: Cape, 1985). Caroline "was in love with a young Che Guevara from the L.S.E. [London School of Economics].... She looked ... full of secret and unscrupulous satisfactions" (288).

5. Robert J. C. Young, *Postcolonialism* (Oxford: Oxford University Press, 2003), 16–20.

6. Charles Townshend, *Terrorism* (Oxford: Oxford University Press, 2002), 5.

7. Noam Chomsky, *9-11* (New York: Seven Stories Press, 2002); Noam Chomsky, *The Culture of Terrorism* (Boston, MA: South End Press, 1988); Edward W. Said, "The Essential Terrorist," in *Blaming the Victims: Spurious Scholarship and the Palestinian Question,* edited by Edward W. Said and Christopher Hitchens (London: Verso, 1988), 149–58. Nonetheless, left-wing Communists are careful to distinguish their form of "collective" revolutionary action from that of "individual" terrorist attacks. In *The Good Terrorist,* Bert, a member of Alice Mellings's terrorist cell, decontextualizes snippets of Lenin's writings on terrorism and violence to justify the group's car bombing (345, 362). However, Lenin clearly noted the difference between the organization and discipline required by a mass communist movement and that of anarchic terrorist cells. See Alice Ridout's "'What Is the Function of the Storyteller?': The Relationship between *Why* and *How* Lessing Writes" in Part Two of this collection for further discussion of Lessing's engagement, then disillusionment, with Communism [editors' note].

8. Friedrich Dürrenmatt's 1980s *The Assignment: Or, On the Observing of the Observer of the Observers,* trans. Joel Agee (New York: Random House, 1988), is a fascinating fictional analysis of arms dealers, spies and counterspies, state terrorists, and insurgents. Dürrenmatt deconstructs the principle of observation and representation in

realist accounts of terrorism (which would include *The Good Terrorist*). "[M]an's bondage [which] consisted of being observed" is situated within "a system of computers, for what was observing was two cameras connected to two computers observed by two further computers and fed into computers connected to *those* computers" (Dürrenmatt, 109). In Dürrenmatt's view, terrorists and other individuals perform within simulations, game-play scenarios, or operational projects, in which frames their acts must be interpreted. See Rubenstein's remarks on how "Lessing has continued to surprise her readers by remaining several steps ahead of their expectations," in "Notes for Proteus: Doris Lessing Reads the *Zeitgeist*," in Part One of this volume [editors' note]. The comparisons with Chomsky's social criticism and Dürrenmatt's novel show her contributing already in the 1980s to the understanding of terrorism.

9. Jean-Paul Sartre, Preface to *The Wretched of the Earth*, by Frantz Fanon, trans. Constance Farrington (New York: Grove Press, 1966), 26.

10. Townshend underscores the importance of Lessing's novel for its discussion of this notion of the "good terrorist" (20–21). For his discussion of the infamous attack on Grand Duke Sergei, see Townshend, 58. "Terrorism" or "terrorist" is a category assigned by others; likewise, Alice "could not remember a point when she had said, 'I am a terrorist. I don't mind being killed'" (*GT*, 367).

11. For a discussion of groupuscular terrorism, see Townshend, 66–73. Lessing has identified the 1983 Harrods bombing as a specific source for the car bombing in *The Good Terrorist*. See Margaret Scanlan, *Plotting Terror: Novelists and Terrorists in Contemporary Fiction* (Charlottesville: University Press of Virginia, 2001), 173–75, for a review of historically specific issues and other incidents related to *The Good Terrorist*.

12. Lessing, *Under My Skin: Volume One of My Autobiography, to 1949* (New York: HarperCollins, 1994), 16.

13. The most repeated pejorative adjective in the text is "shitty," used especially by Alice, but also by the other squat members to refer to "fascists," meaning ordinary British citizens. The group dismisses those who do not share their vision of the end of British colonial rule in Ireland, which they imagine will be shaped by their Communist ideals (especially about shared resources).

14. Scanlan develops a thorough reading of language manipulation in *The Good Terrorist*. In her view, "The welcomed return to earth in *The Good Terrorist* [after Lessing's *Canopus in Argos* series] is accompanied by a renewed sense of speech differences, but also by a heightened sense that the voice in which one speaks may not be a spontaneous authentic expression of a personality but a deception" (79). Scanlan adds, "[w]hat attracts the novelist to her subject is a fascination with the inaudibility of personal voices, with the fragility of printed books in a world where the electronic media accent our speech and feed our violence" (91). In particular, Lessing seems to show how group mentality and above all group language carries Alice and the other members along. See Lessing's comments about this power of group mentality in relation to *The Good Terrorist* in her interview with Claire Tomalin, "Watching the Angry and Destructive Hordes Go By," in *Conversations*, 175, and in her interview with Michael Upchurch, "Voice of England, Voice of Africa," *in Conversations*, 226–27. Also, Susan Watkins in "Writing in a Minor Key: Doris Lessing's Late-Twentieth-Century Fiction" in Part Three of this collection explores how narrative choices affect the politics of terror [editors' note].

5: *London and Kabul*

15. *The Good Terrorist* falls into a long tradition of using the peccant bomb in fictional writings about terrorism. As with Joseph Conrad's *The Secret Agent,* in *The Good Terrorist,* the terrorist's bomb misfires, leaving the symbolic target intact, but killing the bomb carrier. See Conrad, *The Secret Agent: A Simple Tale,* edited by Peter Lancelot Mallios (New York: Modern Library, 2004). One cannot but hear echoes in *The Good Terrorist* of Conrad's *The Secret Agent* Adolf Verloc, in his failed attempt to blow up the symbolic location of the Greenwich observatory. In both Conrad's and Lessing's novels, the effects of the misfired bomb are particularly gruesome. See Barbara Arnett Melchiori, "Peccant Engines," in *Terrorism in the Late Victorian Novel* (London: Croom Helm, 1985), 59–83. American contemporary of Lessing Mary McCarthy similarly uses a peccant device as a means to end her terrorist novel, *Cannibals and Missionaries* (San Diego: Harcourt, 1991), wherein almost all of the members of the terrorist cell, hostages, and famous works of art are conveniently blown away.

It is interesting to see *The Good Terrorist* as demonstrating the workings of reading conventions, which Wolfgang Iser describes in *The Implied Reader: Patterns of Communication in Prose Fiction from Bunyan to Beckett* (Baltimore: Johns Hopkins University Press, 1980). The reader must follow clues, ones that Alice may be missing, in order to judge Alice as the book's "good terrorist" or "bad terrorist." Iser describes the manipulation of the reader in the reading process: "As the literary text involves the reader in the formation of illusion and the simultaneous formation of the means whereby the illusion is punctured, reading reflects the process by which we gain experience" (Iser, 290). The reader's sustained curiosity is necessary for a full appreciation of Alice's amateur terrorist group in No. 43 Old Mill Road, which operates in tandem with No. 45, an arms and information distribution point associated with paramilitary training camps and a Russian spy network. Iser's narrative theory of illusion-puncturing supplements my discussion of secondary meaning revealed in everyday jokes and irony.

16. Lessing seems to satirize Alice's appalling behavior toward Dorothy Mellings, which Alice justifies through her use of bogus language such as calling her mother a "shitty old fascist" (330). Alice is so duped by ideology that she cannot remember her own actions, an enigma that baffles her mother: "Alice could remember nothing of that [calls she made to the estate agent about selling the family home]. Dorothy could not believe Alice did not remember. For the thousandth time the situation was recurring . . . Alice . . . thinking that her mother maliciously made things up; while Dorothy sighed and pursued interesting thoughts about the pathology of lying" (326). See Lessing's comments on her relationship with her mother at the end of the second chapter of *Under My Skin* (15–17), where she also speaks of girls' attitudes toward their mothers and the contemporary sense of entitlement she questions.

17. Jonah Raskin, "Doris Lessing at Stony Brook: An Interview," in *A Small Personal Voice: Essays, Reviews, Interviews,* edited by Paul Schlueter (New York: Vintage, 1975), 71–73.

18. A trestle table, like the one the reader may recall for Communist Party affiliate Anna Wulf's four notebooks in *The Golden Notebook,* is used for Jocelin's bomb preparation in *The Good Terrorist:* "On the long table in front of Jocelin were four nasty little devices, identical, ranged side by side, and looking rather like outsize and complicated sardine tins" (336–37). Other fiction writers and their critics have similarly alluded to and

speculated about the connection between author and terrorist. For an in-depth analysis of the author-terrorist connection through a variety of texts, see Scanlan, *Plotting Terror.*

19. Hanna Segal, *Klein* (Brighton, England: Harvester, 1979).

20. See the Lessing interview by Thomas Frick where he asks Lessing about her "detached realism" in *The Good Terrorist* ("Caged by the Experts," in *Conversations,* 160). Lessing attributes the detachment of the observer in *The Good Terrorist* to her age. "It was probably due to my advanced age. We do get detached" (161). Realist detachment facilitates exploration of the terrorist personality and experience in *The Good Terrorist.* In my dissertation, I argue that Lessing's style of realism changes with *The Diaries of Jane Somers, The Good Terrorist,* and *The Fifth Child,* and one characteristic is the author's increased attention to the way in which "reality" is known and represented in fiction (Sandra Singer, "Doris Lessing's Fiction and Contemporary Cultural Theorists" [PhD diss., University of Cambridge, 1992], 222–46).

21. Lessing in *Our Words* eventually questioned the goals of searching out female resistance fighters: "this interest of ours . . . had come to seem frivolous, even typical western sensationalism, or gimmickry. What did it matter who was fighting? . . . For them it is the fight that counts" (138).

22. Elaine Scarry, *The Body in Pain: The Making and Unmaking of the World* (Oxford: Oxford University Press, 1985). In *The Body in Pain,* Scarry understands war as an "injuring contest" where differences not resolved by language are tackled with damaging force (114). She contrasts inflicting pain in torture and war, which destroys language, with the creation of the world by the return of the sentient being who interprets the physical trials of war through language.

23. *Our Words* depicts the bhurka as clothing for deception: "it goes without saying that this bhurka is used for all kinds of dangerous or shady transactions. The authorities on the frontiers between Pakistan and Afghanistan look at hands and feet: is this a muhjahid or a journalist trying to get in to Afghanistan?" (102).

24. Lessing describes in *Our Words* approaching her agent, Jonathan Clowes, in order to speak against an "Everyman" series presentation on television of "the mujahidin as crazed, drugged fanatics, babbling about their rights to a paradisal bliss" (159). She wanted to repair this distorted television image by speaking about her recent visit to Pakistan, but the television program "and two others said in effect, 'No, Afghanistan is just a bore.' 'No one is interested in Afghanistan.' This neatly illustrates the media's way of sheltering behind attitudes they have themselves created" (160).

25. Hannah Arendt, *On Violence* (New York: Harcourt, 1970), 59–66.

26. Ibid., 80.

27. Fariba Nawa, "Afghan Women Debate the Terms of Their Future," Women's eNews, June 30, 2002, http://www.womensnews.org/story/the-world/020630/afghan-women-debate-the-terms-their-future (accessed March 17, 2010). See also Farah Hiwad, "Afghanistan: Tajwar Kakar—Fighting for Women and Freedom (Part 4)," RFE/RL Newsline, March 5, 2004, http://www.rferl.org/featuresarticle/2004/3/FE443C0B-0B4B-48B8-BEBB-727E653CC158.html (accessed July 12, 2009); and Alexander Smoltczyk, "Afghanistan: Operation Freedom," *World Press Review* 50.4 (April 2003), http://www.worldpress.org/article_model.cfm?article_id=1108&dont=yes (accessed July 12, 2009).

5: London and Kabul

28. Manoel de Almeida e Silva, "Press Briefing," UN News Centre, May 7, 2002, http://www.un.org/apps/news/infocus/afghanistan/infocusnews.asp? NewsID=174&sID=1 (accessed July 12, 2009).

29. State-sponsored terrorism is facilitated, according to Chomsky in *The Culture of Terrorism*, when the "enormous economic and propaganda resources of the dominant (often foreign) society [are] combined with a depressed economy, ethnic rivalries, religious controls, exploitation of fear and ignorance, a mounting cycle of violence and other factors" (83). The "U.S. [in El Salvador and Nicaragua] has organized and directs *a terrorist force* [the Contras in Nicaragua, for example] that must use violence to achieve the ends of the foreign master and the local elites that rely on external power, unable to enter into a political struggle since they have nothing to offer the population beyond a renewal of misery and subordination" (Chomsky, 93, emphasis added).

6

The Porous Border between Fact and Fiction, Empathy and Identification in Doris Lessing's *The Cleft*

PHYLLIS STERNBERG PERRAKIS

As she approaches the end of her ninth decade, Doris Lessing continues to search for new and appropriate forms to express her late-life creativity.[1] Very often these forms are experimental and exploratory, involving the crossing of various kinds of boundaries, of genre, gender, and even of species.[2] These crossings almost invariably involve characters in difficult or painful experiences that detach them from old ways of thinking or being and open them up to the possibility of new kinds of speculation and growth. In this essay I argue that in *The Cleft* (2007)[3] Lessing portrays the porous nature of all three borders (genre, gender, and species) in her fabular tale of the supposedly first people, the all-female Clefts, and their offspring, the first males. The crucial feature of the fable that mediates the reader's response to the gender-stereotyped "pre-people" characteristics of the Clefts and males[4] is its narration through the lens of the older Roman Senator and historian, Transit. Transit's narrative, itself a genre crossing that combines fact and fiction, history and literature, fits what Linda Hutcheon calls "historiographic metafiction."[5] Not only are postmodern novels "intensely self-reflexive but . . . also [they] . . . re-introduce historical context into metafiction and problematize the entire question of historical knowledge."[6] Transit's narrative raises the very questions about the history/literature divide and the borders of truth/fact/fiction that Hutcheon addresses in her discussion of the status of historiographic metafiction. Transit's memoir, set in the context of first-century Rome, both constructs and questions the gender assumptions of his time, while his struggles to narrate the Clefts' story from surviving millennium-old fragments capture a historian's efforts to decipher, verify, and interpret his material. Both narrative layers suggest the porous border between history and fiction. Indeed, we will see below that Transit is self-consciously aware that the ancient scrolls he is working with are already the product of interpretation and fiction-making.[7]

In working with these ancient fragments, Transit must struggle not only with the remoteness of the records of the Clefts but also with the horrific nature of the story they tell—the atrocities that result from the Clefts' sudden new capacity to give birth to male children. Because these records deal with two levels of trauma—the Clefts' response to overwhelming, traumatic change and the males' response to physical and psychological abuse—Transit's role as a historian is a complex one. He must respond with sensitivity to the brutal events described without becoming too implicated in their horrors. Dominick LaCapra calls this difficult narrative task "empathetic unsettlement."[8] This "desirable empathy" involves a "mode of representation . . . that inhibits or prevents extreme objectification and harmonizing narratives."[9] Objectification "denies or forecloses empathy"[10] by distancing or detaching us from others' horrific experiences so that we are not made uncomfortable by their pain. Harmonizing narratives are those narrations of extreme events "from which we derive reassurance or a benefit,"[11] using the terrible suffering of others for our own well-being—for example, for "something career-enhancing, 'spiritually' uplifting, or identity-forming for oneself or one's group."[12] I will argue that Transit, like the responsible historians of extreme events discussed by LaCapra, manages (usually) to create an experience of "empathetic unsettlement" in which he and the reader feel empathy for the traumatic experience of both the Clefts and the Monsters without losing their objectivity or without trying to use the tales for their own advantage. Because we see the Clefts and males' difficult journey to individualized personhood through the lens of Transit's (usually) balanced empathy and detachment, we come to appreciate not only Transit's struggles to understand his material but also the early peoples' own slow development of the capacity to empathize with each other. Further, we gradually also come to understand that in Transit's wrestle with this highly charged, gendered material, his own understanding of his relationship to the gender attitudes of his day is changed.

Before examining further the implications of LaCapra's formulation of empathetic unsettlement for Transit's relationship to his historical material, I want to examine the psychological theory underpinning the concept of empathy. The traditional explanation of empathy rests on the individual's ability to share and comprehend the inner experience of another, particularly if he or she has undergone a similar experience—a "process through which one's experienced sense of basic connection and similarity to other humans is established.... Without empathy, there is no intimacy, no real attainment of an appreciation of the paradox of separateness within connection."[13] Empathy has both an emotional component and a cognitive one. It requires a balance of emotion and thought, objectivity and subjectivity. The individual must be capable of easing up the boundaries of self in order to allow the "trying out quality to the experience, whereby one places one's self in the other's shoes or looks through the other's eyes.... [D]istinctions between self and other blur experientially."[14] However, this vicarious experience of the other's emotions is temporary, and is followed by a return to one's own feelings and needs. Further, one must be objective enough to understand what the other is feeling, not just to experience it emotionally. This balance of identification with the other's emotions and cognitive understanding of them is necessary for successful empathetic response.

To find this balance an individual must have self-boundaries that are not too rigid, and not too open.[15] If the boundaries of the self are too rigid, she will not be sufficiently open to the emotions of the other to experience them. She may misunderstand the other's emotions or project her own onto them. Or she may experience the other's emotions as a threat. Similarly, if an individual's self-boundaries are too open or weak, she will be engulfed by the feelings of the other and will not be able to maintain or return to her own emotions and needs.[16] So a balance between identification with, and detachment from, the other is required for a successful empathetic response. With Lessing's women focalizers the boundaries of self often tend to be porous, and the women are often in danger of losing their self-identity in their empathetic response to the other. Anna Wulf's over-identification with her lovers Michael and Saul Green in *The Golden Notebook*[17] is an extreme example of this.[18] For the male narrator examined here the boundaries of self tend to be more self-enclosed and need to be opened up if he is to feel empathy for the other, especially for the other who is very different.

Lessing expands the dimensions of the empathetic response by developing the possibilities for detachment. Detachment increases the range of aspects of the self and the other with which an individual can feel empathy. By allowing sufficient distance from the demands of the ego or from the limitations in an individual's self-understanding that block his responsiveness to the other, detachment facilitates the connection of empathy to otherwise denied or disassociated parts of the self and to an otherwise alien other.[19] Thus detachment and empathy go hand in hand. Each kind of experience feeds and enables the other. What Lessing adds to this description of detachment is an awareness of deeper levels of self to which an individual can become attuned in both the self and in the other. To reach these deeper levels of self requires discipline and effort and is often associated in Lessing's work with undergoing a difficult or painful experience that detaches the individual from old ways of thinking or being.[20] The acquisition of this kind of detachment frees the individual not only to empathize more widely but also to see his world anew and to speculate and ask questions about it in ways that he could not have done before. We will see Transit undergoing this process of deepening detachment as he becomes exposed to painful aspects of the ancient records and of his own experiences. As a result he becomes capable of wider sympathies and greater questioning. And thus his historical work becomes not only the compilation and interpretation of the Clefts' ancient records but also the discovery (and at times invention) of the meaning of their experience and of his own.

The reader, too, becomes implicated in the sorting out of truth from fiction in Transit's story and his historical work. On one level we read the story of Transit's attempt to accommodate himself to the records left by a people who lived millennia before his time and whose experiences and mind-sets are radically different from his own. The "ancient scrolls and fragments of scrolls" (60) that Transit must order and make sense of contain records of the oral tales of the first females, the Clefts, and the radical disruption of their lifestyle when they suddenly begin giving birth to male children. On another level these records plunge readers into the disturbing world of the highly gendered characteristics of the early Clefts and males. While Lessing gives primacy to the Clefts' ability to nurture and to maintain a cooperative, peaceful lifestyle, she critiques their seeming obliviousness: they are also slow, heavy, porpoiselike creatures who spend much of their time half in and half out of the sea, existing in a dreaming, almost totally unself-conscious state, "an eternal present" (31). It is not by accident that these first females are usually referred to as Clefts, not women, throughout the ancient records. Thus as Lessing herself admits, the work is "not politically correct."[21] Not only are the Clefts physically and mentally different from humans as we know them but also they are types rather than individualized characters, named for the functions they perform; that is, each cave "family" consists of "the Cleft Watchers, the Fish Catchers, the Net Makers, the Fish Skin Curers, the Seaweed Collectors" (10–11). The first males (first called Monsters, later called Squirts) bring another set of stereotypical features into this genetic soup. They are adventurous and daring but initially lack adult language and a full range of emotions. Being already one step away from the first people, they are more self-conscious than the early Clefts, but they also lack individuality. Each group is powerfully driven by biological need. It is only when the two groups begin to mix, first physically and then more slowly culturally, that the resulting hybrid species begins to acquire the traits necessary for individualized human development—not only the ability to care for and perpetuate the species or to explore, adapt, and hunt but also the ability to self-consciously think, understand, and empathize.

Here again as she did in *The Fifth Child* (1988) and *Ben, In the World* (2000), Lessing blurs the boundaries between the human and the animal. In so doing she risks confusing or alienating her readers who do and do not identify with the Clefts and the Monsters.[22] However, I believe Lessing gives the reader a clue on how to read her fable by setting the extreme gender descriptions found in the ancient mythic tales in the context of Transit's metafictional tale of historiography. Thus we encounter the prehuman characteristics of the Clefts and males in the context of Transit's own concern about how to respond appropriately to the disturbing nature of the collection of bits and fragments of records that he has acquired.

From the beginning Transit must struggle with the porous border between fact and event, myth and history in the material with which he works.[23] The ancient scrolls are themselves already an interpretation of the Clefts' response to the sudden birth of the males. As Transit points out, the "official story" recorded by the Clefts—"the one that they taught to their Memories" (those responsible for passing down the oral history from generation to generation)—does not contain all the records that have been saved. A very early fragment, containing a "sickening" account of the atrocities committed by the Clefts on the very first Monsters, was saved separately, presumably by a minority group, and was never considered part of the official record (23–24). We will see below that Transit's response to this contested early record blurs even further the border between fiction and history.

The creation of the new hybrid species, the human race, out of the physical and cultural mixing of the Clefts and males comes only at the price of dealing with the shock and trauma of facing difference, of dealing with the alien other and gradually learning to accommodate to and then empathize with it. The reader too must face this shocking encounter with extreme gendered difference, and it is only Transit's combination of objectivity and empathy toward the ancient records that makes possible the reader's ability to understand and empathize with the slow growth into individualized personhood of the Clefts and males. However, some reviewers, put off by the accentuated, stereotypical sexual differences of the Clefts and the males in the old records, do not respond to Lessing's use of Transit's narrative as the vehicle for the ancient tale's presentation.[24] I will argue that Transit's role is crucial to the metafictional layering of the novel. While Transit self-consciously struggles to make meaning of the ancient records, creating the story of the Clefts and the males' gradual growth through their painful interactions, Lessing's fable captures the way Transit's own self-understanding changes through his encounters with the old records. Both the story of Transit's individual growth in perspective and the story he tells of the specieslike growth of the Clefts and males come together in Lessing's carefully orchestrated narrative of the encounter of genders and cultures and the rich new selfhoods that result. The interplay between Transit's growing empathy toward the women in his life and the lessening of differences between the gender extremes of the Clefts and the males in the story of the ancient records he crafts is, I believe, the whole point of Lessing's fiction—that is, Transit in his life and the Clefts and the males in the records grow in their ability to empathize with the other gender.

Lessing has previously used this pattern of a more evolved narrator who is himself changed by his interaction with a less advanced civilization in *Shikasta*, although Johor is not only affected by his involvement with Shikastan archives but also directly intervenes in Shikastan reality.[25] Transit plays the subtler role of the historian whose attempt to make meaning out of humankind's first records changes both him and the narrative he puts together. In the end it may or may not affect the understanding of his civilization. But as with *Shikasta*, Lessing here seems to be also attempting to influence the understanding of her readers, wryly suggesting that our own gender attitudes may prevent us from acquiring the deeper level of human understanding that sees us all as "One—one Race or People" (24).[26]

The kind of changes necessary for the birth in the Clefts of what Geraldine Bedell calls "person-hood" are not easily accomplished. The written records of the Clefts' oral tales capturing the moment when the females suddenly begin giving birth to males involve horrors of a kind not easily dealt with by Transit or the reader. One of the most interesting features of Transit's role as narrator is his wrestling with the problems of a historian dealing with personal accounts of extreme or limit events. Transit possesses or learns to acquire the balanced empathy that historian Dominick LaCapra advocates for historians dealing with such sensitive material—an empathy that is "responsive to the traumatic experience of others" without appropriating their experience.[27] To do this Transit must engage with the kind of issues raised by LaCapra in dealing with personal accounts of traumatic narratives. For example, LaCapra discusses the danger for the historian of overidentifying with traumatic material, especially eyewitness accounts, and of experiencing a "secondary or muted trauma."[28] LaCapra notes that the use of "objectification within limits" serves as "a protection of the researcher especially in areas in which traumatic suffering is marked and the tendency to identify fully with the victim may be compelling."[29]

Transit confronts this problem when he begins recording the birth of the first Monsters and the Clefts' cruel treatment of them—most were put out to die, a few were kept as pets and mutilated. Transit seems to be consciously working at finding the balance between objectivity and identification advocated by LaCapra. Transit stresses both his identification with and his separateness from his material. He notes, "I am writing this, feeling some of those ancient long ago emotions. I note that Maire [the Cleft narrating this incident] in her account said 'we' and 'us' identifying with the first Clefts, just as I cannot help identifying with the very first males" (23). However, like a responsible historian, Transit is "actively aware . . . of the need to come to terms with . . . [his] implication in, or transferential relation to, charged, value-related events and those involved with them."[30] Thus Transit is able to step back from his identification with the first males and to bring both empathy and objectivity to his account of the early Clefts' cruelty toward the first baby boys. As he concludes, "Shock after shock was felt by this community of dreaming creatures and it was their helpless panic that caused their cruelty" (33). Here Transit seems to satisfy LaCapra's comment that empathy is "on some level necessary for understanding."[31] It seems clear that Transit would not have been able to respond to these early records at all if he had not been capable of both detachment from his identification with the Monsters and some empathy toward the early behavior of the Clefts.

However, the balance of detachment and empathy is not always enough or even possible. The blurring of the relationship between fiction and history, identified by Linda Hutcheon as germane to historiographic metafiction, is intensified by Transit's response to the first brutal fragment already left out of the Cleft's official records. While Transit chooses not to include this first fragment of the Clefts "told by someone in shock" that details the "sickening" ingenuity of "the cruelties thought up by the old females" (21), he does not leave it out because he thinks it is exaggerated or inaccurate. Rather he accepts the authenticity of this record—"there is something too raw and bleeding about the account of the cruelties to be fake" (24)—but still avoids including it. "It is too unpleasant. I am a Monster and cannot help identifying with those long-ago tortured infants, the first baby boys" (21). Here Transit's reaction suggests that this first fragment induces too strong a secondary trauma for him to cope with it. Thus his account reminds the reader of how porous the border is between fiction and history, identification and detachment. Moreover, the fact that the official records of the Clefts had already left out this brutal first fragment suggests exactly what historians beginning with Hayden White have been at pains to point out—that history is based on records that are themselves the product of interpretation.[32]

Transit's self-conscious struggle as he works at turning the ancient scrolls into a comprehensible narrative is highlighted often and variously. Despite his generally empathetic response to the Clefts' early records (with the exception of that first fragment), Transit makes it clear that he feels a certain distance from his material. This distance, I feel, is crucial to the reader's acceptance of Transit's historical efforts. He describes himself as having a tendency toward "scepticism," which, he feels, "has made me able to take on the task of telling the tale of our real origins," a tale that "does have elements of legend" (27). His acknowledgment of the fabular quality of the ancient records aids his detachment and is crucial to his ability to work with the disturbing documents.[33] While a historian's total objectivity in interpreting the past is now viewed with suspicion,[34] Transit's believability is strengthened by his ability to detach himself to some extent from the gender attitudes of his time. He notes, "I have always found it entertaining that females are worshipped as goddesses, while in ordinary life they are kept secondary and thought inferior" (27). This detachment aids Transit's conscious avoidance of overidentifying with his material or assuming the voice of the victim (whether Cleft or Monster)—tendencies mentioned by LaCapra as inappropriate for developing "an ethics of response for secondary witnesses."[35] Transit's skepticism also identifies his sophistication as a historian aware of the at least partially fictive nature of historical narrative.

Transit's sophistication and awareness are immediately seen in his interpretation of the first fragment that he includes: "a record of an interrogation by one of us—that is, the males . . .—of a She, or Cleft" (25). Transit immediately notes that the "interrogator is in a position of power; and that locates it late in our long history" (25), but it is "preserved by the method used by the females, the memorising of a history" and this places it among "very early events indeed" (25). So this is a late example of preserving ancient oral history. Here Transit's response to his material is both sensitive and discriminating. Rather than responding to this material in a purely objective manner, using what LaCapra calls "excessive objectification,"[36] Transit seeks to be sensitive to the subject position and voice of the records.

Transit also acknowledges the role of ideology in preserving historical memory.[37] Noting that the ancient records have been kept locked up in "prison" and some of them even destroyed not only because of the violence they contain but also because of their controversial account of the beginning of the human race, Transit concludes, "[p]erhaps it has been felt that an account of our beginnings that makes females the first and founding stock is unacceptable" (27). Transit's comment here acquires a deeper irony, as some early reviewers of the novel also felt it unacceptable to portray the first humans as porpoiselike females, lacking curiosity or daring.[38] Transit's skepticism and irony are clear in his comparisons of the Cleft's account with two alternative contemporary creation stories. Regarding the official story taught in the Roman schools in which "males were the first in the story and in some remarkable way brought forth the females" (25), Transit ironically comments that it remains "unexplained" how this was accomplished (26). Regarding the creation story current in the new Christian "sect"—"the first female was brought forth from the body of a male"—Transit ironically remarks, "[s]ome male invented that—the exact opposite of the truth" (27).[39] Here Lessing foregrounds the cultural and ideological input in foundational records from the past and deliberately points to her rewriting of the biblical story of Adam and Eve (as well as Roman creation myths). In doing so she uses the kind of parodic postmodern intertexuality associated with historiographic metafiction that "uses and abuses those intertexual echoes, inscribing their powerful allusions and then subverting that power through irony" (Hutcheon, 298). Similarly, Lessing plays with Transit's attachment to the goddesses Artemis and Diana and his use of them to try to understand the power of Maire, the first Cleft to visit and mate with the males. The power of this illusion is then undercut as Transit muses that "[i]t is not possible to imagine anything that could banish Artemis, or for that matter pretty Diana, from their positions in our hearts" (117). The similarity between the names Maire and Mary only deepens the irony of Transit's comment.

Both Transit and his creator are clearly aware that myths of origin have ideological implications. However, it is the ideological implications of Lessing's focus on gender in her mythic story that have bothered some of her critics. Lessing, however, is, I believe, both more sophisticated and more even-handed in her creation of a gendered myth of origins than some of her detractors have realized. The primacy of her first female protohumans is balanced by their links to their sea-creature past. The liveliness and curiosity of the first males is balanced by their neediness and vulnerability. Lessing herself comments on the relationship between the genders in the book by noting that while the males "pep up" the genetic soup of humanity, they were "a haphazard species" who always needed to be looked after and died "much too easy."[40] The real point of her myth of origins, however, as we shall see, is the absolute interdependence of the Clefts and males for the creation and then the evolution of the human race.

6: The Porous Border in Doris Lessing's The Cleft

As in *The Marriages between Zones Three, Four, and Five*,[41] isolation or an attitude of superiority by one group, whether it is defined by gender or by territory, leads to the malaise of all. Indeed, a comparison of *Marriages* and *The Cleft* is very instructional. In both books the boundaries erected by human arrogance or fear must be crossed if the human species is to survive. Thus Al*Ith must leave the security and comfort, but ultimate stagnation, of the seemingly utopian world of woman-centered Zone Three to learn to understand and eventually love the cruder, more militaristic, but also less self-satisfied and more questioning, world of male-dominated Zone Four. Further, Zone Three's arrogance and xenophobia as well as Zone Four's repressive laws and extreme militarization have hurt their own Zone's well-being and that of the whole. Neither the highly evolved women of Zone Three nor the militaristic men of Zone Four, or for that matter the warlike, woman-ruled tribes of Zone Five, can exist without the others. It is only when the boundaries between the territories and the gendered attitudes associated with them begin to give way and there is free movement between the zones that the well-being of the whole can be achieved. What perhaps makes Lessing's later novel harder for some readers to deal with is that the Clefts are more primitive and closer to their sea-creature forebears than the slightly more evolved Monsters. As such the Clefts are more foundational and likely to survive but also less open to change and less creative in adjusting to new circumstances than the males. But, as in the earlier fable, both genders, albeit with modified versions of their characteristics, are necessary to the well-being and advancement of the human race. Boundaries must be literally and figuratively crossed as Al*Ith goes down to Zone Four and Maire goes over the mountain to the valley of the males.

However, unlike the highly imaginative but little individualized storyteller from Zone Three, who is very much in the background of his retrospective narrative, the more factually oriented, conservative historian, Transit, is very much in the foreground of his present-tense narrative. Indeed, Transit's personal experience is crucial to his historical storytelling. From the outset Transit makes it clear that he has been able to empathize with the ancient records in large part because of events in his own experience. He has young children from a much younger second wife, his first wife having died and his first two sons having been killed while fighting with the Roman army in the north. His early career involved little empathy for either his wife or sons. He was too "ambitious," and, as Transit notes, "[I] had very little time for my wife and less for my boys" (55). Aware now of the loss he has experienced in not having really known his first two sons, Transit spends many hours in the nursery observing his second family. It is his observation of his young daughter and son's first discovery of their sexual differences and their different reactions—she is "shocked, envious, repelled"; he is proud and assertive of "his equipment" (60)—that enables Transit to "at least try and take on . . . my history of that ancient, long-ago time" (62). His observation of his children and his study of the ancient texts each make the other more understandable.

We see Transit's openness to his material in his refusal to judge or assert superiority over the very early behavior of the Clefts and males. When Maire and Astre, the first two Clefts to establish relations with the males, leave the valley of the males after their first visit with them, Transit records, "[t]heir time for conception had come and gone (76)—though of course they had no idea of that" (76). But then he immediately adds, "[b]ut when we say things like that now, 'they did not know,' 'they were so primitive,' 'they were too ignorant'—the gamut of dismissing phrases—well I, for one, wonder. How do we know what they knew, and how?" (76). Here Transit captures the "the process of *attempting* to assimilate" the data of the past (rather than the actual assimilation) that Hutcheon claims is "foregrounded" in historiographic metafiction.[42] Transit leaves space in his account for, indeed emphasizes, what he and his civilization do not know or understand about the early Cleft's knowledge.

Transit's self-conscious questioning of how much he really understands the gender relations in the Clefts' story leaks into his telling of his own story. While Transit had laughed at the gender discrepancies in Roman attitudes toward women, he himself initially assumes the superiority of age, knowledge, and experience over his much younger second wife, Julia, whom he describes as "a clever little provincial girl" (56) who "was almost completely ignorant" (57). However, as Transit works with the manuscripts of the Clefts and lovingly observes the development of his second family, he also observes Julia's increasingly nontraditional female behavior—her lack of interest in nurturing her children, her socializing in sophisticated ruling circles, and her sexual promiscuity.[43] At first he judges Julia harshly, comparing her "selfish, self-indulgent, amoral" behavior unfavorably with his mother's virtue, "piety, and strength of character" (59). When this has no effect on her, he settles for warning her to be careful in her promiscuous sexual life.

Transit's final reference to Julia, however, suggests a change in the dynamics of their relationship and in his attitude toward her. On this occasion, it is she who warns him, spelling out the dangers of allowing rumors to circulate about building a new house—prominent people have had their houses confiscated by the current tyrant, Nero, she tells him. She concludes by shaking him and calling him a "foolish old thing" (176). This scene forces Transit to become aware of how Julia really sees him; her exasperated tone and words suggest not the veneration he had assumed but impatience and annoyance at his lack of understanding of the current political realities about which she is very much aware.

Even more interesting is the narrative placing of this personal digression. Transit includes the story of his scolding by Julia only after he has described late in his tale the great "rage" between the Clefts and the males. At this stage in the records the interactions between the Clefts and males are considerably more organized and advanced; young boys stay with their mothers until around five or six, after which time they go off to live with the men and older boys in the valley by the great river. Maronna, the head of the Clefts at that time, and the male leader Horsa increasingly clash over the males' carelessness in taking care of the little children (a number of boys die in the great river and in other ways) and over the men's dislike of the women's scolding and nagging (172). This rage, which Transit comes to realize was the culmination of a series of fights, finally leads Horsa to decide to go away for a while with the men and boys on a great expedition. Transit's ability to connect the Clefts' impatience with the men's behavior to Julia's scolding of him over the rumor of the new house suggests how his work with the records of the Clefts has opened him up to his own gender assumptions.

What is most interesting for my purposes about Transit's account of the great expedition and, in particular, the accident that cripples Horsa, is the porous nature of the history/fiction, detachment/identification divide in Transit's response to Horsa's accident. While Transit's careful empathetic balance of detachment and identification in his treatment of the ancient records had been established in his earlier work, this balance is now temporarily lost. In describing Horsa's feelings when he lies crippled on the sand, thrown back by waves after attempting to reach the far horizon, Transit is overcome with an identification so intense that it is balanced by no corresponding detachment. Exclaiming over the crippled Horsa, "I feel he is my younger self, perhaps even a son" (215), Transit fails to maintain the objectivity identified by LaCapra as necessary to prevent the historian from falling into unrecognized transferences and projections.[44] Transit assumes that Horsa's desire to reach this new land is not because he aspired to "finer dimensions in life," but rather because like the Romans, Horsa was a "coloniser" at heart (216). Here Transit identifies Horsa's pain with that of Rome itself, hurt in its need to expand (216). Thus Horsa's suffering becomes that of Transit's two sons, "lying somewhere in those northern forests" (216), giving their lives so that Rome could "outleap itself . . . grow . . . reach out" (216).

Identifying Horsa's suffering with the pain Rome has endured in its expansionist drive to increase its empire, Transit mourns anew the death of his first two sons even as he celebrates Rome's desire to extend its boundaries "far and further, wide and wider" (216). Transit's projection onto Horsa of his own feelings about the Roman Empire provides the reader with her own experience of ironic detachment from Transit's narrative. As he rhetorically asks, "Why should there ever be an end to . . . Rome, to our boundaries?" (216), the reader, of course, knows that soon enough Rome will fall to the Germanic tribes from the north. Thus after carefully establishing Transit's balanced approach to his material, the novel here undercuts that reliability and "blurs the line between fiction and history."[45] Perhaps in showing Transit's unbalanced identification with Rome's imperialistic goals, Lessing is suggesting that humankind will take longer to come to terms with its imperialistic desires than with immature attitudes toward gender and sexuality that polarize the differences between the sexes. While the dangers of imperialism and sexism are often intertwined in Lessing's work, increasingly in her oeuvre Lessing has come to concentrate more on the dangers of imperialism than of gender discrimination. While the early works seem to detail more fully the difficulties of sexism than of imperialism, the two seem to be balanced in *The Marriages between Zones Three, Four, and Five,* in which the different genders are associated with different territories and stages of development, and the healing of the gender split is linked to the healing of the malaise gripping geographical regions and even species. But increasingly in her outer-space and fabular fictions Lessing has suggested that the aggressive behavior associated with imperial empires plays havoc with humankind's ability to advance and to survive the grave challenges with which it is confronted, especially that of climate change.[46]

Whatever Transit's imperialistic blindness, Lessing parallels the psychological development of mature gender attitudes in Transit's life story to his account of the sexual and cultural evolution of the Clefts and the males. In Transit's personal life story we find a growing awareness that he and Julia are far more equal and in mutual need of each other than Transit originally imagined. Just as Julia presumably saves Transit's life by warning him of the danger of rumors about building a new house, so earlier Transit had warned Julia of the danger of going to her lover's wedding lavishly dressed, riding in an elegant chariot provided by the lover himself (149). Each needs the perspective and understanding of the other to survive.

Similarly, by the end of Transit's narrative of the ancient records, Maronna, having screamed herself hoarse after learning of the death of most of the young boys on Horsa's great expedition, can see and respond for the first time to the real grief that Horsa feels over their loss and can take him in her arms and comfort him. Likewise, Horsa can get beyond his usual perception of Maronna as a critical, scolding presence and see her pain and vulnerability. Thus instead of feeling threatened and wanting to escape, he can reach out with tenderness to comfort her also. This moment of mutual succor and empathy marks the maturing of not only the two individuals, Maronna and Horsa, but also of the two peoples, the Clefts and the males, into one people, the human race. Maronna and Horsa have widened the boundaries of self and become capable of experiencing the feelings of the other without losing their sense of self. Since they are representative figures, their balance of identification and detachment implicitly suggests that the Clefts and the males will begin to understand not only that they need each other but also that they are capable of empathizing with each other. It is at this point that the rock containing the Cleft, the symbol of the one-dimensional identification of the Clefts with their sexuality, is destroyed and the women are forced to move to a more capacious beach symbolizing a more capacious sense of self. This event marks the end of the ancient scripts recording the division of the Clefts and males into two peoples based on their sexual difference. The splendid new beach to which the women move upon the destruction of the Cleft will "soon house all the women and the children and the visiting men too" (257).

The careful balance of identification and detachment acquired by Transit in working with the ancient records of the Clefts (with a few exceptions) details the gradual lessening of the purely sexual identities of the Clefts and males and the growth of empathetic understanding between them. At the same time, Transit reveals his personal progress in dealing with the gendered assumptions of his time. But the historical metafictional penchant for undercutting whatever values are established is still operative. Transit's combined personal memoir and historical reconstruction will not prevent the fall of his society, and his imperialistic attitudes suggest that fall may be necessary. However, despite this obvious irony, Lessing's prophetic voice still emerges from this disturbing fabular fiction to implicitly demand that we cast a speculative and detached eye on the gender assumptions governing our own civilization and that we both see and query the imperialistic patterns obscured by familiarity and by too little distance from the theater of our lives. Here we see the ongoing creativity of Lessing's late-life writing as she continues to try out new experimental forms for goading her culture to question the stories it tells itself about gender relations and imperial ambitions.

NOTES

1. See "Another Model of the Aging Writer: Sarton's Politics of Old Age" by Anne

M. Wyatt-Brown in *Aging and Gender in Literature: Studies in Creativity*, edited by Anne M. Wyatt-Brown and Janice Rossen (Charlottesville: University of Virginia Press, 1993), 49–60. Wyatt-Brown offers three models for writers' late-life productivity. Lessing's creativity in her late 80s seems to fit Wyatt-Brown's second trajectory, that of writers "liberated by the possibility of radical change" (52). See also my article "Navigating the Spiritual Cycle in *Memoirs of a Survivor* and *Shikasta*," in *Adventures of the Spirit: The Older Woman in the Works of Doris Lessing, Margaret Atwood, and Other Contemporary Women Writers*, edited by Phyllis Sternberg Perrakis (Columbus: The Ohio State University Press, 2007), 47–82, in which I argue that Lessing's "move from inner-space to outer-space fiction . . . offers us a fascinating example of midlife creativity" (47).

2. See Susan Watkins's chapter "Writing in a Minor Key" in Part Three of this volume, in which she discusses Lessing's crossing of species boundaries in *The Fifth Child* (1988; repr., London: Flamingo, 1993) and *Ben, In the World* (London: Flamingo, 2000) and its effect on the reader, especially in England. Also, Roberta Rubenstein in "Notes for Proteus: Doris Lessing Reads the *Zeigeist*," the opening chapter of this collection, begins with a discussion of Lessing's amazing generic "shape-shift[ing]" abilities [editors' note].

3. Doris Lessing, *The Cleft* (London: Fourth Estate [HarperCollins], 2007).

4. The phrase "pre-people" comes from Geraldine Bedell's "Women and Children First," review of *The Cleft*, by Doris Lessing, in *The Observer*, January 7, 2007, http://books.guardian.co.uk/reviews/generalfiction/0,,1984239,00.html (accessed August 13, 2007).

5. See Linda Hutcheon's article "'The Pastime of Past Time': Fiction, History, Historiographic Metafiction," *Genre* 20 (Fall–Winter 1987): 285–305, where she defines the postmodern nature of this generic category and then discusses its relation to historical fiction and earlier, traditional notions of the verifiability of history.

6. Ibid., 285–86.

7. See Hayden White's discussion of the fictionality of all texts available to the historian, in "The Historical Text as Literary Artifact," in *The Writing of History: Literary Form and Historical Understanding*, ed. Robert H. Canary and Henry Kozicki (Madison: University of Wisconsin Press, 1978), 41–62, 42.

8. See Dominick LaCapra, *Writing History, Writing Trauma* (Baltimore: Johns Hopkins University Press, 2001). Jeanie Warnock's fine application of LaCapra's theory of "empathetic unsettlement" to Shani Mootoo's novel, *Cereus Blooms at Night*, increased my interest in this theory and encouraged me to invoke LaCapra. See Warnock, "'Soul Murder' and Rebirth: Trauma, Narrative, and Imagination in Shani Mootoo's *Cereus Blooms at Night*," in Perrakis, *Adventures of the Spirit*, 270–98.

9. LaCapra, *Writing History, Writing Trauma*, 102, 103.

10. Ibid., 40.

11. Ibid., 41–42.

12. Ibid., 99.

13. Judith Jordan, "Empathy and Self Boundaries," in *The Women and Language Debate: A Sourcebook*, ed. Camille Roman, Suzanne Juhasz, and Christanne Miller (New Brunswick, NJ: Rutgers University Press, 1994), 153–64, 154.

14. Ibid., 155.

15. Ibid.

16. Ibid.

17. Lessing, *The Golden Notebook* (1962; repr., New York: Bantam, 1973).

18. See my discussion of Anna's precarious sense of self and her tendency to become submerged in the identities of those she loves in "Doris Lessing's *The Golden Notebook*: Separation and Symbiosis," *American Imago* 38.4 (Winter 1981): 407–28.

19. Judith Jordan explains that the empathetic response is not global; the individual may respond to some aspects of the other or self but not others (155). See my discussion concerning accessing deeper levels of the self in "Navigating the Spiritual Cycle" (50–59).

20. See Perrakis, "Navigating," 52–53. Lessing herself discusses this in "An Ancient Way to New Freedom," in *The Diffusion of Sufi Ideas in the West*, ed. L. Lewin (Boulder, CO: Keysign, 1972), 44–54, 54. See Alice Ridout's discussion of Lessing's interest in her later works in detaching her readers from their usual ways of seeing in her chapter "'What Is the Function of the Storyteller?' The Relation between *Why* and *How* Lessing Writes" in Part Two of this volume [editors' note].

21. Quoted in Hillel Italie, "This Writer Won't Settle Down," Los Angeles Times: Calendarlive.com, February 20, 2006, http://articles.latimes/2006/oct/20/entertainment/et-lessing20 (accessed February 27, 2010).

22. In "Writing in a Minor Key," in Part Three Watkins makes a similar point about the effect of Lessing's crossing of species boundaries in *The Fifth Child* and *Ben, In the World* [editors' note].

23. See Whites's distinction between event and fact ("The Historical Text as Literary Artifact," 43–44).

24. See, for example, Ursula Le Guin's "Saved by a Squirt," review of *The Cleft* by Doris Lessing, *The Guardian Unlimited*, February 10, 2007, http://books.guardian.co.uk/review/story/0,,2009447,00.html (accessed August 13, 2007). For a more positive review see Lisa Appignanesi's "Unto Them, a Boy Is Born," review of *The Cleft* by Doris Lessing, in *Times Online*, January 6, 2007, http://entertainment.timesonline.co.uk/tol/arts_and_entertainment/books/fiction/article1289421.ece (accessed August 13, 2007). Like my own reading, Appignanesi recognizes that "[w]hat distinguishes *The Cleft* is the hard edge of mirroring irony provided by her teller, an elderly historian in Nero's Rome who sifts the fragments of ancient manuscripts in his villa while his much younger wife gambols off to orgies."

25. Lessing, *Re: Colonised Planet 5: Shikasta*, vol. 1 of *Canopus in Argos: Archives* (1979; repr., London: Granada, 1980). See my discussion of Johor's transformation in "Navigating the Spiritual Cycle" (63–67). See also my earlier discussion of how Johor is changed in the process of compiling the documents that compose *Shikasta* in "The Marriage of Inner and Outer Space in Doris Lessing's *Shikasta*," *Science-Fiction Studies* 17.2 (July 1990): 221–38, 228–33.

26. See "Navigating the Spiritual Cycle" where I briefly discuss Lessing's concern in *Shikasta* with influencing her readers (75–76).

27. LaCapra, *Writing History, Writing Trauma*, 41.

28. Ibid., 102.

29. Ibid., 100.

30. Ibid., 105.

31. Ibid.

32. See note 7.

33. Readers of Lessing's fable would do well to emulate Transit in this regard and

similarly acknowledge the fabular quality of the tale. Watkins in "Writing in a Minor Key" in Part Three argues that Lessing's more recent fabular works have often been misinterpreted by British critics because they fail to understand Lessing's use of minor genres.

34. See essays by White and Lionel Grossman, "History and Literature: Reproduction or Signification," in Canary and Kozicki, *The Writing of History: Literary Form and Historical Understanding*, 1–40.

35. LaCapra, *Writing History, Writing Trauma*, 98.

36. Ibid., 99.

37. See Hutcheon's discussion of the ideological implications of writing about history in historiographic metafictions (297, 300).

38. As Ursula Le Guin comments in her review of *The Cleft*, "Women are passive, incurious, timid and instinctively nurturant; without men, they scarcely rise above animal mindlessness. Men are intellectual, inventive, daring, rash, independent, and need women only to relieve libido and breed more men" ("Saved by a Squirt").

39. Co-editor Debrah Raschke points out that Transit is referring here to Genesis 2, not Genesis 1, which describes the simultaneous creation of the genders. Neither, of course, is purely Christian, and Transit seems unaware of the New Testament myth of creation, which emphasizes that in the beginning there was the "Word" (John 1: 1–14).

40. "'What Use Are Men?' Asks Lessing," *BBC News/Wales*, June 2, 2007, http://news.bbc.co.uk/2/low/uk_news/wales/6715227.stm (accessed February 9, 2008).

41. Lessing, *The Marriages between Zones Three, Four, and Five*, 1980, vol. 2 of *Canopus in Argos: Archives* (1980; repr., London: Granada, 1981).

42. Hutcheon, "'The Pastime of Past Time,'" 295, emphasis in original.

43. A similar hint of the wide distribution of gender-linked attributes within as well as between sexes is also found in the ancient records. Thus from the beginning there were Clefts who wanted to spend time in the Valley with the males and men who enjoyed caring for children and being with the Clefts in the caves (143–44, 162).

44. LaCapra, *Writing History, Writing Trauma*, 99.

45. Hutcheon, "'The Pastime of Past Time,'" 293.

46. See, for example, the dangers of imperialism in association with climate change outweighing gender problems in *Mara and Dann: An Adventure* (New York: HarperFlamingo, 1999) and its sequel, *The Story of General Dann and Mara's Daughter, Griot and the Snow Dog* (London: Fourth Estate, 2005), as well as in "The Reason for It" in *The Grandmothers* (New York: HarperCollins, 2003), 131–89.

Part Three

DESTABILIZED GENRE AS SOCIAL CRITIQUE

7

love, again and *The Sweetest Dream*
Fiction and Interleaved Fictions

VIRGINIA TIGER

> Just as the supposed subject of *The Golden Notebook,* women and men, was all the reviewers could see, so the immediate subject of *love, again,* love in old age, was surprising and shocking and the fact that the novel has a rather complicated structure was hardly noticed.[11]

My point of departure in discussion of *love, again*[2] (a novel I have never much liked, much less enjoy) is the plaintive, yet accusatory comment in Doris Lessing's *Walking in the Shade,* volume 2 of the autobiography, where she is engaged in her habitual gesture of swatting at critics as though they are irritating blackflies, to modify Coetzee's felicitous phrase.[3] For a writer whose narratives insist on, not artifice, but rather their own artificiality, it is useful to explore *love, again* as well as *The Sweetest Dream*[4] prompted by the observation here and recalling the hybrid nature of the Lessing project. Authorial will-to-power over her own fictive texts Lessing most certainly demonstrates, interrupting narrative with autobiographically sourced digression, "signs of the times" interpolations, summary, parody, pastiche, or interspersed letter. On record as relishing how "prodigiously adaptable"[5] the novel is by nature, it not being bound, indeed having "no rules,"[6] she once remarked, "Nearly all my books have weak patches but that is because I'm the kind of writer I am, which means I'm always trying things out and I'm very seldom interested in a perfect book."[7]

7: love, again, *and* The Sweetest Dream

As a means to examine such elements in *love, again,* I shall turn as well to the 2001 fiction *The Sweetest Dream,* which offers a rich area of comparison by way of representing a reclamation of the Condition of England novel and traditional classic realist text. In contrast, *love, again* (rather like *The Golden Notebook's*[8] rejection of *A Ripple from the Storm's*[9] novelistic form) marks a repudiation of the seemingly obsolete realist form. It must be stressed that, however different in formal modalities, both novels in their fictional representation of the lives of older women mark what will become an increasingly dominant concern in the twenty-first century. Encapsulating the end of one era for the benefit of the beginning of the next, these two salient stories about older women journey toward the millennium in their recasting of both gender and sexual roles.[10] While *love, again* adopts a complex comparative structural frame to provide some detachment from and perspective on its heroine's eroticized obsession, *The Sweetest Dream* places—and therefore makes sense of—its heroine's aging within a specifically political frame of global politics. Another matter to be explored in both books in a comparative way will be the four seemingly simplistic questions I want to pose: When does a novel begin? What's involved in a novel's title? When does a novel end? And how do beginning, title, and ending relate to structure?

The structure of any narrative is like the opposite of—say—the carapace of a turtle. You cannot see it, but it determines the shape and nature of the creature—rather in the way a seagull's skeleton determines its wingspan and thus flight pattern. And the effects of the narrative structure are experienced over time, a long time. *The Sweetest Dream* amounts to 479 pages while *love, again* clocks in at 352 pages. And the reader's experience of those many pages typically oscillates between confident expectation and desultory distance. This is true of most narratives, for, as Frank Kermode has observed, "any fiction of some length and complication . . . contains parts that are ignored when any reader [experiences and] thinks of the whole."[11] Which is to say that a whole sequence amounts to more than the sum of its parts and, certainly, the plot's sequential episodes. For while the *love, again* narrative moves from first to last page without chapter breaks, pursuing a helixlike course, this old sweet song at twilight turns out to be no "love story." And it certainly is not a single or monologic story.

As readers of *love, again* know, the sixty-five-year-old protagonist, Sarah Durham, is handsome, sensible, cool, collected, her daily life revolving round a successful career as a writer/administrator for a London fringe theater. That theater, The Green Parrot, becomes infatuated with a recently recovered feminist Julie Vairon, a late-nineteenth-century Martinique quadroon, living her adult and last years in France's Midi. Her haunting music, and coolly intelligent journals, become the germinating seeds for an operatic play Durham writes while others attend to its production and eventual performances. As casting and then rehearsals for the production get under way in the magical hot summer of 1985, the entire company—not slowly, but surely—surrenders to Julie's erotic enticements. Stephen Ellington-Smith, a wealthy arts patron, confesses to Sarah that he has been—and for some time—desperately in love with the long-dead woman;[12] thus his financial support of as well as engaged commitment to the enterprise. Sarah is described, as few other novelists might have the courage to so depict a woman past her prime, as having reached "the heights of common sense . . . the evenly lit unproblematical uplands where there are no surprises,"[13] thus giving twenty-first-century novelists permission to write of older women beyond such unfavorable platitudes as the haranguing hag, withering widow, or sulfuric witch. Yet Sarah allows herself to become obsessed by a twenty-eight-year-old narcissistic actor, the bisexual Bill who is playing one of Julie's lovers. Following that assaultive *coupe de foudre,* Sarah discovers that Andrew, the forty-year-old actor playing another of Julie's lovers, has fallen in love with her. And she more deeply in love with Henry, the thirty-five-year-old American director of the play. For while Mann's *Death in Venice* is one of a host of intertextual allusions—by my count sixty-five—and an appropriate one for *love, again's* meditation on old age and romantic seizure, Shakespeare's *A Midsummer Night's Dream*[14] or Austen's *Emma*[15] best invokes the atmosphere where the other and many— six more to my count—character actors and producers become besotted with one another, including the actress Molly McGuire playing Julie, who falls in love with the play's patron, Ellington-Smith.

[L]*ove, again's* whole sequence amounts to more than a sum of its parts, for as Sarah—and thus the novelist, Lessing—reflect, we each have our own to-be-excavated story, though it may not occupy a centrality of position, jostling as each does with yet another. Subsidiary characters, Jean-Pierre, a French mayor who sponsors the Julie Vairon festival in Provence, a wealthy American backer, Benjamin Greenfield, who finds his own erotic release in artistic ventures, Sonia, a theater producer (sharp, decidedly young and female and impatient to shake up the Green Parrot's old regime), Stephen's *echt* Oxfordshire wife, Elizabeth, with her lesbian liaison Norah Daniels, are among the subplots, two of which erupt more and more strenuously as the novel moves toward its conclusion—that of Hal, Sarah's pompous, selfish brother, who by any social-class register represents a patriarchal pillar of the British establishment. Then too there is Joyce, his misfit daughter, anorexic, drug-drawn and dirty, whom Sarah—in a recasting of the surrogate mother/

daughter dyad of *The Memoirs of a Survivor*[16] or *If the Old Could*,[17] as well as *The Sweetest Dream*—takes on as her responsibility.

If plot has been defined by a contemporary critic, J. Hillis Miller, as "the neat folding together of elaborate narrative materials [a complication and an unraveling or denouement] in a single resolution, leaving every story line tucked in,"[18] then *love, again*'s plot differs from its structure. The former, with its narrative unity of beginning, middle, and end, is represented by the protagonist's coming of age. Nothing much actually happens to Sarah Durham, though readers nearly smart in the brine of her anguish, into which we are constantly submerged.[19] She inhabits a region of inconsolable need, longing, and grief, entering the state of desire the older woman had thought solely the prerogative of younger ones. The love depicted here can be likened to a fire in the blood, "Lessing align[ing] herself with the medieval pre-romantic tradition that considers love a sickness, from which one must eventually recover."[20] True as this gloss is, readers again are struck by Lessing's millennial prescience in embodying that kind of romantic obsession and inflamed eroticism in a sixty-five-year-old woman. In the ensuing year's inspection of her past, "trying to shine light into the dark places" (349), Sarah Durham will come to recognize that the state of emotional disarray one describes as being in love has its generative source in early infancy: the adult state of anguish is not only "what a baby feels when it is hungry and wants its mother" but also "the baby's longing for something just out of its memory" (350). At the end of her year's ordeal, she remains celibate: the aged female.

Plot, however, must be distinguished from structure, as we remember was limpidly the case in *The Golden Notebook*. [L]*ove, again* is a sister text of *The Golden Notebook*. "Like the story of Anna Wulf, *The Golden Notebook*'s protagonist, Sarah's experience is doubled by that of [Julie Vairon], the imagined woman Sarah is writing about."[21] And this double-decker strategy of storytelling amounts to *love, again*'s narrative structure. Anna's double, Ella, the heroine of Anna's novel "The Shadow of the Third," lives contemporaneously, sharing Anna's historical time and gendered station. Shaped by the nineteenth and very early twentieth centuries, Julie's life (1865–1912) is transparently different from that of the "free woman," whom Sarah embodies. Illegitimate daughter to an upper-class French estate owner in the West Indies and his mulatto mistress, Julie is educated beyond her rank, "her prospects and even her possibilities" (16), only to fall in love with Paul Imbert, an army officer, and accompany him on his return to France. True to the epoch's conventions, his family determines on an appropriate wife, Julie being thrust aside. She falls more deeply in love with Remy Rostand, a French aristocrat, who, in turn, must marry for station, not love. Thenceforth, she lives in solitude, her modest cottage sequestered in a forest of cypress and pine, with a nearby insistent and audible river coursing toward a whirlpool. Occasionally, she tutors the children of surrounding landowners while always she writes music, draws, paints, and keeps a remarkable journal, whose cold intelligence—like her second-period music—makes counterpoint by way of near cruel commentary on erotic raptures and the negative excitement of romantic obsession. Still young when the bourgeois master printer, Phillipe Angers, asks her to marry him, and on the cusp of marriage—the conventional ending to a nineteenth-century novel—Julie kills herself by drowning, thereby fulfilling that other conventional closure to a nineteenth-century novel—as we know from, for example, Kate Chopin's *The Awakening*[22] or Edith Wharton's *The House of Mirth*.[23]

Julie Vairon's life acts as a template for the contemporary romances that do not, of course, run smoothly. While belonging to "the genre of . . . storytelling represented by John Fowles in *The French Lieutenant's Woman* [and] A. S. Byatt's *Possession*,"[24] like the structure of *The Golden Notebook* with its embedded notebooks, *love, again* interleaves the melancholy tales of the (fictional) entries from Julie's journals, written necessarily in the first person, their insertions indicated typographically in italics. The tactic used to shift from Sarah Durham's internal focalizing consciousness to the entries themselves is a narrative voice in the third person, diegetically placing the frame:

> Remarks about her future husband continue, and they are calm, sensible, one could say respectful. There is, however, an entry describing a day in her married life. *I shall wake up in that comfortable bed beside him, when the maid comes in to do the fire.* . . . A week before the mayor . . . was to marry them . . . she drowned herself in the pool where the gossips said she had killed her baby. (25)

In contrast to *The Golden Notebook*'s notebooks, which engender a fictional recasting in "Free Women," Julie's journal fragments engender their duplication in Sarah's life. *[L]ove, again*'s "narrative unfolds on several levels and each level repeats the same patterns . . . [Sarah's] infatuations echo[ing] those of Julie Vairon."[25] Julie's three loves become Sarah's three loves. Julie's music, with its "uncomfortable patterns of sound, continually repeating but not exactly, changed by a note or a tone [with a] sequence of notes [being] changed into a different mode" (71), becomes the pattern for the narrative structure that is provided in *love, again*, with its multiple repetition with variation on the none too innocuous matter of falling in love. Julie's cool and crystalline journals are matched by the dry accusations and critical commen-

7: love, again, *and* The Sweetest Dream

tary Sarah turns upon her own experience of being romantically in love. One example from the perspective of Sarah's monologue with herself:

> I could easily jump off a cliff. . . . People killing themselves for love do it because they can't stand the pain. Physical pain. I have never understood that before. The broken heart. But why should an emotional hurt manifest itself as a physical anguish? Surely that is a very strange thing. (216)[26]

Julie's spinning down into her death in the river's whirlpool is recast in Sarah's descent, deep and deeper into a psychic whirlpool, with "forgotten selves . . . appearing like bubbles in boiling liquid" (212), as she observes and concludes: "She was obviously dissolving into some kind of boiling soup, but presumably would reshape at some point" (212). The Julie Vairon tale acts finally as the inverse template for the conclusion, but not closure, of a contemporary tale about women released from the poison that is love denied. No female fatality, Sarah Durham is a survivor; she knows that, in order to ward against "the dangerous animal that might attack from an unexpected place" (342), she must never relax vigilance.

"When does a novel begin?" was another question I posed. For the reader the novel begins with its opening sentence: "Easy to think this *was* [italics mine] a junk room silent and airless in a warm dusk, but then a shadow moved, someone emerged from it to pull back curtains and throw open windows" (1). This set piece of description of the room gives us the primary psychological setting of the story; readers will come to learn that the inventory of the room is an inventory of the protagonist's sensibility, a sensibility that will undergo change, including the excavation of hypocritical memory. When does a novel's beginning end? Is it the first paragraph? The first chapter? But this novel has no chapters.

Deliberately and as distanced as a camera's long shot, the external narrative voice—what I shall call the Eye/Voice—advises in the second sentence: "It *was* [italics mine] a woman, who now stepped quickly to a door and went out, leaving it open" (1). And fifteen sentences later, still in the past tense and still impersonal, the Eye/Voice observes, "not a young woman . . . a woman of a certain age, as the French put it, or even a bit older" (1). Lucid, measured, objective with ironic implication concealed beneath the dry, cool tone, the Eye/Voice is silenced when it is cut across by a recording of the love plaint of the troubadour, Countess Die:

> I must sing, whether I will or not:
> I feel so much pain over him whose friend I hold myself,

Virginia Tiger

For I love him more than anything that is . . . (2)

Although the not-young woman has yet to be named, the voice of the protagonist herself seeps into the discourse, displacing the judicious voice of the narratorial Eye/Voice. Readers are now placed in the focalizing consciousness of Sarah Durham, experiencing for the first time the novel's adopted narrative strategy of moving from Eye to I, from omniscient narrator to limited consciousness, from the diegetic to the mimetic. "The Countess Die was too disturbing . . . she was altogether too much affected by this old troubadour and trouvere music . . . she was restless, and she was feverish" (2–3). With the arrival of Stephen Ellington-Smith and the second frame of the Julie Vairon tale, *love, again's* beginning ends and the plot proper begins. Without question, the novel has—to quote Lessing again—"a rather complicated structure."[27]

A complicated structure intimately tied to its title. A novel's title is part of its text, the first part of it, in fact, that readers encounter—and therefore has the abiding ability to compel as well as condition our initial response. Here it is not the name of the central character, as in *Moll Flanders*,[28] *Tom Jones*,[29] *Clarissa*,[30] or—for that matter—*Martha Quest*.[31] As title, *love, again* could mark a theme, as do Austen's *Sense and Sensibility*,[32] Golding's *The Inheritors*,[33] and Lessing's *Briefing for a Descent into Hell*.[34] But it has been hitched to a resonant musical quotation: Marlene Dietrich's lifelong signature song. It appears on the front page in this double-decker novel as *"love, again a novel,"* both inscribed deliberately in lower case. Using *a novel* as part of its title is a first, according to my review of past Lessing titles. Is its presence here a pointer to that capaciousness of a literary form that she has, frequently, declared to be "much more truthful" than autobiography?[35] Or is it a gesture toward the mercurial fictiveness of the writing enterprise itself, which in this case demanded the repudiation of the classic realist text?

But before readers begin the beginning of *love, again a novel,* we are made to move through five initial computerlike windows: one-page salaams to eight "great cartographers" of sexual passion, including Proust, Colette, and Goethe. A second window, the acknowledgment page, lists twenty-five writers from D. H. Lawrence through Aphra Behn and Andrew Marvell. A third window opens to quote a verse from William Butler Yeats's "Memory,"[36] his Maud Gonne plaint of unrequited love. A fourth window opens with the title, *sans* its informing double *a novel*. And a fifth and final window quotes a fragment from Dietrich's crystalline *"I'm falling in love again, Never wanted to . . . ."* My guess is these five windows, in conjunction with the double-decker structure and the double-decker narratorial shift from the

7: love, again, and The Sweetest Dream

detachment of the omniscient Eye/Voice to the writhing, burning intensity of the focalizing voice, are directed toward Lessing's long-announced conviction that the personal is never primary.

Precisely such a terrain belongs to the classic realist text whose subject is always the ongoing life of society, where individual lives are enmeshed within political, economic, and historical encomia. And if the sister text of *love, again* is *The Golden Notebook,* then *The Sweetest Dream* gains by being in sororial affinity to *The Four-Gated City.* (In this comparison, however, one must set aside the latter's speculative "APPENDIX".) [37] Responding to cultural, political, psychological, sexual, and intellectual change, both *The Four-Gated City* and *The Sweetest Dream* represent long-standing narrative critiques of postwar Britain, with *The Sweetest Dream* giving fictional shape to large social questions and to the individual's experience of them as either coercive or liberating. A documentation, depiction, and diagnosis of three decades ranging from the so-called Swinging Sixties through the eighties with their ethic of greed, this capacious canvas has characters enough to embarrass a nineteenth-century Russian novel. (By my count, there are thirty-two *named* characters, one of whom, the African President Matthew Mungozi, makes his initial appearance on page three hundred and sixty, *viz.*, ninety-eight pages before the fiction's end.)

The Sweetest Dream's central figure is Frances Lennox, a divorced woman writer in her forties with two adolescent sons. Distinctly different from *love, again's* mapping of its heroine's movement from the whirlpool perils of romantic obsession in her journey toward detachment, *The Sweetest Dream* places the aging of its heroine over three decades in an explicitly political frame. At the same time, in *The Sweetest Dream's* recasting of the Angel in the House,[38] Frances Lennox is figured as the manager of her sons' friends, most of whom are deranged, melancholic, confused, and certainly disaffected. Indeed, it is a carnival cast of misfits that wanders through her house and Lessing's text: druggies; an anorexic stepdaughter; discarded wives; adolescent dropouts swaddled in sleeping bags; indulged and infantile "kids" who shoplift on principle, "liberating" Biba dresses or expensive books because all property is theft; Rose, a vicious tabloid journalist; weak, unhappy sons—such as Colin—who drink too much; corpulent and corrupt African politicians and civil servants; fat cats who work for international agencies such as "Global Money" and "Caring International." Then there is Frances's former husband, Johnny Lennox, a selfish, dishonest, greedy, vain, and all too seductive Communist Party comrade. True to its alignment with the realist text's focus on the forces and institutions that decide the course of lives, *The Sweetest Dream* presents the seventies, which from one end of the (non-Communist) world to the other was to have bred "a race of Che Guevara clones" (188). Here universities—particularly those in London, as the text insists—are presented caustically as in "almost continuous celebration of Revolution, with demonstrations, riots, sit-ins, lockouts, battles of all kinds." Seething everywhere were these young heroes:

> and Johnny had become a grand old man, and the fact that he was an almost entirely unrepentant Stalinist had a certain limited chic among these youngsters who mostly believed that if Trotsky had won the battle for power with Stalin then communism would have worn a beatific face. (188)

Its title suggesting not theme so much as occluded irony and regret, *The Sweetest Dream* represents a plural text where, instead of *love, again's* competing narrative frames, in this novel there are competing narrative focalizations. Disparate, yet interlocking, vocal strands emerge from the constantly shifting points of view. However, three presiding women, each of a different (therefore antagonistic) generation, dominate. Frances Lennox—the text's primary focalizer—is an especially conscientious mother.[39] In the novel's opening episode, she stands in her kitchen, an inviting table set for sixteen before her, cooking potatoes flavored with celeriac, creamed spinach, buttered carrots, wine-basted lamb stew, providing food to youngsters she was convinced "did not eat 'properly' unless it was at this table" (14). Cape gooseberries, lychees, passion fruit, guavas, Stilton cheese will come to follow as the years are transcribed: "These days there would be nothing remarkable in the witty little spread . . . a swallow visiting from the plenitudes of the future," as Frances will come to think (87). (As a self-consciously realist novel about London during the three decades, *The Sweetest Dream* lets us, for example, remember and relish the sixties specifics of Biba mini dresses, Vidal Sassoon haircuts, Elizabeth David recipes for *Poulet farci en cocotte* or *Dindonneau farci aux marrons mode d'Artois*.)

Frances Lennox is the all too familiar Lessing figure, the reliable maternal woman: the middle-aged wise woman who undertakes the responsibilities of households, the fatigued manager who organizes food, spooning out suppers and suggestions and becoming, mostly, a sponge for the discordant needs and demands round her table. To compare Sarah Durham with this character is to recognize just how much the protagonist of *love, again* is, by way of her solitary valiance, a singularly different kind of heroine and how very much the narrative strategies of the two novels differ, despite the fact that each addresses the resolute realities of women as they age.

Kitchen, basement, attic, storied house of many rooms, the once elegant

7: love, again, *and* The Sweetest Dream

Hampstead home *The Sweetest Dream's* extended family inhabits is another familiar trope, that of the house as cultural, political, and economic metonym for nation.[40] Each level, indeed each room, serves as the repository for what amount to the competing political posturings and passions of the sixties—from unreconstructed Stalinism, to libertarianism, the New Left, and women's liberations. The upper regions are occupied by Frances's ex-mother-in-law, the German-born patrician Julia Lennox. The ex-daughter-in-law resides a level below, and the two grandsons, Andrew and Colin Lennox, one more level below.

> No one said, "Why does Julia need four rooms?" The house was hers. This rackety over-full house, people coming and going, sleeping on floors, bringing friends whose names she often did not know, had at its top an alien zone, which was all order. (3)

Frances and Julia are the dominating presences in the first two decades. Frances's ex-husband Johnny Lennox's stepdaughter, Sylvia, presides over the last decade, the novel having abruptly departed for Zimlia, the newly independent African nation, clearly based on Lessing's Zimbabwe.[41] Sylvia, now in adulthood a qualified doctor, flies there as a missionary angel to heal the sick in a village, and to set up a rudimentary school and clinic. Such is the large scope of this novel that readers are pulled into this increasingly corrupt country, where a wholly narratorial voice, neither neutral nor impersonal, judges.

> And Zimlia, ill-governed before on ill-digested Marxism and tigs and tags of dogma, or remembered sentences from textbooks on economics, now rapidly plunged into corruption. Immediately currency began its steady, but rapid devaluation. In Senga [Harare, Zimbabwe's capital city] the fat cats got fatter everyday and out in places like Kwadere [Sylvia's village] money that had descended into a trickle now dried up altogether. (365)

Here the shattered dream implied by *The Sweetest Dream's* title is African liberation, with Sylvia facing daily the fact of greed, poverty, incompetence, and—in her capacity as a physician in an impoverished rural Catholic mission—the slim sickness, which in the early eighties (President Mugabe having declared AIDS an invention of the whites) was misdiagnosed as pneumonia, tuberculosis, diarrhea, skin lesions.

That it is the character Sylvia Lennox who comes to manage this African mission—so far away from the multitudinous gifts, capacities, and excesses of London and starving for food, medicines, books—is particularly apt. For it is through her figure that the novel turns its implicit indictment of the wastefulness and indolence of the non-African world. In adolescence an anorexic, sitting at Frances Lennox's groaning table with its chicken stews, breads, cheeses in Julia Lennox's house with its solidity, safety, permanence, "each room so full of things that had an exact purpose, serving a need among a multiplicity of needs" (367), Sylvia had to be literally nursed back to life through the ministrations of the two competent women, Frances and Julia. That anorexia prefigures the starvation Sylvia will come to know in Africa, Zimlia being the recipient of incompetent ministrations from abroad: donations from a "Global Money" or "Caring International" are as extravagant and useless as, for example, grandiose tractors by the hundreds that will rot and rust for want of spare parts, fuel, know-how.

The terrible waifs, druggies, thieves, and middle-class dropouts who once bickered round Frances's table, subscribing to the various dogmas of universal liberal idealism, become players in the world. In adulthood they are as uninformed, indulgent, and self-absorbed as they were in adolescence. Only now there are dangerous consequences, as we discover when they are reintroduced in *The Sweetest Dream's* African section. Andrew Lennox has become a preening, besuited "Caring International" delegate living in luxury hotels, while Rose Trimble has grown fat as a muckraking journalist who (for a purpose) pleases Zimlia's Marxist regime, slandering the family she had sponged off in earlier years to satisfy her adolescent envy of and rage against the privileged Lennox household. Thus, to further her career, Rose ends Sylvia's work at the Mission hospital by writing a smear piece charging Sylvia with being a close associate of a deported South African spy. "Sylvia was a doctor, people knew she had created a hospital in the bush where none had existed. She had fallen foul of the government, too bad," as the narrative voice stonily summarizes (446).

Unproblematic as is *The Sweetest Dream's* chronological narrative, its title announces its overall agenda, one set to debunk inherited habits of mind, first fostered by the Communist Party where—according to Lessing's longheld position—the habit of polarization came to contaminate critical judgment. Thus does this novel anticipate twenty-first-century preoccupations with political correctness and those contrarians who expose its inflexible reductiveness. More unsparingly than in any other of the works, *The Sweetest Dream* is fueled by the conviction that cant must be exposed and prevailing orthodoxies laid bare. So the vainglorious slogans of sixties radicals are stripped clean along with the self-serving shibboleths of seventies feminists and the righteous rhetoric of eighties anticolonialists. In this densely inhabited Condition of England novel, the consistent object of vilification is the unthinking adherence to dogma that leads believers to commit heinous acts in pursuit of one utopian dream or another.

And how does this huge, brave, contradictory novel end? Returning to the questions first posed, that endings may mark critical points for analyses of plot as well as structure, I would suggest that—in contrast to *love, again*, which merely stops—*The Sweetest Dream* concludes. To the earlier death of Julia—and her representative meaning as an individual shaped by the legacies of two world wars—is added that of Sylvia, whose dream of making a better world had been so sweet she worked herself to death. A chilled and chilling novel, it does show the importance of individual acts of charity—most frequently that unsung labor that is the work of women: Rebecca, the Zimlian housekeeper at the Mission, or Sister Molly, the fiercely independent Irish nun. For all its derisive debunking of politically correct feminism, *The Sweetest Dream* is really about women who simply get on with it. (In keeping with the novel's conviction that cant must be exposed, neither Rebecca nor Sister Molly would ever describe their work as the kind conventionally expected of women; nor would they countenance the notion of women's roles, a phrase of which they would not so much disapprove, as deplore.) Julia, Frances, Sylvia: these are the women who engage in small but sustaining acts of philanthropy. So readers are persuaded that the novel's resolution is a life-affirming one. The novel closes some thirty years after it has begun—in the Hampstead kitchen with a newly configured family group round the deal table—and Frances's granddaughter Celia, fourth-generation Lennox female, spinning, spinning, spinning. "The little girl did not want to be gathered in and held, she spun around on herself, singing for herself and to herself . . ." (479).

Turning back to *love, again*, *The Sweetest Dream*'s contrasting companion, let me reiterate the question, "When does a novel end?" Conclusions are so frequently the least real part of a novel; "But it wasn't an end, it wasn't *a real end*"—as a young child in A. S. Byatt's *A Whistling Woman* fiercely protests at the conclusion of a long, intricate, and magical tale.[42] *Northanger Abbey*'s narrator may famously observe that her "readers will see in the telltale compression of the pages before them that we are all hastening together to perfect felicity"[43] as the final chapter—in characteristic Austen fashion—summarily winds up lives and loves. [L]ove, again* does not offer such a windup, but something of an open-ended ending. Lessing has her novel stop in the middle of a conversation between Sarah and her two nieces. Apparently they have been talking about their recently divorced father, who is Sarah's demanding, infantile, and confident brother Hal: "'*Please* don't be too nice to him,' Briony said to Sarah, 'or we'll never get him married again'" (352). It is the novel's last sentence.

Readers are left resonantly but ambiguously up in the air. Can this then be the ending of a novel about lust and love in old age? To be sure, readers have revisited the very room we entered on the first page: Sarah discarding the accumulated mementos, thus symbolically stripping away false memories. Just as she has inspected herself before the mirror at the novel's beginning, so at its ending she interrogates her image, seeing a woman now, after merely one year, ten years older. To be sure, the reader has been offered an epiphanic moment in a penultimate scene where, alone in a London park, Sarah "witnesses a mother whose brutal . . . preference for one of her children [her son and not the older daughter] awakens a suppressed memory [that she too had been] rebuffed and unloved."[44] Her unquenchable craving for love had this source. So even *love, again* is informed, even infused, by the figure of Lessing's mother, the author—then in her seventh decade—still picking at a festering wound long since in need of benign neglect.[45] I remain convinced that such a reductive explanation for the yearnings of erotic need—mapped we will remember by those acknowledged cartographers Proust, Goethe, Richardson—represents yet another of those "weak patches" of a Lessing enterprise. *[L]ove, again* is a work powerfully strengthened by structural design, thus moving a novel about an older woman's experience well beyond merely bathetic inventory of the anguished loins of old women.

NOTES

1. Doris Lessing, *Walking in the Shade: Volume Two of My Autobiography, 1949 to 1962* (New York: Harper Collins, 1997), 339.

2. Lessing, *love, again* (New York: HarperCollins, 1996).

3. J. M. Coetzee, "The Heart of Me," review of *Under My Skin*, by Doris Lessing, *New York Review of Books*, December 22, 1994, http://www.nybooks.com/articles/2034 (accessed July 26, 2009). (This Web site does not have pagination.)

4. Lessing, *The Sweetest Dream* (2001; repr., New York: HarperCollins, 2002).

5. Lessing, "A Writer Is Not a Professor," interview by Jean-Maurice de Montremy, in *Doris Lessing: Conversations*, edited by Earl G. Ingersoll (Princeton, NJ: Ontario Review Press, 1994), 196.

6. Lessing, "Writing as Time Runs Out," interview by Michael Dean, *Conversations*, 91.

7. Ibid., 93.

8. Lessing, *The Golden Notebook* (London: Michael Joseph, 1962).

9. Lessing, *A Ripple from the Storm*, vol. 3 of *Children of Violence* (London:

7: love, again, *and* The Sweetest Dream

Michael Joseph, 1958).

10. With their thumb on the wrist of a population well beyond its first prime (yet healthy and wealthy enough to purchase self-help specialties), publishers have produced a battery of books on many aspects of aging since 2000, including *The New Love and Sex after 60* by Dr. Robert N. Butler and Dr. Myrna I. Lewis (New York: Ballantine Books, 2002). On August 23, 2007, *The New England Journal of Medicine*, in its most comprehensive national survey of sexuality among older Americans, *Love and Sex after 60*, reported that some are active sexually well into their early eighties and many through their sixties. Providing the first clear picture of sexuality in later life, the survey was based on interviews that researchers at The University of Chicago and the University of Toronto undertook with 3005 Americans from fifty-seven to eighty-five years of age. John H. J. Bancroft, "Sex and Aging," *The New England Journal of Medicine* 357.8 (August 23, 2007): 820–22.

11. Frank Kermode, "Sensing Endings," *Nineteenth-Century Fiction* 33.1 (1978): 145.

12. "Sarah's male counterpart and close friend . . . [is] so completely in love with his fantasy image of the long-dead Julie that he sees no alternative to suicide" (John Hobbs, "Love, Again," *America* 175.18 [1996]: 25). One of the germinating seeds for the novel, the nature of grief, came to Lessing (as she remarked during an interview) when she spoke with a friend who had fallen in love with his great-aunt, on seeing her portrait. "When someone tells you something like that, of course, you smile. But it was no laughing matter. I tried to make practical remarks to him, but he wasn't going to have it. In fact [he] committed suicide." Helena de Bertodano, "Life Is Stronger than Fiction," *Daily Telegraph*, April 11, 1996, 5.

13. Lessing, *love, again*, 43.

14. William Shakespeare, *A Midsummer Night's Dream* (New York: Washington Square Press, 1967).

15. Jane Austen, *Emma*, vol. 2, *The Complete Novels of Jane Austen* (New York: The Modern Library, 1992).

16. Lessing, *The Memoirs of a Survivor* (London: Octagon Press, 1974).

17. Lessing, *The Diaries of Jane Somers* (London: Michael Joseph, 1984).

18. J. Hillis Miller, "The Problematic of Ending in Narrative," *Nineteenth-Century Fiction* 33.1 (1978): 5.

19. "The basic situation in the novel . . . cannot but seem mundane, compared to Anna's political and sexual evolution [in *The Golden Notebook*]," writes Paul Schlueter, "Review of *love, again*," *Doris Lessing Newsletter* 18.1 (1996): 1.

20. Anna Latz, "The Quest for Freedom in *Love, Again*," *Doris Lessing Newsletter* 18.2 (1997): 7.

21. Millicent Bell, "Possessed by Love," *Partisan Review* 64.3 (1997): 487.

22. Kate Chopin, *The Awakening* (Chicago: Herbert S. Stone & Company, 1899).

23. Edith Wharton, *The House of Mirth* (New York: Charles Scribner's Sons, 1905).

24. Maureen Corrigan, "Improbably Star-Crossed," review of *love, again*, by Doris Lessing, The *Nation*, May 6, 1996, 63.

25. Latz, "Quest," 3.

26. Describing an inexplicable grief from which she suffered for several months, Lessing observed: "What is interesting is that it expresses itself in physical pain—a heart-

ache so appalling that you could throw yourself off a cliff to get away from it" (de Bertodano, "Life," 5).

27. Lessing, *Walking in the Shade*, 339.

28. Daniel Defoe, *Moll Flanders* (London: Dent, 1977; repr., New York: Dutton, 1977).

29. Henry Fielding, *Tom Jones* (Harlow, Essex, England: Addison Wesley Longman, Ltd., 1999).

30. Samuel Richardson, *Clarissa* (Oxford: Basil Blackwell, 1930).

31. Lessing, *Martha Quest*, vol. 1, *Children of Violence* (London: Michael Joseph, 1952).

32. Austen, *Sense and Sensibility*, vol. 1, *The Complete Novels of Jane Austen* (New York: The Modern Library, 1992).

33. William Golding, *The Inheritors* (London: Faber and Faber, 1955).

34. Lessing, *Briefing for a Descent into Hell* (London: Jonathan Cape, 1971).

35. "[T]o my surprise, I discovered—in writing my autobiography—that fiction is much more truthful: it's a question of memory, what is remembered and the huge stuff of what isn't," Lessing remarked in an October 1997 reading (which I attended) at New York City's 92nd Street Y. On the subject of autobiography and the confessional mode, Lessing has been famously cranky, dismissing biographical parallels in works as obviously autobiographical as the Martha Quest series while admonishing critics for not attending to its encoding in *The Memoirs of a Survivor*, whose title page includes "an attempt at an autobiography."

36. Yeats, "Memory" (1919; repr., in *The Collected Works of W. B. Yeats*, London: Macmillan Company, 1977), 168.

37. Lessing, *The Four-Gated City*, vol. 5, *Children of Violence* (London: MacGibbon and Kee, 1969), 560.

38. Coventry Patmore, "The Angel in the House" (1854–62; excerpted in *The Norton Anthology of English Literature*, 7th ed., vol. 2, ed. M. H. Abrams and Stephen Greenblatt [New York: Norton, 2000]), 1723–24.

39. The speculative pleasure of matching fiction to biographical fact is provided, once again. An "Author's Note" introduces the text, instructing readers that "I am not writing volume three of my autobiography because of possible hurt to vulnerable people. Which does not mean I have novelized autobiography." Lessing, *The Sweetest Dream*, n.p. That disclaimer would seem to follow directly in the footsteps of the last paragraph of her second volume of autobiography, *Walking in the Shade*. "For about six years," Lessing writes of life from 1962 to 1968 (during which time was written, not coincidentally, *The Four-Gated City* with a middle-aged Martha Quest supervising a household of disoriented lives), "I proved my rapport with the times by becoming a housemother—now that is a sixties' word—for adolescents or young adults who either lived at 60 Charrington Street or came and went. All of them were in some kind of trouble: were 'disturbed,' were being seduced by drugs, were alcoholic, were having serious breakdowns, were known to the police" (403). Despite the author's caveat, novel and autobiography should be conflated, the fictive enterprise merging with Lessing's life-long engagement in autobiographical fiction. See Robin Visel's chapter 3 in Part One of this collection, "House/Mother: Lessing's Reproduction of Realism in *The Sweetest Dream*," which also talks about Lessing's reference to cultural artifacts of the 1960s [editors' note].

40. Such a metonym for nation is a particularly appropriate trope for the realist novel in its depiction of the social, the political, and the historical. Recalled in this context is not only the Victorian squat in *The Good Terrorist* (London: Jonathan Cape, 1985) but also the Bloomsbury edifice in *The Four-Gated City* and the seemingly sturdy block of flats in *The Memoirs of a Survivor*.

41. Here a consistent authorial gesture in Lessing's fiction occurs. The novel's author savagely indicts Zimbabwe's President Robert Mugabe, depicted in the character of Comrade President Matthew Mungozi, whose seduction into greed—like that of Mugabe—is likened to other "immensely rich, dissolute and corrupt rulers of the new Africa and new Asia" (365).

42. A. S. Byatt, *A Whistling Woman* (New York: Alfred A. Knopf, 2002), 13.

43. Jane Austen, *Northanger Abbey,* vol. 2, *The Complete Novels of Jane Austen* (New York: The Modern Library, 1992), 526.

44. Bell, "Possessed," 491.

45. See Ruth Saxton's discussion of this same theme of maternal deprivation as the source of Sarah's frustrations in love in her chapter "Sex after Sixty: *love, again* and *The Sweetest Dream*" in Part Four of this volume [editors' note].

Writing in a Minor Key

Doris Lessing's Late-Twentieth-Century Fiction

SUSAN WATKINS

As we travel further into the twenty-first century, the effects of decolonization and globalization are felt in ever more complex and contradictory ways, and debates about "race," nation, and ethnicity have become increasingly central. In the past (with some notable exceptions) readers and critics have paid less attention to Doris Lessing's continued engagement with such ideas than to reading her work in relation to Marxism and feminism.[1] Lessing's work has also been discussed comparatively rarely in relation to postcolonial theory and criticism, as Anthony Chennells suggests.[2] Doris Lessing's late-twentieth-century fiction, specifically *The Fifth Child* (1988), its sequel *Ben, In the World* (2000), and Lessing's 1999 novel *Mara and Dann*, have been controversial precisely because of the way she writes about "race" and nation. Readers have been disturbed by her appropriation of racially marked stereotypes of the animal, the primitive, and the atavistic in each text.[3] A secondary and related concern surrounds the success of Lessing's choices of genre and narrative technique; Lessing deploys in unfamiliar and disturbing ways what might be termed the "minor" genres of urban gothic, picaresque, and disaster narrative in her late-twentieth-century work. Certainly, genre and "race" are connected issues in Lessing's work, and it is only when those connections are understood that we can make an assessment of this fiction and understand Lessing's attack on dominant cultural and ideological formations in the late twentieth century. This attack is a clear response to the cultural climate of the period in which the novels were written, a climate in which "race" issues were of increasing concern.[4] In the twenty-first century, issues of "race" and nation are, of course, even more to the fore, and Lessing's prescience in dealing with such questions is evident.

In analyzing Lessing's late-twentieth-century "fabular" fictions in relation to ideas about genre and "race," Gilles Deleuze and Félix Guattari's discussion of "minor" literature proves instructive. Deleuze and Guattari define minor literature as exhibiting three main characteristics: "the deterritorialization of language, the connection of the individual to a political immediacy, and the collective assemblage of enunciation."[5] Thus, minor literature has a partial relation to nationality both linguistically and, I will argue, generically. The "social milieu" (18) is not merely background or context for the individual protagonist or author; rather, her relation to that context is directly, explicitly political. The concept of the author as "master" of the text or gifted individual is replaced by a "collective, and even revolutionary, enunciation" (17). Of particular relevance to Lessing's late-twentieth-century fiction is the conception of "becoming animal," which constitutes an *absolute deterritorialization . . . an immobile voyage*" (35). Deleuze and Guattari suggest that in Kafka's work the "becoming-human of the animal and the becoming-animal of the human" are part of a "single circuit" (35) that deliberately resists metaphoricity, symbolism, and allegory. This attempt to block the impulse to read the human/animal metaphorically is clearly related to the resistance of the territoriality of genre in Lessing's late-twentieth-century fiction. When reading this work, we are unable to secure or anchor our response to identity in terms of the well-worn distinction between the animal and the human; we are equally unable to find a safe home in familiar genres.

Although its disturbing qualities were often noted, *The Fifth Child* was far better received than *Ben, In the World* and *Mara and Dann*. Lessing's blend of elements of fantasy, horror, fable, and fairy tale within the realist fabric and framework of the text was generally seen as successful and as an explanation for "the visceral response the novel has engendered."[6] Those who admired the play with generic convention also appreciated the text's ambiguous treatment of Ben's "difference." Throughout the text, Harriet, Ben's mother, seeks to explain his behavior in terms of the animal, the primitive, and the atavistic, suggesting that he may be an alien, goblin, troll, or monstrous changeling. Most significantly, Harriet repeatedly returns to the interpretation of Ben as a Neanderthal genetic throwback.

Despite praise for the novel, many critics saw its message as profoundly conservative and potentially racist. Louise Yelin, for example, argues that in representing Ben as a throwback Lessing evokes the threat of the "enemy within" or racial "other." She links this process of racial "othering" to contemporary British politics, particularly to the increasingly racist elements of British Conservative Party ideology during Margaret Thatcher's governments of the 1980s, which made use, she suggests, of the figure of "the enemy within."[7] Yelin concludes that Ben's attacks on Harriet represent an alien invasion of the white British motherland by black people: "[i]n the national narrative that unfolds in *The Fifth Child,* the alien invader, a version of the enemy within, is Ben—that is, the discursive construction of Ben's difference reproduces the discursive construction of racial difference common to Powellite 'new racism' and 'Thatcherite ideology'" (104). Enoch Powell was a Conservative Member of Parliament famous for his "rivers of blood" speech of 1968, in which he argued that infiltration of white British culture by non-white peoples in the post–World War II period would inevitably produce social tension and ultimately violence. Enoch Powell gave his speech on April 20, 1968, to the Annual General Meeting of the West Midlands Area Conservative Association. Shoring up his remarks with classical allusions, Powell spoke of the future of "race-relations" in Britain thus: "As I look ahead, I am filled with foreboding; like the Roman, I seem to see 'the River Tiber foaming with much blood.'" The speech was substantially quoted in the *Birmingham Post* on April 22, 1968. Powell subsequently lost his position as shadow cabinet minister under the leadership of Edward Heath.[8] Although Yelin conflates two very different periods in Conservative Party politics and ideology (the 1960s and the 1980s), it is the case that in the 1980s many commentators saw rioting and social unrest in inner-city areas of London, Bristol, Liverpool, and Birmingham as evidence of the accuracy of Powell's prophecy rather than a legitimate response to deindustrialization, escalating unemployment, and social deprivation.

Yelin's argument constructs *The Fifth Child* as one of a number of texts that establish Lessing's "exclusionary concept of national identity."[9] Yet this reading of the novel as profoundly racist is possible only because she ignores the generic complexity and ambivalence of narrative perspective in the text. In this respect, Yelin's negative assessment of *The Fifth Child* more closely resembles critical opinion about Lessing's sequel, *Ben, In the World,* which is more often seen as inferior. Michiko Kakutani argues that whereas the first novel worked because it "created a perfect balance between naturalistic detail and fablelike allegory," the sequel is an artistic failure because it "reads entirely like a fairy-tale, and a not very compelling one at that."[10] Other reviewers have commented negatively on the novel's fabular, allegorical, and picaresque qualities and have doubted the wisdom of switching the point of view to Ben himself.[11] Kakutani describes the novel as exhibiting a "primitive, knee-jerk brand of story-telling."[12]

8: Writing in a Minor Key

The negative response to Lessing's choices of genre, style, and narrative technique in *Ben, In the World* corresponds with judgments about the novel's treatment of issues of "race." Alex Clark writes: "We are given to understand, over and over again, that Ben does in fact belong to a branch of the species that has long since died out."[13] Kakutani suggests that the novel's animalistic descriptions of Ben "make him out to be some sort of generic creature, endowed with only the most instinctual reactions and responses, and Ms. Lessing does nothing to give him a discernible personality."[14] The concern here is that Lessing's style, technique, and generic choices encourage readers to objectify Ben and position him as animal, nonhuman, and unfathomably "other" in ways that are subtly and disturbingly racially coded.

Responses to *Mara and Dann*, published the year before *Ben, In the World*, suggest similar anxieties about both form and content. Many reviewers note the fairy-tale or fabular plot of orphaned siblings who make a long journey to safety through trials and tribulations.[15] The consensus seems to be that the novel is a failure as science fiction, either because of its "iffy technology"[16] or because of its "clichéd" message of industrialized culture's dependence on technology and indifference to global warming.[17] The suggestion persists that Lessing never quite manages to jettison her realist roots, which remain as unhappy traces of unrealized characters and unfortunately clumsy style. She would have been better off, as Michael Upchurch suggests, sticking to "her greatest strength as a writer: her ability to dissect the vacillations and delusions of 20th-century people living in a 20th-century world."[18]

The "tribal" treatment of character in the novel and its implicit racial marking of physical difference also provoke comment. Kakutani points out that "virtually all the bad people Mara and Dann meet are short, thick and ugly; virtually all the good people they meet are tall, thin and gracious ... the minor characters in the novels are crude types, not individuals."[19] Erica Wagner also remarks on the "tribal" nature of difference in the world of Ifrik: "Mara and Dann, dark-haired, brown-skinned Mahondis, move northwards, encountering different tribes along the way; the controlling, sybaritic Hadrons; the clone-like, sinister Hennes; the pale-skinned Albs, who claim their origin in the frozen continent of Yerrup."[20] At its most extreme, a tribe of look-alikes represents, according to Upchurch, one of a number of "menacing racial varieties."[21] This apparently "lazy" characterization is most apparent in what is believed to be the swift recourse to the idea of the tribe as a way of grouping and naming people in the novel.

The ease with which some readers have made these three texts occupy racist positions results from a failure to appreciate what Lessing has attempted in each case in terms of genre and narrative perspective. These novels make much more sense if they are seen as "minor" genres that ultimately critique racist narrative. As Deleuze and Guattari suggest, "A minor literature doesn't come from a minor language; it is rather that which a minority constructs within a major language" or, to rephrase, "what a minor genre constructs within the territory of a major one" (16). Lessing utilizes characteristics of urban gothic in *The Fifth Child;* she uses the picaresque tradition in *Ben, In the World;* and she works in the subgenre of the disaster narrative in *Mara and Dann.* Thus, Lessing uses these minor narratives to call attention to the racial implications that underlie the narratives of family values and evolutionary progress and then, in doing so, works toward dislodging them.

The representation of Ben in *The Fifth Child* is, as Yelin suggests, intimately related to the decade of the 1980s and what it signified in British culture. However, rather than evoking a white British motherland threatened by "the enemy within" in order to construct an "exclusionary concept of national identity,"[22] Lessing attempts something rather different: something that closely resembles what has come to be known as the urban gothic. According to Roger Luckhurst, in his account of "London gothic," British gothic fiction in the late 1980s and 1990s began to respond in new ways to ideas of the metropolitan and the urban, creating "a newly Gothicized apprehension of London."[23] Gothic fiction of the last two decades of the twentieth century, he argues, responds to debates over how best to govern contemporary London. During the 1980s the abolition of ILEA (the Inner London Education Authority) and the GLC (Greater London Council), the principal local authority for London, was a key part of a Conservative ideological agenda that sought to remove conflict with central government and eradicate challenges from implicitly subversive (and left-leaning) local government. Luckhurst claims that we can witness the "deliberate evisceration of London's democratic public sphere marked out on the physical landscape of the city" (539) and also read it in the period's gothic fiction. Placing *The Fifth Child* in this context allows us to interpret it as a family "romance" in which the gothic convention of the return of the repressed is deliberately deployed in order to generate a critique of 1980s Conservative Britain and its defensive focus on family values and fear of inner-city social unrest. Margaret Thatcher famously denied the existence of such a thing as "society," suggesting that there were no larger social groups than the family.[24] In this way, she rejected any larger-scale explanation for social problems that sought to find answers in the consequences of unemployment and inner-city deprivation rather than in individual and family breakdown.

At the opening of the novel we are told that when Harriet and David met, they both recognized something familiar in the other: "conservative, old-fashioned, not to say obsolescent; timid, hard to please . . . they defended a stubbornly held view of themselves, which was that they were ordinary and in the right of it, should not be criticized for emotional fastidiousness, abstemiousness, just because these were unfashionable qualities."[25] The use of the word "conservative" here primarily suggests a fundamental timidity and traditionalism rather than any specific political position, but the core values of the couple are, more importantly, positioned as *defensive*. Specifically, they are defensive of their normality and typicality in their adherence to family values and traditional sexual propriety during the 1960s (when the novel opens), a decade in which such values were being challenged. The couple feel similarly "abstemious" about establishing their home in London: "Not possible to find the kind of house they wanted, for the life they wanted, in London. Anyway, they were not sure London was what they needed—no, it wasn't, they would prefer a smallish town with an atmosphere of its own" (13). Given that the couple represent family and suburban commuter values, it is not surprising (since this is a gothic novel) that their fifth child is born with the opposite inclinations: he has an aggressively animalistic, violent, and physical nature, coupled with, as he gets older, an affiliation to youthful gang or street culture that represents an antifamily and stereotypically urban stance: "These days the local newspapers were full of news of muggings, hold-ups, break-ins. Sometimes this gang, Ben among them, did not come into the Lovatts' house for a whole day, two days, three" (147). Ben represents everything the couple repudiates in their rejection of the urban: sexuality, violence, the city, the gang, and the animal.

The reader necessarily shares Harriet's fear of Ben and her near inability to define him as human, but identification with Harriet is only ever partial. The text encourages readers to reach beyond surface meanings and construct allegorical ones, but it then deconstructs those allegories so that, as Collins and Wilson suggest, "the novella actually undermines its own legitimizing allegorical dimension and that of other legitimizing narratives." This happens partly as a consequence of what Collins and Wilson term "genre-boundary trespass"[26] and partly through the clever use of narrative perspective. In other words, if readers are encouraged by Harriet to interpret Ben as a genetic throwback to a more "primitive race," they are also encouraged to question this interpretation by the novel's textual and generic strategies of "deterritorialization" of genre. Although the narration is in the third person, the point of view is closely but not exclusively aligned with Harriet's; this shifting focalization both encourages and resists the complete identification of the reader with Harriet. Throughout the text we see the explanations that various characters offer for Ben's "difference" as powerful but ultimately insufficient. This involvement of our most as well as our least reactionary responses is, I believe, one of the strengths of Lessing's use of genre and one of the ways in which the novel makes very uncomfortable reading. Luckhurst argues that the fiction he terms London or urban gothic cannot be described as a "coherent political analysis of London ills"; it can just as easily create "nostalgia for those very spaces of unregulated violence or disorderly conduct."[27] In other words we might feel an almost pleasurable revulsion when Ben is found eating raw meat because we feel (temporarily at least) able to position him as securely "other" and animal. The serious engagement with deeply disturbing beliefs is characteristic of the genre and explains why critics such as Yelin can interpret *The Fifth Child* as endorsing a racist agenda. As David Punter remarks when discussing *The Good Terrorist*: "What is not shirked . . . is that parts of ourselves, as readers, as social beings, as terrorists, may be bound up in these liminal depictions. It is this admission of involvement which saves Lessing's text from . . . the inevitability of complicity, the feeling of voyeurism, the colouring of the salacious." He continues: "It is, seemingly paradoxically, the case that while we continue to depict the terrorist as uncompromisingly 'out there' . . . we remain at the mercy of our own projections, always running the risk of revelling in a fear which we can justify as representative of a State legal system 'in terror.'"[28] In other words, because we have been forced to share Harriet's response to Ben we are unable to repudiate it prematurely. We have to acknowledge how we are implicated in fear of difference and thus come to understand this fear and question it.

Harriet's decision to rescue Ben from the institution where he has been incarcerated (after an unspoken family agreement made without her knowledge) demonstrates that she is unable literally to expel Ben from the family, the human, and the suburban: she is unable to make him "become animal." At the point where she decides to take him home, she thinks that "he looked more ordinary [read "human"] than she had ever seen him" (100). Becoming human–becoming animal is, as Deleuze and Guattari suggest, a "single circuit" (35).[29] In returning him to the family she takes his place as scapegoat and endures the resentment and blame (but also the pity) of her husband and children (and the reader). This mobility in the figure of the "other" within the family unit is more disturbing than the simple fear of Ben. Who might be rejected next? The text's strategies thus involve a more complex critique of family values and the place of the mother within them.

Like many writers before her, Lessing uses Ben, her picaro figure, as a way to comment on a society experiencing intense social upheaval. As Angela Hague remarks, the critical consensus is that "picaresque literature flourishes when a society is in a state of flux."[30] Her article analyzes a number of 1950s novelists who have been retrospectively grouped with the "angry young men" movement and notes that their use of features of the picaresque novel is important in establishing their critical, "outsider" stance on 1950s Britain. According to Hague, the typical hero of these novels and those of the picaresque tradition is a marginal figure, critical of society but unable to find a space outside it. Other important features are the emphasis on "the material level of existence[,] . . . where existence and subsistence are discussed in terms of 'sordid facts, hunger, money' and a profusion of objects and details," all of which project contemptuous attitudes toward art.[31] In the 1950s Lessing was aligned with many of the writers Hague discusses; she contributed her well-known essay "A Small Personal Voice" to the 1957 volume *Declaration*, which was associated with the "angry" stance,[32] so perhaps it is not surprising that she might exhibit an interest in the possibilities of the picaresque, even if decades later.

The picaro is a semi-outsider figure, but Ben's isolation is far more severe, and his ability to survive by his wits and turn a series of exploitative situations to his advantage (another feature of the genre) are far more in doubt. The emphasis on the material becomes, in this novel, a frequent detailing of Ben's animalistic urges for meat, violence, and sex. Contempt for elite art forms and the idea that the picaro's own life *is* his art form are pushed to extremes when Ben is taken up by a film director, Alex, who imagines making a film about a Neanderthal in which Ben will star as himself: "Alex was saying quietly to himself that Ben was not human, even if most of the time he behaved like one. And he was not animal. He was a throwback of some kind. If the company of ancient men were only a kind of animal how was it that Ben could live the life of human beings—well, for most of the time?"[33] The aim of *Ben, In the World* is satirical. Lessing uses Ben as a device to question how we define humanity and how we separate ourselves from the animal and the atavistic. Some, such as Alex or the director of the research institute in which Ben is imprisoned for the purpose of scientific experiment with other animals, attempt to quantify the difference between themselves and Ben as that between the primitive and the cultured or the animal and the human. This taxonomic attitude, Lessing implies, intensifies the racist attitudes that lie not far beneath the lip service paid to diversity in contemporary Western industrialized cultures. The distinction between animal and human makes use of pseudo-Darwinian hierarchies or distinctions that position white masculinity at the apex of an evolutionary chain ascending from the apes to Africans (often figured as "gorillas" and "apes" or with ancient human ancestors, particularly Neanderthals) and finally to white European peoples. In collapsing such distinctions, Lessing also challenges the late-nineteenth-century positivist narrative that sanctioned colonization. As Brickman suggests: "the idea of 'the primitive' and its network of associated meanings played a critical role as a central trope of colonialist discourse and its evolutionary approach to racial and cultural difference. The colonialist designation of conquered peoples as 'primitive' was an attempt to cloak as scientifically respectable the domination of human beings considered as Europe's racial others."[34] Indeed, it might be argued that the evolutionary thinking implicit within such distinctions between "the primitive" and "the evolved" is still in play in the United States' various efforts to export its traditional narrative of democracy around the world.

If it is a feature of the picaresque novel to negotiate the opposition between nature and civilization, *Ben, In the World* resembles other contemporary "neo-picaresque" texts that exaggerate and parody the very opposition between nature and culture in order to demonstrate the fully cultural, indeed linguistic, construction of ideas of the natural, the animal, and the freakish.[35] It is for this reason that, though often aligned with Ben's, the point of view in *Ben, In the World* is not confined to his first-person narration as in many early picaresque texts. The narrator is thus able to demonstrate how those around Ben develop their perceptions of him and to show how Ben acquires an understanding of himself through the responses of others. Indeed, the questionable reliability of perception in the novel extends to the "objectivity" of the narrator's own voice, which is parodied through the humorous device of prolepsis.[36] To take just one example, we are told that Alfredo and Teresa had a strong understanding that "ended in their marrying, some months in the future. So their story at least has a happy ending: things turned out well for them" (134). Lessing is here exaggerating to the point of ridicule the device of omniscience, associating our naïve belief in what the narrator tells us with the acceptance of "common sense" judgments about Ben's difference from others and questioning both.

In *Mara and Dann,* Lessing returns to science fiction, a genre that Luckhurst argues underwent resurgence in the late 1990s. At this specific historical moment, he suggests, governmental rhetoric was focused on incorporating previously oppositional cultural industries such as avant-garde fine art and popular music into the work of the New Labour government. Science fiction was one of the few genres (others are gothic and fantasy) that "could still find spaces outside the general de-differentiation or 'mainstreaming' effect sought by the strategy of cultural governance."[37] One specific SF subgenre he considers is the disaster narrative, which has always formed a significant part of the British SF tradition. Critics such as Fredric Jameson and Peter Nicholls have claimed that such narratives are often concerned with "imperial anxiety."[38] What is striking about *Mara and Dann* is the way it attempts to rewrite the construction of an embattled but surviving England that is key to such texts as *The Day of the Triffids* (1951) and *The Midwich Cuckoos* (1957).[39] In this novel the ice age that has completely redrawn the map of the world has obscured Europe, or Yerrup (and presumably the rest of the industrialized West). The action takes place in Ifrik (Africa), where drought is threatening all but the northern parts of the continent. In many disaster narratives there is a reversion to a folkloric, pastoral idyll associated by implication with reactionary class and race formations, or as Luckhurst suggests, a return to "conservative narratives of belonging to some ancient tradition inhering in the land."[40] Lessing alludes to this tradition at the novel's opening, where Mara and Dann are forced, as children, hurriedly to leave home with changed identities, for their own (and, it is strongly implied, their tribe's) protection. At this time Mara's main sense of the world around her is tribal—her sense of her (superior) Mahondi People as opposed to the (inferior) Rock People. We are encouraged to believe throughout the novel that Mara and Dann are special, "chosen" and being watched and kept for a unique destiny. Toward the end Mara and Dann's "true" identities as Mahondi royalty are revealed. However, when urged to marry her brother Dann and form a new dynasty capable of ruling Ifrik when the ice finally retreats, Mara responds, "I don't know why you are so anxious to rule Ifrik. . . . It is a desert of dust and death below the River Towns."[41] Instead of gracefully and gratefully accepting their future, she and Dann run away and continue their journey north. The novel ends with them forming a small self-sufficient farm on the temperate northern coast, joined by several others from a number of different tribes or "races." Suggestively, Dann asks Mara a question that concludes the novel: "Mara, tell me honestly, no truthfully, the real truth: when you wake up in the morning, isn't it the first thing you think of—how far you're going to go up today, one foot after another, another little bit of the way up Ifrik?" (407). Mara admits that this is true. The novel's final emphasis on process rather than conclusions refuses a mythic narrative trajectory that should conclude with racial and class difference confirmed as absolute, hierarchical, and bound up with a notion of nation and land. Equally, the focus on Mara's point of view, on the details of sexuality and reproduction, which she contends with during her journey, and on her relationship with her brother, serves to challenge the patriarchal focus and structure of such narratives.

In deploying and disrupting the features of a number of what Deleuze and Guattari might term "minor" literary genres, Lessing aims to challenge the implicitly racist cultural constructs of the animal, the primitive, and the tribe that were becoming significant in late-twentieth-century Britain. It is obvious that Lessing's long career as a writer has not merely echoed or provided a commentary on, but often initiated, developments in British fiction. What is noticeable about her writing is the progressive challenge she offers to realism as the century progresses, accompanied by her "eternal (partial) return" to it. As Gąsiorek suggests, "Lessing disrupts realist narrative modes from within and turns to other genres in her search for ways to mediate contemporary social life."[42] As Alice Ridout notes in her essay "'What Is the Function of the Storyteller?': The Relationship between *Why* and *How* Lessing Writes," Lessing's initial attachment to realism was a political one, as is suggested in "The Small Personal Voice," but as her enthusiasm for Communist politics waned so did her belief in the realist mode as necessarily progressive. As early as 1987 Hanson sees her work as typically postmodernist in its challenge to "the authority of identity and the identity of the author" and in its rough, unresolved style,[43] what Deleuze and Guattari term "sobriety of language" rather than "intensities, reversals and thickenings of it" (58). I would also argue that her periodic and deliberate choice of minor genres suggests a growing awareness that the formal strategies of "expressive realism" can be aligned with reactionary positions that have attempted to silence and exclude the feminine and the minority ethnic. Lessing's movement in and out of realism (what Gąsiorek terms an experimental realism rather than an outright rejection of it) is an attempt not merely to raise issues about form, style, and technique, but also to explore the political implications of certain generic and stylistic choices, particularly in relation to those issues that have dominated the late twentieth century and continue to dominate the twenty-first: "race," nation, and ethnicity.

NOTES

1. See my account of the reasons for this emphasis in two recent articles: "'Grande Dame' or 'New Woman': Doris Lessing and the Palimpsest," *LIT: Literature, Interpretation, Theory* 1.3–4 (2006): 243–62 and "Remembering Home: Nation and Identity in the Recent Writing of Doris Lessing," *Feminist Review* 85 (2007): 97–115.

2. Anthony Chennells, "Postcolonialism and Doris Lessing's Empires," *Doris Lessing Studies* 21.2 (2001): 5.

3. See also Phyllis Sternberg Perrakis's discussion of species crossing in "The Porous Border between Fact and Fiction, Empathy and Identification in Doris Lessing's *The Cleft*" in Part Two of this collection [editors' note].

4. See Pat Louw's "Domestic Spaces: Houses and Huts in Doris Lessing's African Stories" in Part Four of this collection for additional commentary on Lessing's concerns with race [editors' note].

5. Gilles Deleuze and Félix Guattari, *Kafka: Toward a Minor Literature,* trans. Dana Polan, fwd. Reda Bensmaia (Minneapolis: University of Minnesota Press, 1986),

18. Further references are to this edition and appear in the text.

6. S. Dean, "Lessing's *The Fifth Child*," *Explicator* 50.2 (1992): 122.

7. Louise Yelin, *From the Margins of Empire: Christina Stead, Doris Lessing, Nadine Gordimer* (Ithaca, NY: Cornell University Press, 1998), 104.

8. The full text of the speech is available on several Web sites, including http://www.sterlingtimes.org/powell_speech.doc (accessed April 23, 2004).

9. Yelin, *From the Margins of Empire*, 106.

10. Michiko Kakutani, "Books of the Times; His Weirdness Attracts Types Even More Weird," *The New York Times*, August 8, 2000, http://query.nytimes.com/gst/fullpage.html?res=9A04E2DB103CF93BA3575BC0A9669C8B63 (accessed November 15, 2005).

11. See Alex Clark, "Growing Pains: Alex Clark Finds Lessing's Sequel as Freakish as Its Hero," *The Guardian*, June 17, 2000, http://books.guardian.co.uk/reviews/generalfiction/0,,332971,00.html (accessed November 15, 2005); and M. Pye, "The Creature Walks Among Us," *The New York Times*, August 6, 2000, http://query.nytimes.com/gst/fullpage.html?res=9D06E4DE163DF935A3575BC0A9669C8B63 (accessed November 15, 2005).

12. Kakutani, "His Weirdness Attracts Types Even More Weird."

13. Clark, "Growing Pains."

14. Kakutani, "His Weirdness Attracts Types Even More Weird."

15. See, for example, H. Barnacle, "On Thin Ice," *Sunday Times*, April 4, 1999, 9; Michiko Kakutani, "Books of the Times; Where Millenniums Are Treated like Centuries," *The New York Times*, January 26, 1999, http://query.nytimes.com/gst/fullpage.html?res=9D0DE2DD1539F935A15752C0A96F958260 (accessed November 15, 2005); and Michael Upchurch, "Back to Ifrik," *The New York Times*, January 10, 1999, http://query.nytimes.com/gst/fullpage.html?res=9C05E2DD1E3FF933A25752C0A96F958260 (accessed November 15, 2005).

16. Barnacle, "On Thin Ice," 9.

17. Among those to use this term about the novel were Brian Aldiss, "My Sort of Fairy Tale," *The Guardian*, April 17, 1999, 8; and Erica Wagner, "Good on Science," *The Times*, March 25, 1999, 42.

18. Upchurch, "Back to Ifrik."

19. Kakutani, "Where Millenniums Are Treated like Centuries."

20. Wagner, "Good on Science," 42.

21. Upchurch, "Back to Ifrik."

22. Yelin, *From the Margins of Empire*, 106.

23. Roger Luckhurst, "The Contemporary London Gothic and the Limits of the 'Spectral Turn,'" *Textual Practice* 16.3 (2002): 527–28.

24. Margaret Thatcher, interview by D. Keay, "AIDS, Education and the Year 2000," *Woman's Own*, October 31, 1987, 8–10.

25. Doris Lessing, *The Fifth Child* (1988; repr., London: Flamingo, 1993), 7. Further references are to this edition and appear in the text.

26. J. Collins and R. Wilson, "The Broken Allegory: Doris Lessing's *The Fifth Child* as Narrative Theodicy," *Analecta Husserliana: The Yearbook of Phenomenological Research* 41 (1994): 281, 289. See Phyllis Sternberg Perrakis's essay, which also accentuates the importance of genre-crossing in Lessing's work in "The Porous Border between

Fact and Fiction, Empathy and Identification in Doris Lessing's *The Cleft*" in Part Two of this collection [editors' note].

27. Luckhurst, "The Contemporary London Gothic," 540.

28. David Punter, *Gothic Pathologies: The Text, the Body and the Law* (Basingstoke, England: Macmillan, 1998), 98–99. See also Sandra Singer's timely essay on Lessing's assessment of terrorism in "London and Kabul" in Part Two of this collection [editors' note].

29. See Phyllis Sternberg Perrakis's discussion of how integrating the narrative of the Other changes discourse in "The Porous Border between Fact and Fiction, Empathy and Identification in Doris Lessing's *The Cleft*" in Part Two of this collection [editors' note].

30. Angela Hague, "Picaresque Structure and the Angry Young Novel," *Twentieth Century Literature* 32.2 (1986): 211.

31. Ibid., 213, 216.

32. See Tom Maschler, *Declaration* (London: MacGibbon and Kee, 1957). Lessing's essay is reprinted in *A Small Personal Voice: Essays, Reviews, Interviews,* ed. Paul Schlueter (London: Flamingo, 1994), 7–25.

33. Lessing, *Ben, In the World* (London: Flamingo, 2000), 82. Further references are to this edition and will appear in the text.

34. Celia Brickman, "Primitivity, Race, and Religion in Psychoanalysis," *The Journal of Religion* 82.1 (2002): 55.

35. Thomas Pughe, "Reading the Picaresque: Mark Twain's *The Adventures of Huckleberry Finn,* Saul Bellow's *The Adventures of Augie March,* and More Recent Adventures," *English Studies* 77.1 (1996): 59–70.

36. This use of prolepsis was commented on negatively by many reviewers. See, for example, Kakutani, "His Weirdness Attracts Types Even More Weird"; and Pye, "The Creature Walks among Us."

37. Roger Luckhurst, "Cultural Governance, New Labour, and the British SF Boom," *Science Fiction Studies* 30.3 (2003): 425.

38. Luckhurst, "Cultural Governance," 425.

39. John Wyndham, *The Day of the Triffids* (London: Michael Joseph, 1951) and *The Midwich Cuckoos* (London: Michael Joseph, 1957).

40. Luckhurst, "Cultural Governance," 428.

41. Lessing, *Mara and Dann* (London: HarperFlamingo, 1999), 374. Further references are to this edition and appear in the text.

42. Andrzej Gąsiorek, *Post-War British Fiction: Realism and After* (London: Edward Arnold, 1995), 93.

43. Clare Hanson, "Doris Lessing in Pursuit of the English; or, No Small, Personal Voice," *PN Review* 14.4 (1987): 42. See also Alice Ridout's essay in Part Two of this collection, "'What Is the Function of the Storyteller?': The Relationship between *Why* and *How* Lessing Writes," where she discusses the political implications of Lessing's turn from realism to utopian and science fiction genres [editors' note].

Part Four

REFLECTIONS ON EARLY, MIDLIFE, AND LATER-LIFE LESSING

9

Domestic Spaces

Huts and Houses in Doris Lessing's African Stories

PAT LOUW

Doris Lessing's African Stories, set in the 1930s, reflect a particular historical moment of colonialism in Zimbabwe. Lessing's own early life can be seen as a microcosm of the settler life, in particular of the process of relocation and also dislocation that is inherent in colonialism. In this discussion of domestic spaces, I would like to focus on two main aspects of Lessing's early experience of houses and huts that seem to be significant in her constitution of these spaces in her narratives. One is the relationship between the house and the natural environment, that is, between the domestic space and external wild spaces of the African bush. The other is the relationship between house and hut. Both relationships involve the intrusion of the foreign power into indigenous spaces, affecting both the human and nonhuman environment. In this analysis, space is seen not as simply a background against which the action is played out but as a means to articulate an understanding of "the multiplicity and flexibility of relations of domination."[1]

HOUSES AND HUTS IN LESSING'S EARLY LIFE

The importance of houses in Lessing's early childhood development emerges clearly in *Under My Skin*. Her early years were marked by transitions. Born in Kermanshah, Persia, she was taken back to England for a few months and thence to Africa before she was six years old. This meant that although she experienced living in different houses and different countries, there were periods in her life when she had no home. For instance, when they had moved to Africa and her parents were looking for a farm to settle on, she was left under the supervision of an Irish governess at a place called Lilfordia, near Salisbury. Lessing reports that she experienced extreme anger at that time, and began to lie and steal meaningless objects. Her parents realized that this behavior was related to the need for a home: "They knew what I needed was a regular nursery routine, an ordered life, but how and when? Before that could happen, there must be a home, and it wasn't built yet."[2]

The crucial importance of a home in the form of a built structure is clear from this passage. Perhaps it is because Lessing experienced such unhappiness during this unsettled time that she placed so much value on the house that was later built for the family on their farm, "the house on the hill." She says: "no house could ever have for me the intimate charm of that one."[3] Apart from the need for a home, the charm of this house also issues from the fact that it is built almost entirely from elements of the bush: thatch from the vlei grass, poles cut from trees, mud for walls, and dung for floors. She seems to delight in its temporary and organic nature: "In London you live in houses where other people have lived, and others again will live there when you have moved or died. A house put together from the plants and earth of the bush is rather like a coat or dress, soon to be discarded, for it probably will have returned to the bush, from fire, insects, or heavy rains, long before you die."[4] The image of the dress speaks of the intimacy of the domestic space of Lessing's childhood. She has the sense of being enfolded by the house in a very personal way, but at the same time being vulnerable to the surroundings.

Some important points are raised by Lessing's description of the family house. First, the house has very little impact on the landscape. In spite of the house being a colonial intrusion that could be expected to clash with the natural bush, it merges with it. Lessing writes: "What impresses me now is not how much effect our occupancy had on the landscape of the farm, but how little."[5] The wild bush began only a few yards from their house, and it was normal for them to have wild cats, porcupines, or buck visiting their garden. She liked to look out at the bush while she was in bed: "I used to prop the door open with a stone, so that what went on in the bush was always visible to me—it was only a few paces away down the steep slope. I fought with my mother to have this door open."[6] This conflict between mother and daughter marks a pronounced difference in their attitudes toward the wild African environment. While Lessing as a child was open to that environment, her mother was more conservative and fearful. Victoria Rosner remarks that

Lessing's mother "was deeply committed to maintaining the structural integrity of the house, preserving a barrier against the bush."[7]

Another example of contrasting attitudes toward the outside spaces is found in the amusing phenomenon of the little tree that grew up through a crack in the linoleum on Lessing's bedroom floor. Her mother would attempt to get rid of it, but it would reappear the next season.[8] It is as if the mother's attempt at "civilizing" or suppressing nature by the thin layer of linoleum was foiled by the irrepressible force of the bush. Lessing's delighted amusement in the strength and persistence of this force of nature contrasts strongly with her mother's attitude, which one could say exemplifies a middle-class colonial stereotype: fear of the wild environment and a determination to keep it out of domestic spaces. In opposition to her mother, Lessing provides a different model of colonial interaction: one that favors openness and curiosity about the natural environment.

With regard to the relationship between the house and the hut, Lessing disrupts some of the colonial stereotyped ideas and assumptions about housing. One of these ideas is that that there was always a clear distinction between African homesteads and "white" homesteads, that white homes were wealthier and better than African homes. It may indeed be true that the settlers aspired to having homes that were superior to African huts, but in fact early settlers' first homes were initially built as huts. For instance, Caroline Rooney describes the similarity between a Rhodesian farmhouse and some African huts in two watercolor paintings, saying: "Although the farmhouse is distinct in style, it yet shares features with the huts and exists in a continuum with them."[9]

Lessing uses the terms "houses" and "huts" interchangeably for both settler and African dwellings. She points out the similarities: "The most attractive houses of those early days were like the Africans'. An African family had a group of huts, each hut for a different purpose, and early settler houses were often half a dozen thatched huts, or brick or pole-and-mud, sometimes joined together by pergolas covered with golden shower or bougainvillea."[10] The pergola joins the different huts together to form a unit, thus forming a transitional structure from hut to house. This could indicate insecurity in the settler mentality, feeling the need to protect the inhabitants from external threats in the unknown country. In contrast, the traditional African homestead with its cluster of separate dwellings reflects the social organization of the African family. Each wife in a polygamous family would have her own hut. The connection between outdoor and indoor space is an important distinguishing feature of African architecture. These two spaces blend together as people spend time preparing food, working on crafts, or cooking between

9: Domestic Spaces

FIGURE 1. Typical African hut in rural Zululand, South Africa. Photograph by Anita de Villiers.

the structures. This contrasts strongly with settler housing, where living space is mainly contained within the walls.

In architectural terms, "hut" is used to denote an African vernacular one-celled structure. In the area of Banket, where Lessing lived, the Shona built "cone-on-cylinder" styled huts that were circular structures with mud walls and deep-eaved, thatched conical roofs made from local timber poles and bark string[11] (figure 1). Early settlers had to use local building materials because of lack of funds, building materials, and the skills of European builders. When these became available, however, the settler houses developed into the style of a bungalow: a single-story building surrounded by a veranda that connected the indoor and outdoor spaces and helped to keep the interior cool in summer (figure 2). In British colonial architecture, "the bungalow was to become the imperial domestic dwelling. Its origins lay in India, but its adaptability and convenience were to take the basic idea to the ends of the earth."[12]

Although African and settler housing had a great deal in common in the early stages of colonial habitation, "hut" eventually took on a derogatory association in colonial terms.[13] Dwellings convey a relationship with the environment, and the settler's dwellings demonstrate a complex relationship with Africa in that they are constructed from the materials of Africa but impose a foreign ideology on these structures.

Pat Louw

FIGURE 2. Samarang: colonial house in Eshowe, Zululand. Photograph by Anita de Villiers.

For the settler, the building of a house was a way to create a sense of belonging. David Parkin writes: "The juxtaposition of locality and belonging immediately raises the question of whether one can belong to a group which does not also have a territorial reference point."[14] Houses act as important "territorial reference points" for the settlers. The boundaries drawn around domestic spaces are also an expression of a claim to the land. This involves negotiation with other social groups, especially in a colonial situation where ownership is contested. Shannon Jackson describes the concept of "space" as "a historically and socially constructed set of boundaries, [which] can be analyzed in terms of the models that evolve out of the constant navigation between social groups and the built environment."[15]

The contestation of boundaries found in Lessing's childhood is represented in various ways in her stories. While Lessing's spatial metaphors can function as external manifestations of an inner, psychic space,[16] Victoria Rosner sees Lessing's childhood home as "emblematic of Southern Rhodesia settler culture."[17] She highlights the importance of boundaries in relation to these spaces: "boundary markers were deployed to police the doctrine of racial hierarchy."[18] The continual negotiation of social and political boundaries generates a tension between different racial, ethnic, class, and generational groups. Patricia Chaffee uses the analogy of "a world of occasionally overlapping circles of individuals"[19] to indicate how groups in Lessing's stories set up boundaries within or in spite of the physical ones. The proximity of African servants in settler houses, for example, can lead to invisible boundaries being drawn up inside the physical perimeter of the house. These are the boundaries of social norms that were strongly enforced in the settler community. In *The Grass Is Singing,* these boundaries fail to be enforced, leading to scandal, breakdown, and death.

The architectural images in Lessing's African Stories play a key role in her representation of colonial society. I have used a selection from the collected volumes, *This Was the Old Chief's Country* and *The Sun between Their Feet,*[20] to accentuate Lessing's commentary on ideological tensions inscribed in colonial architecture.

THE HUT AS INVADED SPACE

The hut is particularly vulnerable to the colonial process, but it also provides a challenge to settler society in that it represents a different way of life. As the process of colonialism unfolds, the hut becomes a space under threat for the black inhabitants of the land, but when it is inhabited by settlers it can become threatening in turn to the norms and values of settler society. The hut can therefore involve transgressions of the norms of settler society and can also be seen to provide a microcosm of the broader transgression perpetrated by the colonial system against the indigenous population. I have chosen three stories to illustrate this point: "The Old Chief Mshlanga," "The Second Hut," and "The Story of a Non-Marrying Man."

In "The Old Chief Mshlanga," Lessing uses the traditional hut to focus attention on the destructiveness of colonial displacement. The process of colonialism is focalized through the young girl in the story, who grows in her understanding of this process after a chance meeting with Chief Mshlanga on her father's farm. She is so struck by the dignity and presence of the Chief that she begins questioning the history of the farm and her family's claim on it. The Chief's son works for them as a domestic servant, and her curiosity about his "other life," outside the domestic space of the kitchen, leads her to walk across the farm in search of the homestead of the Old Chief Mshlanga. In doing this she moves into a transgressive space beyond the borders of designated settler space, invading traditional African space. For white people to enter the private domain of the hut is a transgression of the social norms of both settler and African society.[21]

The girl's visit to the chief exemplifies the encroachment of white society on the most sacred and intimate space of black society and foreshadows the final act of displacement when the process of colonialism forces the Chief and his people to leave their homestead to make way for white settlers. She is, however, privileged to have a glimpse of his dwellings that are as yet untouched by colonialism, "lovingly decorated with patterns of yellow and red and ochre mud on the walls."[22] The girl remembers the dirt and neglect of the housing area for workers on the farm, and the contrast confronts her with the effect of colonialism on domestic spaces. The "sense of belonging" is clearly evident in the care that is taken with the construction and decoration of the huts, whereas the sense of rootlessness is evident in the neglect of the compound area on the white farm. Until this moment, the girl has had no means of comparison between the housing for laborers on the farm and the authentic homes of the Africans. It is as if she realizes for the first time that they are real people and simultaneously that she has no place with them: "you walk here as a destroyer."[23] This feeling is confirmed a year later when she again visits the Chief's homestead, only to find that they have been moved and that the village is a ruin of mud and rotting thatch. Ironically, the ruined huts are covered by pumpkin plants: "The pumpkin vines rioted everywhere, over the bushes, up the lower branches of the trees so that the great golden balls rolled under foot and dangled overhead: it was a festival of pumpkins."[24]

This image of the ruined huts with the ironically festive "golden balls" of pumpkins makes an eloquent statement about the upheaval caused by colonialism. It speaks of the care the people took in planting food for their families, food that would be sorely missed by them in their allotted area, while the abundance accrues to some randomly picked settler who has no connection with the land. In witnessing this change in the huts, the girl is able to see with greater clarity how colonialism invades and destroys the domestic spaces of the indigenous people, thus making a powerful critique of colonialism in general.

In "The Second Hut," the invasion is more subtle. If one takes the hut as emblematic of the colonized group, then placing a white man in that type of abode constitutes invasion, even if the building is not actually occupied by the native people at the time (as in the previous story). One could say that the settlers invade African space by taking over their style of building and then compound the invasion by compelling black people to build such an abode for a white person whom they resent. This changes the whole context of hut-building. In many traditional African societies, hut-building is a communal experience. People help their neighbors to build their homes. It can also have religious significance.

In this story, the farm owner, English-speaking Major Carruthers, employs a poverty-stricken Afrikaans-speaking man, Van Heerden, to help him with the farming operations. Van Heerden belongs to a group of landless white settlers who were known as "poor whites" in Rhodesian settler society: "The 'poor white problem,' as it came to be called, was one of the central bogies of colonial society, rivaling the black peril in its power to induce anxiety."[25] In terms of Chaffee's spatial patterning, the closed groups of the English- and Afrikaans-speaking settlers remain in separate ethnic, social, and economic circles, while they overlap racially and politically.

Carruthers decides to place Van Heerden in a vacant hut on the farm rather than share his domestic space with him: "Major Carruthers knew that if his new assistant had been an Englishman, with the same upbringing, he would have found a corner in his house and a welcome as a friend."[26] However, by putting Van Heerden in a traditional African dwelling, Carruthers is placing him in a difficult situation. A white man in settler society living in an African dwelling possesses an ambivalent status. He is placed in authority over the black laborers and yet lives in a situation similar to theirs. This is probably one reason for Van Heerden's harsh treatment of the laborers, as his authority is not backed up by the status of his housing establishment. When the farmer discovers that Van Heerden has a large family, he instructs the laborers to build a second hut for him. The laborers' resentment of this order emerges in the construction of the hut: "The grass was laid untidily over the roof-frame, still uncut and reaching to the ground in long swatches. The first layer of mud had been unevenly flung on."[27] The racial tension reflected in the building of the second hut prefigures the final catastrophe when the hut is destroyed. It is burnt down, and one of Van Heerden's children is killed. This does not result in Van Heerden's leaving the farm, as one might expect. He is used to hardship and accepts it, looking ahead to the birth of another child. It is Major Carruthers who is defeated by the attitude of Van Heerden and who decides to leave Africa. Thus, racial tension and conflict engendered by the colonial system is expressed in this story through a focus on the domestic space of the hut, which is violated by its connection with the settler group. The building and destruction of the hut becomes a medium through which the resistance of the indigenous people toward colonialism is channeled.

In "The Story of a Non-Marrying Man," Lessing presents another case of a white man living in a hut, but this time the "invasion" takes a different form, as it involves a polite request for a white man to be accepted into tribal society. It is the story of Johnny Blakeworthy, and it represents a significant movement away from the house and from settler society. He transgresses the norms of the society not only by living in a hut but also by living in an

African community with an African woman. At first he alternates between living in settler society, with different (white) women at different times in a kind of serial polygamy, and wandering around the wild countryside, living under the stars. Finally he asks permission from an African chief to live in his community and is given an African woman "with whom he lived in kindness."[28] He, in other words, went "native."[29] Kennedy expands on this concept: "The symptoms of degeneration ranged from a relatively mild 'mental inertia,' through a more serious alcoholic profligacy, to the terminal depravity of 'going native.' This final stage was typified by adopting African dress, housing, customs, and especially by taking an African wife—becoming, in effect, a white African in European eyes."[30]

Lessing points out that the reason for Blakeworthy's rejection of settler society is its excessive consumerism. His philosophy is: "If you don't spend a lot of money then you don't have to earn it and you are free."[31] The house here is an image of entrapment for the man, not the woman, as is often the case. Between the extremes of living entirely without the shelter of domestic space and living within the confines of settler society is the option of the hut, which in traditional African society offers domestic space without the clutter of modern consumerism. It provides a challenge to the norms and values of the settler as it represents a different way of life.

In transgressing the norms of settler society, Blakeworthy is not representing a social group but rather is an eccentric, struggling against the stream. Lessing clearly enjoys eccentrics, as can be seen in the interview with Roy Newquist in 1964. She says: "People who might be extremely ordinary in a society like England's, where people are pressed into conformity, can become wild eccentrics in all kinds of ways they wouldn't dare elsewhere . . . I don't think my memory deceives me, but I think there were more colourful people back in Southern Rhodesia because of the space they had to move in."[32]

The hut as invaded space serves to illustrate the tension between the settler community and the indigenous people as well as the conflicts and tensions within the settler group. From the point of view of the black inhabitants of the land, it becomes evident that their most private domestic space is appropriated in different ways by the settler community.

THE VERANDA AS MARGINAL SPACE

The veranda is a significant feature of colonial architecture because it unveils the way the settler conceptualizes the relationship between the external world and the internal domestic space. The veranda acts as an extension of the interior of the house, with furniture such as chairs, settees, and tables on it. But it can also be thought of as part of the garden, as plants can be found in pots on a veranda, or they can actually form a wall themselves, as we see in the opening passage of *Martha Quest*: "Two elderly women sat knitting on that part of the veranda which was screened from the sun by a golden shower creeper . . . They were Mrs Quest and Mrs Van Rensberg; and Martha Quest, a girl of fifteen, sat on the steps in full sunshine, clumsily twisting herself to keep the glare from her book with her own shadow."[33] Lessing places Martha on the steps of the veranda. She is thus on the outermost boundary of the domestic space—as close as possible to the external, outside space. Although she opens herself to the sun's power, her body is twisted in the effort to shade her book, suggesting that her allegiance is also divided between the intellectual world and the natural world. Socially, Martha's distance from the women makes it very clear that she is a marginal figure in this group. Being an adolescent, she is not included in the adult conversations, and not being a child, she tries to show her maturity by engaging in intellectual activity and not simply running outside to play. The veranda is a metaphorical reflection of her intermediate position, in terms of gender, age, and space. She is placed on the margin between the interior domestic space of the women's domain and the exterior space of the men's domain. This applies equally to the figure of the adolescent girl, who recurs frequently in the African Stories.

Lessing plays on the veranda's marginal space in much of her writing. In some ways it gives settlers a space to be *in* Africa but not *of* Africa, thus providing a metaphor for the colonial's alienated psyche. It provides a safe space from which to survey the African landscape without getting dirty or taking any risks, and enables people to follow their cultural traditions while reaping the benefit of the African setting. We can see this in the opening scene of the story "The De Wets Come to Kloof Grange" where the owners of the farm, Major and Mrs. Gale, watch the sunset: "The veranda, which was lifted on stone pillars, jutted forward over the garden like a box in the theatre . . . There sat Major Gale and his wife, as they did every evening at this hour, side by side trimly in deck chairs, their sundowners on small tables at their elbows, critically watching, like connoisseurs, the pageant presented for them."[34]

Lessing invests this scene with imagery taken from European culture: the theater box, the connoisseur, and the pageant. It is significant that the veranda is lifted above the plants below, as if it were maintaining a distance between the soil of Africa and the human construction. The human beings are critical observers, as the word "connoisseur" implies, but what is notable here is their passivity. They simply sit back and wait for the "show" to be presented to them. Their relationship with the surrounding land is clearly indicated by their separation from it and their elevation above it. There is a sense in which they do not want to be tainted by the mess and dirt of the earth, but nevertheless wish to have it at their feet as they contemplate the sunset. Through this description of the veranda, Lessing conveys the couple's sense of superiority to Africa and their complacency about their life there.

The sense of superiority conveyed by the veranda scene is carried over into the ethnic or cultural divisions between the English- and Afrikaans-speaking settler. This comes to the fore when Major Gale employs an Afrikaans-speaking white man, Mr. De Wet, to help him with his farm management. De Wet's new wife is a girl of seventeen years who suffers from loneliness on the farm. There is a clash between Mrs. Gale and this couple, as they have different values and attitudes in a number of spheres. First, differences emerge between Mrs. Gale and Mrs. De Wet with regard to gardens. The young woman's lack of interest perplexes Mrs. Gale, who "could not imagine anyone not being fond of gardens."[35] Robert Balfour describes the garden in colonial Africa as "the European translation of an alien space."[36] For Mrs. Gale, the garden forms a buffer between her and the "alien space" of the African bush, and the veranda is part of this buffer region.

The veranda space is replicated in the garden by the bench, which is set on a rocky ledge overlooking the valley. In the same way that the veranda lifts the Gales above the soil, allowing the couple to view the aesthetic qualities while keeping their distance from them, Mrs. Gale sits on her garden bench viewing the mountain scene across the valley. She abhors the "alien space" of the wild valley below, with its rank smells and dangerous river. Mrs. De Wet, however, prefers the valley. She is not inclined to sit watching passively from a distance. Not only does she ignore Mrs. Gale's call to appreciate the beautiful view of the mountain; she goes down into the valley, where she enjoys the feel of the water and the smell of the vegetation.

Ultimately, the "veranda attitude" is what divides them as women. It is the lack of physical contact that the veranda ensures that is attractive to Mrs. Gale but unacceptable to the younger woman. What Lessing suggests here is that Mrs. De Wet, as a representative of the Afrikaans-speaking settler subgroup, is in many ways more integrated with Africa than the Englishwoman. Although her youth is an additional factor, it is part of her Afrikaner culture that Mrs. De Wet has a more open way of responding to the outdoor environment than does Mrs. Gale. Contrary to the opinion of Antony Beck, who accuses Lessing of "tolerance for the elite whilst treating the more outspoken Afrikaners and white working-class immigrants with greater dislike,"[37] I argue that she delivers a subtle but deliberate critique of upper-class English snobbery in her use of the veranda as symbol in this story. The "veranda attitude" associated with Mrs. Gale is a measure of the artificial life she has created for herself in Africa. The attitude of an art connoisseur is difficult to uphold in the middle of the bush, and what goes with it is an English upper-class snobbishness that Lessing humorously conveys in Mrs. Gale's closing statement: "'Next time you get an assistant,' she said finally, 'get people of our kind. These might be savages, the way they behave.'"[38] These words encapsulate the "veranda attitude" and unwittingly convey Mrs. Gale's own racism toward both Africans and Afrikaners.

THE HOUSE AS GENDERED SPACE

In settler society, as in patriarchal societies in general, the home is the woman's domain. She may be denied political and economic power in other areas of society, but in the home she is in charge. For first-generation settler women in particular, it is important for a woman to be able to exercise her power in this way, because having left her original home in her mother country, she has a strong need to establish a place of belonging in the new country. The settler house is a territorial marker of this place of belonging. It also gives the settler woman status in the settler community, and ultimately it becomes part of her identity, the new identity she has to forge in the new land.

The settler house is thus a site of gendered power in Lessing's work. She gives an insight into the way in which children are socialized into accepting the house as the female domain in "Traitors." She also shows how the struggle of the adolescent for recognition as an adult is reflected in the attempt to become mistress of a house in "The New Man." Finally, she shows how this gendered space can be contested in the colonial situation, by black women ("Traitors") and by black men (as in *The Grass Is Singing*).

In "Traitors" we are shown that it is not "natural" for girls to restrict themselves to the domestic spaces of house and garden. The two little girls in this story have a strong impulse to explore the "male" domain of the wild bush that lies beyond their familiar area. They cross the boundary into this area with much excitement and trepidation, partly because it is unknown, and partly because they know they are going against their mother's wishes.

In crossing the barrier between the wild and the domestic, the little girls in the story are being traitors in a sense to white female ideology, and yet they cannot discard its influence. When they do venture into the bush, they find the ruins of an old house and they proceed to create their own imaginary house on that site. Even though they are in the male domain, the bush, they obey the female imperative to create a house: "We sat under a blazing sun, and said in our Mother's voice: 'It is always cool under thatch, no matter how hot it is outside.' And then, when the walls and the roof had grown into our minds and we took them for granted, we played other games, taking it in turn [sic] to be Mr Thompson."[39]

The power of the mother's voice is so great that it dominates their imagination, transforming the reality of the heat into coolness as they sit and play. It is significant that Lessing uses prepubescent girls as the protagonists in this story, as they seem to be rehearsing both male and female roles.[40] They are not yet bound to the colonial project and the role that women play in settler society. Their building of the phantom house in the wilderness demonstrates how they simultaneously transgress gender boundaries and also enforce them.

Apart from showing how children are socialized into their roles in a society, this story also demonstrates the way that the settler house becomes a contested space. In discovering the ruin of the old Thompson house, the children become involved in a gender conflict that goes beyond their understanding. It is an adult conflict based on the isolation and loneliness that many settler women feel, contained in their domestic spaces and away from the actual work of the farm. What makes it uniquely African compared with other gender struggles is the racial element. As the title "Traitors" implies, the betrayal of white women by their husbands is perceived as doubly treacherous if it is as a result of an interracial relationship. It challenges women in their domestic roles and makes them dispensable.

It seems that before Mr. Thompson's house burned down he was living with a black woman. This woman suddenly appears at the ruined site while the little girls are playing there and frightens them by staring at them and asking about Boss Thompson. When they shout at her, she laughs at them. By her behavior and her previous intimacy with Mr. Thompson, this woman contests the ownership of the house, even in its ruined state. The children cannot act out Mr. Thompson any longer: "We no longer knew him: that laugh, that slow, insulting stare had meant something outside our knowledge and experience. The house was not ours now."[41]

The contested aspect of this domestic space becomes even more evident when the new Mrs. Thompson insists on being taken to the site of the old house. In spite of the fact that it is ruined and broken, it remains a threat to the present Mrs. Thompson, who is anxious to find out about her husband's past and to be in control of it. She is supported by the girls' mother, who sympathizes with Mrs. Thompson in female settler solidarity. The white woman feels the need to stamp her mark on the house in order to possess his past and to wipe out the traces of the "other woman." Thus the house is a profound expression of ownership for the woman. It not only provides the domestic role for the woman in the society but also gives her a sense of being "mistress" of the house and the man. The house confers a sense of social identity on the woman, which is why it is a hotly contested arena especially when that identity is threatened by a black woman.

While "Traitors" illustrates two young girls being socialized into the importance of the house for gender and social identity, "The New Man" gives an example of this process of socialization being taken a step further. The protagonist in this story is an adolescent girl whose burgeoning sense of her womanhood is set against her mother's insistence on seeing her as a child. When the girl has to share a seat with a lonely and struggling young farmer to whom her parents give a lift, the man embraces the girl and she is simultaneously repulsed and attracted by him. However, her attraction is not so much to him as a person, but to his house. She later walks over to the man's house and goes through it in his absence. When she goes a second time, the man arrives but she is not pleased: "For now she was wishing not that she had not come but that he had not come. Then she could have walked, secretly and delightfully, through the house, and gone, secretly."[42] It is as if she wants to rehearse the role of mistress of the house without having to become involved with the man, although the physical contact with the man is something that she remembers. The title of the story, "The New Man," initially refers to the man being new in the neighborhood, but clearly also refers to the girl's first experience of a man's desire for her. The house becomes a channel for her response to this situation. It is also a means of separating herself from her mother's perception of her. Being the mistress of a house would confer adult status on her and prove to her mother that she is no longer a child. She has internalized the importance of the house as a defining characteristic of a woman's identity and wants to adopt it as a way of establishing her identity as an adult.

However, even this small, pathetic, neglected, fly-ridden house is a contested space. The girl wants to take charge of it, but she is prevented by her father, who comes to fetch her and take her home. He does not allow her to move out of the adolescent space to the adult space at this stage, and he does this by denying her access to the house. Second, he makes sure that Rooyen, the man, finds a wife by helping him to fix up his house. Once the house is in a reasonable condition, Rooyen is able quite easily to find a wife, who then takes over the space that the girl wished to control.

Finally, the contested aspect of the settler house is dramatically played out in the domestic servant realm. The relationship between a white woman and her black male servant is particularly prone to tension and conflict because of the gender issue involved. For a man from a patriarchal tradition to submit to the authority of a white woman is to experience both racial and gender domination. The domestic space can become a site of resistance in a variety of different ways in the stories, but it is in *The Grass Is Singing* that we have a dramatic and extreme example of such resistance.

From the outset, Mary Turner is locked into a battle with her servants. She seems to take on a different identity when she instructs them, finding fault with everything: "Dick saw all this with increasing foreboding. What was the matter with her? With him she seemed at ease, quiet, almost maternal. With the natives she was a virago."[43] The old servant, Samson, who was prepared to work under Dick's rule, gives notice and leaves as a result of Mary's treatment of him. She has problems with the subsequent servants, as well, punishing them severely for any transgression and expecting them, unreasonably, to understand the finer points of English domestic life, such as the difference between a dinner plate and a pudding plate.[44]

The reason for Mary's harsh and unreasonable treatment of the servants seems to be bound up with the way in which the domestic space supports and defines her identity. The more threatened and powerless she feels in the male-dominated world of the farm, the more strenuously she enforces her authority in the domestic space. Her identity is also threatened by the poor standard of the dwelling, with its cramped spaces and lack of ceiling. She seems to be desperate to keep up "standards" and tries to force her servants to produce the right cutlery as a way of doing this.

Ultimately, Mary loses the battle of domination in the domestic space as she engages in the power struggle with Moses. The physical space of the house contributes to Mary's loss of power, partly because it allows the heat to aggravate the situation through the thin corrugated iron roof and also because the smallness of the spaces result in a lack of privacy. This lack of privacy subsequently invites an intimacy that is never fulfilled but which creates tension. Control of the domestic space is contested as Moses slowly begins to assert his power over Mary. Their relationship develops a pathological quality as the social boundaries are crossed and power relations reversed.

Lessing shows how colonialism not only damages the indigenous people but can also damage the settler, especially in situations of contestation where the relationship becomes pathological and almost surreal in its transgression of boundaries. She breaks down traditional colonial definitions of gendered space and shows the fragility of the colonial situation. The settler house proclaims the presence of the settlers, but it is inadequate to create the power relations they wish to achieve.

CONCLUSION

Just as Lessing fought against the imposition of boundaries in her childhood, most of the stories selected for this study involve crossing boundaries. The invasions in the first section emanate from a crossing of socially prescribed boundaries of settler culture. The physical space traditionally associated with African culture, the hut, provides both a challenge and a resource for settlers. It is adopted and used by them but is also an instrument of class discrimination, as in "The Second Hut." From the point of view of the black community, the hut becomes a threatened space as settlers encroach on it in different ways. While Blakeworthy's eccentric move into the hut in order to become part of the black community seems to bring no negative repercussions, the girl's innocent visit to the bush in "The Old Chief Mshlanga" is followed by the relentless appropriation of African space during colonial settlement. These cases involve a transgression that is either interracial or intraracial.

In "The Traitors," "The New Man," and "The De Wets Come to Kloof Grange," Lessing also accentuates the unformed and unsettled stage of adolescence where questions of identity and gender roles are still being defined, so that when spatial barriers are crossed, new territory is explored as both geographical space and social space. The more fluid sense of space experienced by these young people unveils the fixed identities and fixed roles of adults in terms of gender, ethnicity, and race. Older people seem to be trapped in their retrospective gaze toward England, whereas younger people are more open to Africa and can thus move beyond the house with greater freedom. This means that the younger generation of settlers are better able to make a direct connection with Africa than the first-generation settlers were. Thus, Lessing seems to be suggesting that future generations could become successfully integrated with the land and its people.

Lessing's use of space in these stories disrupts the smooth flow of colonial culture and strikes a discordant note in settler society. In this way she makes a protest against the prejudice and class consciousness of the settler, reaching out toward a broader sense of humanity and freedom. Lessing invests dwellings with a multiplicity of meanings that go beyond their primary purpose and contribute significantly to her full and complex representation of the colonial world of Rhodesia in the 1930s. Her insight into the complexity of that world helps contemporary readers understand the roots of some of the problems of postliberation Zimbabwe. It also adds poignancy to the troubled state of affairs in contemporary Zimbabwe, as the more positive side of her analysis holds out some measure of hope for a future society that is able to overcome the barriers of race, class, and gender.

NOTES

1. Michael Keith and Steve Pile, *Place and the Politics of Identity* (London: Routledge, 1993), 1.
2. Doris Lessing, *Under My Skin: Volume One of My Autobiography, to 1949* (London: HarperCollins, 1994), 51.
3. Ibid., 54.
4. Ibid.
5. Ibid., 55.
6. Ibid., 70.
7. Victoria Rosner, "Home Fires: Doris Lessing, Colonial Architecture, and the Reproduction of Mothering," *Tulsa Studies in Women's Literature* 18.1 (1999): 74.
8. Lessing, *Going Home* (St. Albans: Panther Books, 1968), 53.
9. Caroline Rooney, "Narratives of Southern African Farms," *Third World Quarterly* 26.3 (2005): 431–40.
10. Lessing, *Under My Skin*, 56.
11. Rowan Roenisch, *Encyclopaedia of Vernacular Architecture of the World*, ed. Paul Oliver (Cambridge: Cambridge University Press, 1997), 2147.
12. Robert Fermor-Hesketh, *Architecture of the British Empire* (London: Weidenfeld and Nicolson, 1986), 193.
13. Susan Denyer, *African Traditional Architecture* (London: Heinemann, 1978), 1.
14. David Parkin, Foreword, *Locality and Belonging*, ed. N. Lovell (London: Routledge, 1998), ix.
15. Shannon M. Jackson, "Cape Colonial Architecture, Town Planning, and the Crafting of Modern Space in South Africa," *Africa Today* 5.4 (2005): 34.
16. Rosner, "Home Fires," 85. See also Robin Visel's chapter 3, "House/Mother: Lessing's Reproduction of Realism in *The Sweetest Dream*," in Part One of this collection where she discusses domestic and maternal spaces [editors' note].
17. Rosner, "Home Fires," 59–89.
18. Ibid., 59.
19. Patricia Chaffee, "Spatial Patterns and Closed Groups in Lessing's African Stories," *South Atlantic Quarterly* 43.2 (1978): 126.
20. Lessing, *This Was the Old Chief's Country*, vol. 1, *Collected African Stories* (1973; repr., London: Paladin, 1992). Lessing, *The Sun between Their Feet*, vol. 2, *Collected African Stories* (1973; repr., London: Flamingo, 1994).
21. Dane Kennedy, *Islands of White* (Durham, NC: Duke University Press, 1987), 77. See also Susan Watkins, "Writing in a Minor Key: Doris Lessing's Late-Twentieth-Century Fiction," in Part Three of this collection for further discussion of Lessing's critique of racial narratives [editors' note].
22. Lessing, "The Old Chief Mshlanga," *Chief's Country*, 21.
23. Ibid., 23.
24. Ibid., 25.
25. Kennedy, *Islands of White*, 168.
26. Lessing, "The Second Hut," *Chief's Country*, 48.
27. Ibid., 60.
28. Lessing, "The Story of a Non-Marrying Man," *The Sun between Their Feet*, 47.

29. Ibid.

30. Kennedy, *Islands of White*, 173.

31. Lessing, "The Story of a Non-Marrying Man," *The Sun between Their Feet*, 47.

32. Roy Newquist, "Talking as a Person," in *Putting the Questions Differently*, ed. Earl Ingersoll (London: Flamingo, 1994), 3.

33. Lessing, *Martha Quest*, vol. 1, *Children of Violence* (New York: HarperPerennial, 1995), 1.

34. Lessing, "The De Wets Come to Kloof Grange," *Chief's Country*, 75.

35. Ibid., 93.

36. Robert Balfour, "Gardening in Other Countries: Schoeman, Coetzee, Conrad" (presented at CSSALL conference, University of Durban–Westville, 1995), 8.

37. Antony Beck, "Doris Lessing and the Colonial Experience," *Journal of Commonwealth Literature* 19.1 (1984): 66–67.

38. Lessing, "The De Wets Come to Kloof Grange," *Chief's Country*, 103.

39. Lessing, "Traitors," *The Sun between Their Feet*, 86.

40. Kay McCormick, "The Child's Perspective in *Five African Stories*," *Doris Lessing Newsletter* 9.2 (1985): 13.

41. Lessing, "Traitors," *The Sun between Their Feet*, 87.

42. Lessing, "The New Man," *The Sun between Their Feet*, 221.

43. Lessing, *The Grass Is Singing* (London: Michael Joseph, 1950), 83.

44. Ibid., 81.

~10~

The Challenge of Teaching Doris Lessing's *The Golden Notebook* in the Twenty-First Century

SUZETTE HENKE

> It seems curious to me again and again that . . . this book [*The Golden Notebook*] produces such an echo everywhere in the world. . . . What was still considered taboo in 1962 is no longer so today. . . . On the other hand, this response also shows me . . . that a book is a living thing which can bear many kinds of fruit.[1]

Can one still teach Doris Lessing's masterpiece, *The Golden Notebook,* at the beginning of the twenty-first century? Is Lessing's work politically relevant (and meaningful) to an American student audience for whom the defining moment of adulthood was the tragedy of 9/11/01? And how can contemporary readers relate to the outmoded sex-role stereotypes and self-destructive patterns of personal relationships portrayed in Lessing's opus? For those of us who came of age in the 1960s, *The Golden Notebook* has survived as a sacred feminist text, enshrined in our pedagogical projects as one of the great works produced in the twentieth century. But how can Lessing's epic narrative, rooted as it is in midcentury politics, African colonialism, and British historical struggle, prove meaningful to younger readers teethed on rap music, MTV, and computer hypertexts? What has Lessing to say to students in the new millennium?

10: The Golden Notebook *in the Twenty-First Century*

In an interview with Bill Moyers for a PBS *Now* broadcast on January 24, 2003, Lessing reminisces about her father, Alfred/Michael Tayler, who was traumatized by the loss of a leg during World War I. He and his compatriots, she observes, were "terribly damaged people," as were the veterans of World War II and the Vietnam War. She made the accusation that "your lot—your [American] warmongers" don't understand the psychological price of warfare.[2] People are so badly wounded emotionally and psychologically that they never recover. In fact, Lessing believes that the sixties generation vehemently protested the Vietnam War because they themselves were the children of veterans who had been damaged by World War II. Somewhat wistfully, she notes that nothing at all remains of the world into which she was born, since the British Empire, like all empires, was doomed from the start.

In a February 2003 interview with Billy Gray, Lessing confessed: "I've spent my entire life . . . thinking 'this cannot be happening' because it's so stupid. I mean, crisis after crisis after crisis. The whole of the Second World War[,] I remember thinking 'this cannot be happening, this waste,' . . . but of course it was happening, and now it's happening again. . . . I just can't believe that people can be so stupid."[3] Baby Boomers like me, who came of age in the era of the Vietnam War, can attest to a sense of *déjà vu*, as we witness the postwar occupation of Iraq, a proliferation of insurgency bombings, and a conflict between Sunni and Shiite religious factions.

As Lessing declares in her preface to *The Golden Notebook*, "We have not yet evolved a system of education that is not a system of indoctrination. . . . Those who stay [in this self-perpetuating system] . . . are being moulded and patterned to fit into the narrow and particular needs of this particular society."[4] In this essay, I would like to argue that with sufficient motivation, enticement, elucidation, and pedagogical enthusiasm, a twenty-first-century instructor can offer *The Golden Notebook* to his or her students as a rich treasure trove of historical, political, psychological, moral, and ethical insights—all served up in an intriguing postmodern porridge of scintillating narratives. Here are some examples of the Gordian knots encountered on this pedagogical journey, delineated via the "four P's": Global Politics, Sexual Politics, Psychoanalysis, and Postmodern Narrative.

GLOBAL POLITICS AND CULTURAL HISTORY

> In *The Golden Notebook,* I really tried to write a book which would capture certain vital ideas that were all to do with socialism in one way or

another. . . . It was so ambitious, it couldn't help but fail.⁵

In a new millennium dominated by American power politics of preemption and Christian/Islamic controversies, few readers have any idea of the political antagonisms that dominated "free world" consciousness in Europe and America at midcentury. In order to contextualize *The Golden Notebook,* one must begin with a mini history lesson that highlights the McCarthy hearings, the execution of the Rosenbergs, the death of Stalin in 1953, STASI repressions in East Germany, and Nikita Khrushchev's "secret" denunciation of Stalin at the Twentieth Congress of the Communist Party of the Soviet Union in 1956. As Suzanne Clark, author of *Cold Warriors,* has reminded me, contemporary students have little or no familiarity with the cold war. "How," she asks, "has our memory of the Iron Curtain been erased so quickly?"⁶ After all, it was little more than fifteen years ago that the Berlin Wall was razed, amidst great jubilation. Now that the cold war, along with its attendant political anxieties, has faded into historical memory, we face an entirely different enigma—the emergence of a Middle Eastern damask curtain, so to speak.

What seems to me ironic is that the kind of moral epic Lessing constructed in the middle of the twentieth century has more to say to us now than it did, perhaps, in the 1980s or 1990s. With the advent of the U.S. Patriot Act, we saw the ghost of McCarthyism invidiously resuscitated and attended by many of the political dangers similar to those earlier associated with the Red Menace of Communism. It all comes round again, and this time, in the form of grim governmental machinery that threatens to limit basic civil liberties. During the 1950s cold war, the American Immigration and Naturalization Service (INS) was empowered to round up foreign-born Communists for deportation and to detain them without bail. Analogously, foreign nationals currently perceived as potential threats to U.S. security have been (un)systematically rounded up from far-flung geographical locales such as Afghanistan and Pakistan and detained at Guantanamo military base in Cuba without criminal charges, and without the right to trial or appeal. The open-ended sentences imposed on these prisoners are so stressful that the International Red Cross reports rapid mental deterioration of detainees. In 2003 alone, 305 cases of "self-harm" were reported, including more than one hundred suicide attempts, the majority by hanging. Amnesty International, on the basis of American FBI reports, has brought allegations of prisoner torture and abuse comparable to the brutalities documented at Abu Ghraib prison in Iraq. And physicians from around the world issued a March 2006 appeal in *The Lancet*⁷ urging that American doctors refuse to engage in the force-feeding of Guantanamo prisoners on hunger strike. Do civil rights, one might ask, no longer apply to foreign nationals?

Nor is Lessing's searing critique in *The Golden Notebook* limited to cold war politics. Anna Wulf's Black Notebook explores the "dark continent" of Africa and forces readers to consider the lives and welfare of black citizens geographically isolated and culturally remote. She acerbically reminds us that we avert our attention from the continent of Africa at our peril. Dare we ignore virtual genocide in the Congo and Darfur, the starvation of our fellow human beings in a global village, or the uncontrolled plague of HIV-AIDS decimating populations in Africa and Indonesia? Lessing's political debates in *The Golden Notebook* are shockingly relevant at the dawn of the twenty-first century. One witnesses impending disaster with a sense of impotence and disbelief. And one cannot help sharing Lessing's frustration and incredulity at contemporary examples of world leaders' obliquity in the face of political mayhem.

SEXUAL POLITICS

> I'd constructed this whole book on my experience, . . . but it never crossed my mind that I was writing about feminism or what is now called Women's Lib.⁸

> I learned that I had written a tract about the sex war, and fast discovered that nothing I said then could change that diagnosis.⁹

One of the cultural consequences of the tragedy of 9/11/01 seems to have been a sudden posttraumatic reconfiguration of the way in which we value personal relationships. In the weeks following the shock of 9/11, I recognized symptoms of posttraumatic stress in my own life and among Americans everywhere attempting to translate the bizarre television spectacle of planes crashing into the World Trade Center from the simulacrum of a made-for-TV disaster film into the register of historical reality. In the eighteen months after 9/11, five of my university colleagues gave birth to babies—perhaps as a sign of renewed hope after unimaginable disaster. A surprising number of unanticipated marriages, including my own, seemed partially motivated by an implicit confrontation with mortality and with the daily perils of life on a moving planet that appears to be spinning vertiginously out of control.

Doris Lessing claimed in her 2003 interview with Billy Gray that she has experienced the romantic sensation of being "in love" only once, and she decries the shattering effect that such erotic infatuation can have on one's psyche. "What," she asks provocatively, "is the reason for falling in love? . . . It has no purpose whatsoever. I mean, for centuries people did very well with arranged marriages . . . and the whole concept of romantic love hardly existed except in poetry."[10] Biographers have argued about the identity of Lessing's unique paramour, who might have been the American writer Clancy Sigal, with whom she experienced an intensely conflicted, emotionally violent liaison, mirrored in Anna Wulf's relationship with Saul/Milt in *The Golden Notebook*.[11]

Analogously, Lessing insists that "there are a lot more important battles than the sex war" and that everything she dislikes about politics is "enshrined in the women's movement."[12] In interviews she repeatedly articulates the conviction, expressed in her 1971 preface to *The Golden Notebook,* that "this novel was not a trumpet for Women's Liberation."[13] In 1969 she declared testily: "I'm impatient with people who emphasize sexual revolution. I say we should all go to bed, shut up about sexual liberation, and go on with the important matters."[14]

I would like to argue that *The Golden Notebook* is not so much a *feminist* novel as it is a text that offers a great deal of historical evidence suggesting why it was that women at midcentury *needed* to be liberated by the second wave of feminism—a movement that effected monumental political changes in the 1960s and 1970s. As Ellen Morgan shrewdly observed in her 1973 article "The Alienation of the Woman Writer in *The Golden Notebook,*" Lessing's female characters sacrifice themselves on the altar of traditional sex roles, even as they invent illusory personae of the sexually free women they would like to be. Ignoring the ideological state apparatuses that regulate their lives, all the women in the novel enact archaic sex roles as faithful, devoted, and altruistic partners. The epithet "free women" is clearly—and bitterly—ironic, since "they feel incomplete and inferior as persons" and "share a minority-group psychological orientation which compels them to depreciate their femaleness and their friendship and seek approval from and identification with men."[15] "'Free women,' said Anna, wryly. . . . 'They still define us in terms of relationships with men.'"[16] The real problem, however, is that even Lessing's independent women continue to *judge themselves* via criteria of male approval. In assessing her protagonists Anna and Molly, Lessing calls them "very courageous—for the circumstances of that time—albeit rather crazy in their experimenting with liberation."[17]

I first read *The Golden Notebook* in the 1970s, when it was assigned by Tillie Olsen in an inspiring course, "Women in Literature," at Stanford Uni-

10: The Golden Notebook *in the Twenty-First Century*

versity. I immediately devoured Lessing's novel and have taught it religiously in women's studies courses ever since. The 1970s, however, constituted an era of turbulence and transition, especially in the realm of sexual politics. Although women felt suddenly liberated from reproductive anxiety by access to oral contraceptives, prescriptions for the Pill had to be cannily negotiated by unmarried "bachelor girls." Single women in America approached scornful pharmacists with trepidation, purchased Woolworth wedding rings to flash while traveling in company, and cautiously restricted access to phone numbers if apartments were shared with housemates of a different gender. Although social change occurred rapidly, it demanded enormous psychological resilience on the part of the generation of "flower children" who were engaged in political demonstrations against American imperialism and the Vietnam War. Protestors confronted squads of helmeted policemen, faced weapons of gas destruction, and proclaimed, in echoes of popular songs by the Beatles, that they preferred to make love rather than war. What startles me, in retrospect, is that Doris Lessing belongs to the same demographic cohort as *my mother.* When the 1970s generation began experimenting with liberated lifestyles, most people my parents' age looked on with disapproval, if not downright horror, at such scandalous behavior.

The Golden Notebook proved to be a sacred text for the second wave of the feminist movement, but it could not be construed as a reliable handbook for women's liberation. In the 1970s my own disappointment with Lessing's novel aggregated around three categories: 1) a lack of reproductive realism, 2) Lessing's perpetuation of Freudian models of female sexuality, and 3) her ostensibly restricted vision of queer politics. In women's literature classes, my students patiently plough through 666 pages in which the author/narrator analyzes the most intimate details of female experience—premenstrual tension, the insertion of a tampon, lovemaking, orgasm (two kinds), and the draining responsibilities of single parenthood. In "For the Etruscans," Rachel Blau DuPlessis praises Lessing's candor and relentless "self-questioning. . . . The first Tampax in world literature."[18] The first Tampax, perhaps, but *not* the first Durex. The author of *The Golden Notebook* never broaches issues of contraception and woman's reproductive vulnerability. In the 1970s, it troubled me considerably that Lessing stops short of conceiving a protagonist whose womanhood entails a perplexed struggle with the problematized choices of childbearing and nurturance.

In the fairy-tale landscape of *The Golden Notebook,* Anna Freeman and her lover Max Wulf wake up one morning and hear a baby crying in the next flat. Inspired by the infant's crooning, Max proposes that they have a child. Then they make love and make a baby: "Max said: 'Perhaps we should have a baby?' I said: 'You mean having a baby would bring us together?' . . . Then I suddenly thought: Why not? . . . [A]nd so I turned to him and we made love. That was the morning Janet was conceived."[19] Only the most curious of readers might wonder what Anna and Max had been doing about fertility control prior to this particular encounter. During World War II there were fairly few options. Did the couple use condoms? Did Max withdraw? Did Anna use a diaphragm? We do not know. Nor does the author tell us. She suggests, with a distinctly male-oriented voice, that reproduction is, and always has been, a matter of volition. Women in this novel are surprisingly passive about reproductive planning, a concern that subtly slips through the gaps in their sexual discourse. The free women in Lessing's fiction never feel sufficiently liberated to articulate either maternal desire or sexual need. Although Paul and Ella in the Yellow Notebook share bed and bodily intimacy for nearly five years, it is only when Paul predicts futuristic technological cloning, via the application of ice to women's ovaries, that Ella cries out: "My God, Paul, if at any time during the last five years you'd asked me to have a baby, I'd have been so happy . . . Don't you know that ever since I've known you I've wanted to have your child?"[20] But how *could* he know if she were too timorous to *tell* him?

In the Yellow Notebook, Paul preaches to Ella that the "real revolution" of our time is that of "women against men."[21] Fundamentally conservative in her notions about gender, Ella disapproves of the nascent sexual revolution erupting at midcentury because she believes that "sex is essentially emotional for women." And the litmus test for the viability of heterosexual relationship, she insists, is vaginal orgasm—"the orgasm that is created by the man's need for a woman, and his confidence in that need."[22] As her relationship with Paul deteriorates, Ella resents the fact that he begins to "rely on manipulating her externally, on giving Ella clitoral orgasms," because such practices contradict her Freudian sexology. She believes that the "vaginal orgasm is a dissolving in a vague, dark generalised sensation like being swirled in a warm whirlpool. There . . . is only one real female orgasm and that is when a man, from the whole of his need and desire, takes a woman and wants all her response. Everything else is a substitute and a fake."[23] When Paul cites "eminent physiologists who say women have no physical basis for vaginal orgasm," Ella quickly demurs: "Then they don't know much, do they?"[24] After a group of incensed female physicians walks out of a lecture on sexology by the learned Professor Bloodrot, Paul's colleague Stephanie explains that "women of any sense know better, after all these centuries, than to interrupt when men start telling them how they feel about sex."[25] "Integrity is the orgasm,"[26] Ella insists. And then she asks herself: "Am I saying that I can never come except with a man I love? Because what sort of a desert am I condemning myself to if that's true?"[27]

Thirty-five years ago, these pages in *The Golden Notebook* seemed liable to do more damage to the popular understanding of female sexual response than anything written since Freud's infamous essays on female sexual psychology, which describe the mature woman's eager substitution of vaginal pleasure for clitoral excitation at the outset of puberty. After all, it simply did not make physiological sense to Freud that female pleasure might be focused on a smaller version of the male penis—even though a number of African tribes realized this centuries ago and inaugurated the practice of female genital mutilation to control projected male fears of insatiable female appetites.

Admittedly, Doris Lessing did not have the advantage of Masters and Johnson's study of *Human Sexual Response*[28] or Shere Hite's revolutionary *Hite Report*.[29] Alfred Kinsey had described some fascinating scientific discoveries in *Sexual Behavior in the Human Female*[30] in 1953, but his work was largely ignored by bourgeois couples. It was only in the 1970s that a significant number of women, liberated by contraceptive practice, began freely to explore their sexual desires and to communicate more openly with partners of both genders. Although Kinsey reported that 90% of all women experience sexual pleasure and orgasmic response via clitoral stimulation, a majority of females at midcentury were diagnosed "frigid," by physicians and spouses alike, if they failed to achieve simultaneous orgasm during intercourse. It was commonly agreed that a female preference for clitoral stimulation warranted psychiatric counseling, if not surgical intervention. Throughout the 1960s marriage counselors instructed male clients to stimulate spouses to a point of high excitement and then quickly switch to the missionary position. Such ill-conceived advice must surely have destroyed countless marriages and left a number of women feeling sexually inadequate, if not legally divorced.[31]

In the 1970s women started speaking more frankly to one another, and feminists began to share information about emotions, relationships with men and with other women, lesbian or bisexual experiences, and heterosexual mating. For the first time in centuries (or perhaps millennia), a majority of females on the planet raised their voices in heretofore silenced choruses to expose what Anne Koedt called "the myth of the vaginal orgasm." It now seems remarkable that women, in the course of a single generation, were able to discover and acknowledge so much about their own erotic *jouissance*.

How does one broach the topic of Lessing's Freudian constructions of female sexuality in conversation with twenty-first-century students? The only viable course would seem to be a bold confrontation with the historical controversy. For a bit of comic relief, I sometimes cite James Joyce's allusion, in the "Circe" episode of *Ulysses,* to Rualdus Columbus (a.k.a. Realdo Colombo), the anatomist who claimed to have discovered the female clitoris in the sixteenth century, though many women undoubtedly had discovered this crucial organ long before the above-named gentleman. As one male graduate student commented about this latter-day Columbus: "I'll bet his girlfriend was happy!" So perhaps one shouldn't worry too much about dispelling Freudian myths when teaching *The Golden Notebook* in the twenty-first century. New-millennial students appear to have acquired their own, more sophisticated thoughts on the matter.

Finally, how does one deal with the novel's apparently stereotyped vision of homosexuality in the caricatured figures of Ivor and Ronnie? A number of scholars, including Ellen Morgan, Claire Sprague, Joseph Allen Boone, and Judith Kegan Gardiner, have offered keen assessments of Anna Wulf's postwar homophobia that disinter hints of female self-loathing disguised in emotional revulsion.[32] When Anna speculates about the relationship between her daughter and their homosexual boarder Ivor, she expresses concern that "Janet needs a man in her life," but worries about exposing the impressionable child to a queer guy who fails to meet heterosexist criteria for male authenticity. She grudgingly admits that "he's charming" and asks herself, "so what do I mean by 'A real man'? For Janet adored Ivor. And she adored—or said that she did—his friend Ronnie."[33] When Ivor and Ronnie indulge in sardonic mockery and mimic traditional romantic postures via a ludicrous performance of chivalric behavior, Anna interprets their charade as still another example of perverse and ugly spite. The couple soon find themselves expelled from Anna's heterosexist haven of cozy domesticity.

In his 1998 novel *The Hours,* Michael Cunningham portrays Clarissa Vaughan, a child of the 1960s, taking inspiration for her iconoclastic lesbian lifestyle from Doris Lessing. Clarissa's bedtime reading conspicuously includes *The Golden Notebook,* from which she manages to wrench a late-century script for personal liberation and the free choice of (homo)sexual identity. Such literary intertextuality seems somewhat ironic, insofar as Lessing provides a penetrating critique of traditional marriage, conservative politics, and cultural conventions of every kind, but appears to exhibit a glaring blind spot in her representation of homosexuality as a deviant lifestyle. Hence the implicit revulsion expressed in Anna's snide allusion to the "gaggle of little queers" who exploit Marion when she opens a dress shop in Knightsbridge at the end of "Free Women."[34]

In her recent essay "Historicizing Homophobia in *The Golden Notebook,*" Judith Kegan Gardiner compares Lessing's novel with an earlier short story, "The Day Stalin Died," to contravene Joseph Allen Boone's attribution of homophobia both to Lessing's fictional protagonist in *The Golden Notebook* and to the author herself. Contrasting Anna Wulf's midcentury homophobia with her resilient acceptance of gay and bisexual comrades in Africa during World War II, Gardiner concludes that Anna, as a citizen of postwar England, "internalizes a culturally-dominant misogynistic heterosexuality that aligns femininity, women, and abjection under the alibi of an inborn nature" and "uses her gay male tenant as a way of feeling better about herself." Gardiner concludes that Lessing implicitly satirizes homophobia in her novel, since the "emotions the gay men invoke in Anna, especially her 'effeminophobia,' reveal the grounding of her postwar heterosexual passions in a historicized misogyny that condemned the feminine in both women and men" and "record Anna's progress toward psychological crackup."[35]

PSYCHOANALYSIS

> [S]ometimes when people "crack up" it is a way of self-healing, of the inner self's dismissing false dichotomies and divisions.[36]

> People who are called mentally ill are often those who say to the society, "I'm not going to live according to your rules. I'm not going to conform." Madness can be a form of rebellion.[37]

> The essence of neurosis is conflict. But the essence of living now, fully, not blocking off to what goes on, is conflict. . . . People stay sane by blocking off, by limiting themselves.[38]

For a twenty-first-century audience familiar with psychoanalysis, *The Golden Notebook* needs to be interpreted in the context of Freud, Jung, and R. D. Laing, as well as through the more contemporary lens of Deleuze and Guattari's notion of "schizoanalysis."[39] As Laing proposed in *The Politics of Experience,* so-called madness might not entail a psychological "breakdown" so much as a revelatory, healing "breakthrough" into expanded forms of consciousness and self-integration.[40] Laing told his biographer Bob Mullan that he had given Doris Lessing LSD over the course of six visits, but Lessing "has never publicly acknowledged such treatments," despite her willingness to speak openly about her experience with mescal.[41] She explains that it is "very easy to send oneself round the bend for a couple of days" and that she "did it once, out of curiosity," through a "technique medicine men and witch doctors were quite familiar with, going without eating or sleeping for several days."[42] In deliberate experiments with protracted food and sleep deprivation, Lessing suffered hallucinations and psychological dissociation, as well as a traumatic confrontation with a "figure she calls the 'self-hater.' The voice repeatedly listed her weaknesses and sins in sharp accusatory tones. . . . A horrifying encounter, being told over and over how dreadful a person she was, not worthy of being alive."[43]

As Anna Wulf in *The Golden Notebook* descends into the unconscious and battles the turbulent upheavals of psychological fragmentation in the company of Saul Green, she seems to reach a new focus of self-integration via immersion in the tormented landscape of corporeal abjection. Saul, a tough American writer based on Clancy Sigal, appears to be suffering from megalomania (with the emphasis on *mania*), as well as from a condition that might be diagnosed as narcissistic borderline personality disorder (with the emphasis on *narcissistic*).[44] Spattering a relentless, machine-gun volley of "I's," he lacks cathexis for other human beings, whom he persistently sees as objects to be manipulated to his own advantage. Hence Saul's truculent fabrications in the face of Anna's hysterical jealousy. He angrily denies sexual involvement with a long list of women named in his secret diary. When Saul and Anna surreptitiously begin reading one another's private notebooks, they embark on an intriguing exercise in life-writing as titillating performance. But the game proves emotionally perilous, driving both players into deeper strata of mental confusion and dysphoria. Locked in a state of permanent anxiety, the two exacerbate their collaborative madness through obsessive-compulsive cycles of tenderness and bullying.

Anna's dissociative breakdown entails a vertiginous descent into the unconscious, evocative of visceral anxiety and an overwhelming sense of shame and corporeal abjection. Accosted by feelings of self-loathing and revulsion, idiosyncratically identified as "homosexual disgust," she envisages her body in the monstrous guise of a voracious female spider, devouring her mate in an ecstasy of postcoital cannibalism. Animal images prevail in this atavistic landscape, as Anna hallucinates an encounter with a predatory tiger hovering on the ceiling of her bedroom, with emerald eyes and a bestial, hypnotic gaze reminiscent of the green-eyed Saul. Although this feline predator seems crouched to spring, Anna feels protective of the powerful beast, whom she recognizes as a metaphorical emanation of Saul.

As the invisible "projectionist" of a rich, surrealistic dream that fuses history with fiction, nightmare with biographical reality, Saul metamorphoses in the interior Golden Notebook from tiger/lover into an inner conscience enabling Anna to *name* and to reify the events of her past—to revisit painful memories and work through the resonance of psychological dysphoria. The speeded-up film is a composite personal history that fuses biography and art in therapeutic amalgamation. Through oneiric strategies of narrative reformulation, Anna is able to envisage the aesthetic reintegration of past experience, as segments of her life begin to coalesce in a new dramatic scenario. The dream-film opens up a "breakthrough" path to self-knowledge by forcing Anna creatively to integrate the people, ideas, and emotions from her past into a poignant, healing, and meaningful script. As Paul Tanner and Anna's lover Michael are conflated in a single character, they triumphantly cling to a common goal as idealistic "boulder pushers," post-Sisyphean laborers in the cause of social justice, whose efforts propel humanity slightly forward in the direction of enlightenment.

In *The Golden Notebook,* through a psychoanalytic exercise that resembles Laing's antipsychiatry, Anna Wulf acknowledges the potential violence and masochistic tendencies embedded in her psyche, as well as the traumatized self-hurter and self-hater emotionally repressed and heretofore denied. Arising from what Laing might identify as the fifth dimension of mystical/schizophrenic revelation, in which ego boundaries temporarily dissolve, Anna is able to piece together fragments of her shattered psyche and engender a coherent narrative in the role of creative agent. As author/protagonist of *The Golden Notebook,* she overcomes artistic blockage and begins writing the "Free Women" sections of the convoluted text we are in the process of reading.

POSTMODERN NARRATIVE

> [M]y major aim was to shape a book which would make its own comment, a wordless statement: to talk through the way it was shaped.[45]

> I was working out the shape of *The Golden Notebook.* As you know, there's this framework, the absolutely conventional novel. Five bits of conventional novel and all this chaos in the middle. One thing I was saying was this feeling of despair, which every writer feels when they've finished a novel, that you haven't been able to say it because life is too complex ever to be put into words. That's one thing I was saying through the structure of this book.[46]

As Katherine Fishburn points out in her essay "Teaching Doris Lessing as a Subversive Activity," ever since Lessing published her 1971 Preface to *The Golden Notebook,* "it is as though she asks us if we dare teach this novel at all . . . without institutionalizing it." Fishburn argues that Lessing's "method of teaching is not didactic but Socratic, by which she engages her readers in a progressive dialogue that leads them through a series of multiple realities to a new view of the world." Her Socratic pedagogy takes rich inspiration from the "literature of Sufism and the philosophy of Marxism. From the Sufi canon she has learned the art of teaching indirectly, through parables and . . . conundrums. . . . From Marxism she has learned the related art of dialectical thinking."[47]

Lessing's palimpsestic postmodern technique is the dimension of the novel that many of my students initially find intimidating. In commentaries provided by graduate students in a Modern Literature seminar that I taught at the University of Louisville in spring 2003, one young woman wrote: "When I first read *The Golden Notebook,* I had looked at a few preliminary sources to get some idea of the modern and postmodern dimensions. About three-quarters of the way through, when the narrative structure began to fold in on itself, I realized that I had drastically oversimplified the notebooks. This ultimately became the biggest puzzle for me. . . . I'd be interested in reading the novel a second time to see if bringing different expectations to the text would result in a different reading." Another student commented: "I had never read anything by Lessing before, even though I have a B.A. in English. Reading *The Golden Notebook* was a revelation to me. In class, you compared it to Joyce's *Ulysses.* Now that I've finished the book, I agree that it's one of the great masterpieces of the twentieth century. Why isn't it taught more frequently?"[48]

The Golden Notebook unfolds as a post/modern narrative of metafictional experimentation, with diverse, contradictory, diegetic dimensions that require sophisticated exercises in narratological unpacking.[49] The book mimics a Möbius strip folding back on itself: there *is no original story* or experiential ur-narrative to serve as reassuring epistemological referent. As new-millennial readers face the uncertainties of a post-9/11 world, Lessing's experimental text might tacitly reassure them that it is "okay" not to "observe the forms" of straightforward, formulaic thinking that constitute cultural dogma. *The Golden Notebook* forces its audience to confront the fragmented, contingent nature of modernity. Lessing "utilizes the Marxist model of dialectical progression, . . . whereby her readers learn how to escape institutionalized thought."[50] Lessing's challenging narrative implicitly encourages us to question the kind of utopian schemata that characterize twenty-first century Anglo-American political rhetoric—a rhetoric of optimism contingent on a straightforward "plotline," as well as on a "horserace mentality"[51] culminating in the triumph of cowboy-style democracy throughout the world.

As Lessing acerbically suggests, the kind of psychic fragmentation evinced by radical behavior that "breaks the old forms" and challenges traditional values might simply prove too threatening to fundamentalist values. In *The Golden Notebook,* Molly Jacobs prophetically predicts a reactionary neoconservatism taking precedence at the end of the twentieth century: "I thought that the generation after us are going to take one look at us, and get married at eighteen, forbid divorces, and go in for strict moral codes and all that, because the chaos otherwise is just too terrifying."[52] Hence the moralistic platform of "guns, God, and gays" that prevailed in the U.S. presidential election of 2004. As Katherine Fishburn observes, by teaching *The Golden Notebook,* we are encouraging our students to acknowledge "that there are several ways of looking at the world, that no one social, religious, or political institution has a monopoly on truth."[53]

Approaching the limits of postmodern praxis, Lessing intentionally sets out to create a metafictional nest of decentered narratives whose illusory core (an always-already absent ur-narrative) balances precariously over the void. The center of this series of Chinese boxes proves to be the textual equivalent of an aesthetic "black hole." An (in)finite series of Russian *babushka* dolls implodes from the pressure of diverse, contradictory, and thoroughly fragmented diegetic worlds. As Beth Boehm assures us, "the relationship between the real and the fictional, rather than being irrelevant, is 'unknowable.'"[54] What I sometimes do to increase my students' confidence and understanding of Lessing's challenging postmodern text is to play a tantalizing game by handing out an in-class "quiz" filled with self-contradictory multiple-choice answers that expose the complex scaffolding of Lessing's novel. This ludic academic exercise helps my audience come to terms with the apparent contradictions in Lessing's text and better comprehend the involuted postmodern structure of her narrative.[55]

CODA

> Consciously or unconsciously we keep two-thirds of mankind improperly housed and fed. This is what [my fiction] is about—this whole pattern of discrimination and tyranny and violence.[56]

"We must prevent another major war," Lessing warns. "We're already in a time of total chaos, but we're so corrupted that we can't see it. The world is rocking."[57] As Anna Wulf observes in *The Golden Notebook,* the second half of the twentieth century seemed to offer, for the first time in human history, wildly divergent possibilities—for apocalyptic disaster evinced by the H-bomb, on the one hand; and for previously unimagined technological miracles, on the other. At the beginning of the twenty-first century, the options seem even more staggering: weapons of mass destruction that could wipe out the human race in cataclysmic explosions, versus bionic reconstruction of the biological body and stem-cell research that could cure Parkinson's disease, Alzheimer's, and juvenile diabetes. In utopian fantasy, one might envisage a government budgeting $400 billion to feed and clothe every citizen on the planet, wipe out AIDs and world hunger, and support a global population in dignity and well-being. In contrast, one faces the political nightmare of terrorism, insurgency, and the ongoing occupation of Iraq by coalition forces, as well as a multimillion-dollar budget allocated for U.S. military expenditures in Afghanistan. Many awestruck citizens cannot believe that world leaders could choose the latter scenario. Considering Lessing's current political relevance, I trust that university professors will continue to take up the challenge of teaching *all* Lessing's subversive oeuvre, especially *The Golden Notebook*, well into the twenty-first century—and beyond.[58]

NOTES

1. Doris Lessing, "Placing Their Fingers on the Wounds of Our Times," interview by Margarete von Schwarzkopf, in *Die Welt*, May 9, 1981, trans. Earl G. Ingersoll and Heidrun Neth, in *Doris Lessing: Conversations*, ed. Earl G. Ingersoll (Princeton, NJ: Ontario Review Press, 1994), 102–3. Hereafter cited as *Conversations*.

2. "Bill Moyers Talks with Doris Lessing," interview by Bill Moyers, *Now* (January 24, 2003, PBS videotape).

3. Lessing, "A Conversation with Doris Lessing," interview by Billy Gray, *Doris Lessing Studies* 24.1 and 2 (2004): 26.

4. Lessing, "Preface to *The Golden Notebook*," in *A Small Personal Voice*, ed. Paul Schlueter (New York: Vintage, 1974), 36–37. Hereafter cited as *A Small Personal Voice*. The 1971 preface to *The Golden Notebook* is also called Introduction 1971 [to *The Golden Notebook*] [editors' note].

5. Lessing, "Writing as Time Runs Out," interview by Michael Dean, *Conversations*, 90.

6. Author's conversation with Suzanne Clark, August 2005. See Roberta Rubenstein's "Notes for Proteus: Doris Lessing Reads the *Zeitgeist*" in Part One of this collection, where she describes further challenges for any Lessing reader—including critics—encountering her large opus for the first time [editors' note].

7. D. J. Nicholl, H. G. Atkinson, J. Kalk, W. Hopkins, E. Elias, A. Siddiqui, R. E. Cranford, and O. Sacks, on behalf of 255 other doctors, "Forcefeeding and Restraint

10: The Golden Notebook *in the Twenty-First Century*

of Guantanamo Bay Hunger Strikers," *The Lancet* 367.9513 (March 11, 2006): 811. In January 2009, President Barack Obama signed executive orders banning torture and closing Guantanamo. The fate of most prisoners, however, still remains indeterminate.

8. Lessing, "Writing as Time Runs Out," 90.
9. Lessing, "Preface to *The Golden Notebook*," 27.
10. Lessing, "A Conversation with Doris Lessing," 24.
11. See for example, Carole Klein, *Doris Lessing* (London: Duckworth, 2000).
12. Ibid., 192–93.
13. Lessing, "Preface to *The Golden Notebook*," 25.
14. Lessing, "Doris Lessing at Stony Brook," interview with Jonah Raskin, *A Small Personal Voice*, 71.
15. Ellen Morgan, "Alienation of the Woman Writer in *The Golden Notebook*," in *Doris Lessing: Critical Studies*, ed. Annis Pratt and L. S. Dembo (1973; repr., Madison: University of Wisconsin Press, 1974), 55–57.
16. Lessing, *The Golden Notebook* (1962; repr., New York: Bantam, 1973), 4.
17. Lessing, "Placing Their Fingers on the Wounds of Our Times," 103.
18. Rachel Blau DuPlessis, "For the Etruscans," in *Feminist Criticism: Essays on Women, Literature, and Theory*, ed. Elaine Showalter (New York: Pantheon Books, 1985), 279.
19. Lessing, *The Golden Notebook*, 231–32.
20. Ibid., 213–14.
21. Ibid., 213.
22. Ibid., 214–15.
23. Ibid., 215–16.
24. Ibid., 216.
25. Ibid., 217–18.
26. Ibid., 325.
27. Ibid., 326.
28. William H. Masters and Virginia E. Johnson, *Human Sexual Response* (Boston: Little, Brown, 1966).
29. Shere Hite, *The Hite Report: A Nationwide Study of Female Sexuality* (New York: Macmillan, 1976).
30. Alfred C. Kinsey et al., *Sexual Behavior in the Human Female* (Philadelphia: Saunders, 1953).
31. Rereading Anne Koedt's 1970 essay on "The Myth of the Vaginal Orgasm" forty years after its initial publication is a fascinating historical exercise. Koedt cites Marie Bonaparte's suggestion, in *Female Sexuality*, that if a woman's "clitoral fixation" remains obdurate into adulthood, "a clitoral-vaginal reconciliation might be effected by surgical means" (qtd. in Koedt, 2). Koedt also quotes Frank S. Caprio, whose book on *The Sexually Adequate Female* remained a popular marriage manual throughout the 1960s: "whenever a woman is incapable of achieving orgasm via coitus, . . . she can be regarded as suffering from frigidity and requires psychiatric assistance" (qtd. in Koedt, 2). Koedt observes that, "[o]nce having laid down the law about the nature of our sexuality, Freud [and followers] not so strangely discovered a tremendous problem of frigidity in women" (2). See Anne Koedt, "The Myth of the Vaginal Orgasm," in *Notes from the First Year* (New York: The New York Radical Women, 1968), http://www.cwluher-

story.com/myth-of-the-vaginal-orgasm.html?q=myth+vaginal+orgasm (accessed March 17, 2010).

32. See Morgan, "Alienation of the Woman Writer in *The Golden Notebook*"; Claire Sprague, "*The Golden Notebook:* In Whose or What Great Tradition?" in *Approaches to Teaching Lessing's* The Golden Notebook, ed. Carey Kaplan and Ellen Cronan Rose (New York: The Modern Language Association, 1989), 78–83; Judith Kegan Gardiner, "Historicizing Homophobia in *The Golden Notebook* and 'The Day Stalin Died,'" *Doris Lessing Studies* 25.2 (2006): 15–17; Joseph Allen Boone, *Libidinal Currents: Sexuality and the Shaping of Modernism* (Chicago: University of Chicago Press, 1997). See Rubenstein's comments on contemporary students finding validity in Lessing's narrative representations of sexuality and emotional vulnerability, in "Notes for Proteus: Doris Lessing Reads the *Zeitgeist,*" in Part One of this volume [editors' note].

33. Lessing, *The Golden Notebook*, 391.

34. Ibid., 665. See Michael Cunningham, *The Hours* (New York: Farrar, Straus and Giroux, 1998).

35. Gardiner, "Historicizing Homophobia," 15–17.

36. Lessing, "Preface to *The Golden Notebook,*" 24.

37. Lessing, "Doris Lessing at Stony Brook," 69.

38. Lessing, *The Golden Notebook*, 469.

39. See Roberta Rubenstein, *The Novelistic Vision of Doris Lessing: Breaking the Forms of Consciousness* (Urbana: University of Illinois Press, 1979); and Linda S. Kauffman, *Special Delivery: Epistolary Modes in Modern Fiction* (Chicago: University of Chicago Press, 1992).

40. R. D. Laing, *The Politics of Experience* (New York: Ballantine, 1967), 133.

41. Klein, *Doris Lessing*, 197. See Lessing's 1964 interview with Roy Newquist, "Talking as a Person," in *Conversations*, 11–12; and her 1969 interview with Jonah Raskin, "The Inadequacy of the Imagination," *Conversations*, 13–14.

42. Klein, *Doris Lessing*, 204.

43. Ibid., 205.

44. Roberta Rubenstein, Robert Rawdon Wilson, Gayle Greene, and Linda S. Kauffman all suggest that Saul may be one of Anna's fictional creations, a masculine double or alter ego. See Robert Rawdon Wilson, *The Hydra's Tale: Imagining Disgust* (Edmonton: University of Alberta Press, 2002). Greene speculates that "Anna 'invents' Saul, fabricates him from all the men she has known, a kind of composite male who expresses her own 'masculine' potential (in Jungian terms, her animus) and guides her through breakdown" (123). See Gayle Greene, *Changing the Story: Feminist Fiction and the Tradition* (Bloomington: Indiana University Press, 1991). For further discussion of R. D. Laing's "antipsychiatry" as an influence on Lessing, see Jean Pickering, "Philosophical Contexts for *The Golden Notebook,*" in *Doris Lessing: The Alchemy of Survival*, ed. Carey Kaplan and Ellen Cronan Rose (Athens: Ohio University Press, 1988), 43–49; Marion Vlastos, "Doris Lessing and R. D. Laing: Psychopolitics and Prophecy," *PMLA* 91.2 (1976): 245–57; and Linda Kauffman, *Special Delivery*. Kauffman argues that Saul is an imaginary projection of Anna's consciousness and "does not exist" (145). "Saul's function parallels the Lacanian Imaginary, which relies on the image of the counterpart (the specular ego—*another who is me*)" (146n).

45. Lessing, "Preface to *The Golden Notebook*," 32–33.

46. Lessing, "Writing as Time Runs Out," 90.

47. Katherine Fishburn, "Teaching Doris Lessing as a Subversive Activity: A Response to the Preface to *The Golden Notebook*," in Kaplan and Rose, *Alchemy*, 82–83. For a discussion of Lessing and Sufism, see Müge Galin, *Between East and West: Sufism in the Novels of Doris Lessing* (Albany: State University of New York Press, 1997). See also *Spiritual Exploration in the Works of Doris Lessing*, ed. Phyllis Sternberg Perrakis (Westport, CT: Greenwood Press, 1999).

48. Thanks to Dana Nichols and Ann Marie Pedersen for their thoughtful email responses on the experience of reading *The Golden Notebook* for the first time.

49. See Patricia Waugh, *Metafiction: The Theory and Practice of Self-Conscious Fiction* (London: Methuen, 1984); Gayle Greene, *Changing the Story*; and Beth Boehm, "Reeducating Readers: Creating New Expectations for *The Golden Notebook*," *Narrative* 5.1 (1997): 88–97.

50. Fishburn, "Teaching Doris Lessing as a Subversive Activity," 86.

51. Lessing, "Preface to *The Golden Notebook*," 34.

52. Lessing, *The Golden Notebook*, 510.

53. Fishburn, "Teaching Doris Lessing as a Subversive Activity," 90. Lessing, says Fishburn, "has peppered her text with conflicting information, calculated to remind us that there is no final reality in the novel" (90).

54. Boehm, "Reeducating Readers," 95.

55. *The Golden Notebook* quiz:

    1) Anna's first husband was:
       a. Willi Rodde.
       b. Max Wulf.
       c. Both of the above.
       d. Stephen.
       e. George.

    2) Richard Portmain and Marion:
       a. Have one son, Tommy.
       b. Have three daughters.
       c. Have three sons.
       d. Both "b" and "c."

    3) Tommy Portmain:
       a. Shoots and blinds himself.
       b. Does national service by working in the coal mines.
       c. Marries a girl who is doing a dissertation on the Chartists.
       d. Goes to Sicily with Marion.
       e. All of the above.

    4) Saul/Milt:
       a. Is divorcing his wife because he loves her.
       b. Has an affair with Anna.
       c. Has never been married.
       d. All of the above.

    5) Anna, at the end of the novel:

a. Gets a job with Dr. North as a "matrimonial counselor."
   b. Decides to stop writing.
   c. Overcomes her writer's block.
   d. Composes a novel entitled *Free Women*.
   e. All of the above.
6) Molly, at the end of the novel:
   a. Opens a dress shop.
   b. Marries a wealthy man with a house in Hampstead.
   c. Becomes a psychiatric social worker.
   d. Shoots and blinds Tommy in a fit of rage.

56. Lessing, "Talking as a Person," 10–11.
57. Lessing, "Doris Lessing at Stony Brook," 71.
58. In the past, Doris Lessing has expressed profound disgruntlement with scholars who make a cult of her canon, and she has been particularly dismissive of *Doris Lessing Newsletter/Studies*. I thus apologize in advance should anything in my critique offend her. I long considered Lessing England's best and most worthy candidate for the Nobel Prize in literature and felt enormously gratified when this "sweetest dream" was finally realized in 2007.

11

Sex after Sixty

love, again and The Sweetest Dream

RUTH O. SAXTON

Old women have always inhabited the fiction of Doris Lessing. They have existed around the edges, in the background, in fiction that portrays them through the eyes of a younger female protagonist to whom even middle-aged mothers seem old and to whom the elderly are nearly invisible. Martha Quest, reading Havelock Ellis at age fourteen in Southern Zambezia, sees her mother and Mrs. Van Rensberg as matriarchs with varicose veins and outdated notions about female sexuality.[1] In her own middle-aged years in London, Martha continues to view women of her mother's generation as asexual, a perhaps convenient fiction each generation visits upon the previous one. Not until *The Diaries of Jane Somers*[2] does Lessing create a middle-aged female protagonist who truly *sees* the elderly, albeit from the outside. Janna, through a chance encounter and then a growing and complex relationship with ninety-two-year-old Maudie Fowler, comments: "I was so afraid of old age, of death, that I refused to let myself see old people in the streets—they did not exist for me.... I did not see old people at all. My eyes were pulled towards, and I *saw,* the young, the attractive, the well-dressed and handsome. And now it is as if a transparency has been drawn across that former picture and there, all at once, are the old, the infirm."[3] And not until *love, again* and *The Sweetest Dream*[4] does Lessing portray the world from *inside* the point of view of protagonists over sixty.

In these novels, Lessing reworks familiar tropes from her earlier fiction—a woman's relation to her body, as reflected in confrontations with her mirror, and as revealed in the rooms she inhabits and the choices she makes.[5] Lessing creates sharply contrasting figures in Sarah Durham, who is aged sixty-five in *love, again,* and Frances Lennox, who is in her seventies by the end of *The Sweetest Dream,* exploring two quite different ways for her aging protagonists to inhabit their bodies, their "rooms," and their lives. In creating women of "a certain age" as protagonists and in bringing her astute analysis to bear on Sarah and Frances, Lessing extends fictional attempts to "tell the truth about a woman's body," as Virginia Woolf exhorts.[6] We have rarely seen older women protagonists struggle with their sexuality. It has too often been assumed that women simply outgrow sexual desire, becoming spiritual crones who shed the "weight" of the body and of erotic pleasure. In these two novels, Lessing explores loss and change in terms of the *Zeitgeist* of the times in which they are set, idealism, and the disappointing failures of vision in the realms of the personal and the collective. In this essay I explore the ways in which Lessing articulates this terrain of loss and change in relation to the older woman's response to her body in general and to sexual desire in particular.

Sarah, widowed and with two grown children, finds joy in her creative work and in the solitude of her London flat: "She was finding herself in moments of quiet enjoyment, drawing vitality as she had all her life from small physical pleasures, like the feel of a naked sole on wood, the warmth of sunlight on bare skin, the smell of coffee or of earth, the faint scent of frost on stone" (*la,* 341). She enjoys sensual pleasure, but she denies herself sexual pleasure. Ultimately equating "falling in love" with a baby's longing for the mother from whom she has been exiled since childhood, Sarah celebrates the stoicism inherited from her grandmother and mother (348). Rejecting sexual pleasure in spite of a brief, highly eroticized theatrical summer, she ends the summer feeling "lighter and freer," but looking ten years older (349). Lessing suggests that Sarah, in recognizing her unmet need for maternal intimacy coupled with her discomfort about her aging body, sees sex as a burden. Sarah even wonders whether falling in love when "elderly and old" is "one way of [being hustled] . . . off the stage, to make way for the new" (350). Contrasting the embodied woman with the thinking or creative woman, Lessing suggests that a woman—even in her sixties and seventies—cannot mend the paradoxical rifts between mind and body, solitude and community, creative work and family life.

Sarah avoids physical intimacy as a thing of the past and accepts the double standards and negative attitudes of the larger society toward the aging female body. She believes that she is "in exactly the same situation as the innumerable people of the world who are ugly, deformed, or crippled, or who have horrible skin disorders. Or who lack that mysterious thing sex appeal" (141). She experiences her body as "a husk without colour, above all without the luster, the shine" (140) of youth, and she feels "like a miserable old ghost" (141). She experiences her aging female body as pathological, a dry shell, spectral. Sexual activity for such a no-body or carapace is rendered simultaneously pitiful and abject. It is thus no surprise that in the closing lines of *love, again,* Sarah relishes the autonomy of her single state, appreciates the return to her sensible quotidian self, whose physical pleasure is limited to the sensual and singular, and looks back on her summer of romantic upheaval with the relief one experiences upon recovery from major illness.

In contrast to Sarah's choice to avoid sexual relationships and to live alone, Frances Lennox, divorced mother of two sons, gives family life priority over creative work; her repeated choice to put children first requires steady income rather than the thrill of the theater (her avocation), and leads her to live under the roof of her mother-in-law. Her nurturing extends as far as one can see into her future. For most of her adult life she writes sensible articles and books for a living. However, by the novel's end, she has fallen in love again, keeps writing, and gets to act in *Romeo and Juliet*. Lessing allows her happiness in family, work, love, and sex—for the first time creating an older heroine who gets a second chance at love.

While Lessing exposes with unflinching clarity the dangers of romantic enthrallment in *love, again,* she revisits the importance of physical as well as emotional intimacy in *The Sweetest Dream,* suggesting not only the possibility of remarriage in one's sixties but also that "to be so thoroughly out of phase with the times" one must have "a certain bravado: a man and a woman daring to love each other so thoroughly—well, it was hardly to be confessed, even to each other" (*SD,* 473). In sharp contrast to Sarah, Frances chooses love, again, in her sixties with a second husband ten years her junior, and, while not expecting a fairy-tale romance, she enjoys the marital bed as a place of comfort and pleasure in the middle of a life that includes constant involvement with children, stepchildren, surrogate children, and a granddaughter. Frances reveals none of the disgust toward her body that Sarah feels so acutely.

I recognize the multiple levels at which readers construct meaning in Lessing's texts—including the possibility that she is exposing sexual intimacy, political engagement, and humanitarian responses to world illness *all* as illusions and dreams; nevertheless, I suggest that life without dreams, without sweetness, is bleak and unbearable. I celebrate Lessing's hint that physical pleasure, that sex, for women over sixty is not just a memory that reappears in deathbed scenes or dementia as a vestigial organ in the fantasies of old women, that the aging female body need not be equated with disgust and distaste, that women do not necessarily outgrow sexual desire, and that laughter, rather than eternal youth, can be an excellent aphrodisiac.[7]

Lessing's young and middle-aged female protagonists are nearly always highly aware of their bodies, are easily sexual, and take for granted their own vitality as well as the presence of men in their lives.[8] They manage to be sexy without effort, and they take for granted the attention that comes their way. They often become pregnant unwittingly, marry for all the wrong reasons, and then either divorce or are widowed; however, they manage to stay housed and fed through their own efforts, although sometimes a well-to-do former mother-in-law provides the basics—for the sake of the children. In *The Summer before the Dark*[9] and *The Diaries of Jane Somers,* Lessing explores her characters' body consciousness and sexual desires well into their forties, not restricting the complexities of erotic desire to the young.

Therefore, when I first read *love, again* I was angry with Lessing in that she portrays sixty-five-year-old Sarah Durham as falling in love, aroused by desire, and yet does not allow her any sexual pleasure. Sarah has internalized societal messages about the aging female body and, like Janna in *The Diaries of Jane Somers,* she avoids sex entirely rather than be naked and have a man see her no-longer-youthful body. Because Lessing's female characters have always embraced their sexuality, I expected sexual pleasure to continue as they aged. Puritan values are not the cause of their denial of sex, nor are notions of faithfulness in marriage. Lessing's earlier protagonists have certainly engaged in affairs, and in *love, again,* Sarah pokes fun at "good wholesome ethical Americans" (285) who consider issues of morality in such situations. It is pride, embarrassment in no longer inhabiting the bodies of their youth, that causes Janna and Sarah to avoid opportunities for sex. My initial response to Sarah as I entered my sixties revealed my fear of losing sensuality, or avoiding sexuality, or internalizing the prevailing cultural distaste for the aging female body.

It has taken me several years to recognize that my discontent is not based on Sarah's avoidance of sexual intercourse with any of the mismatched men for whom she feels desire; rather, I am disconcerted by the extent to which Sarah reveals ageist reactions to her own body. Sarah is nostalgically in love with her younger body, and while she continues to be vitally engaged with her work as she ages and still attracts positive attention from men, she avoids physical intimacy because of her distaste for her changing body.

Although the narrator of *love, again* states that it goes without saying "that a woman's interaction with her mirror is likely to go through some changes during the decades" (198), readers familiar with passages in which Lessing's earlier female protagonists dispassionately examine their bodies in mirrors, recognize the usual catalogue of areas most severely critiqued: hair, shoulders, back, breasts, legs. What's new in Sarah's encounter is the attention to her skin's "fine velvety wrinkles" like the surface of "an elderly peach," and her horrible recognition of "the irrevocableness of it. There was nothing to be done." While at one level "she could sincerely say" that she "did not care about this aging carcass," at another level she views her body "as vulnerable as the flesh of roses" (242–43). When she imagines making love with a younger man, who clearly desires her, she recalls how her younger self would have recoiled at the thought of an older woman in bed with a younger man, and realizes that "not even she—whose careless frankness in matters of love had more than once done her harm"—would admit how long she has gone without sex and that "for the first time in her life she would ask to have the light off" (44–45). Rather than face the danger that he will turn on the light, she avoids sex entirely.

I wonder if Lessing plays on her readers' inability to imagine continuing sexual pleasure for women over sixty by having Sarah repeatedly fall "in love" while insisting that such fantasies are less reliable than Sarah's everyday self. Is she trying once again—here as in the two volumes of her autobiography[10] and *The Memoirs of a Survivor*[11]—to make sense of the little girl's love of her younger brother combined with the absence of maternal love? Is she once again suggesting that the yearning that haunts so many of her female protagonists is actually a profound, unmet yearning for maternal love mistaken for "love" of a man, love that is ultimately unsatisfying because misplaced? Lessing juxtaposes Sarah's discomfort with her aging body with Sarah's psychological awareness about her childhood loss of maternal love. Although it may be useful to recognize the complex experiences that affect and limit adult heterosexual intimate relationships, to conclude that such limits make love and desire a malady for an old woman—more so than for a young woman—is suspect and sad.

Wondering how female protagonists over fifty fare in novels by other contemporary women writers, I began research that eventually led me to create a graduate student seminar, "Coming of Age, Coming to Age: Fictions of Female Possibility." Before teaching the seminar, I failed to notice how comparatively positive Lessing's portrait of Sarah is in contrast to those by her contemporaries. Lessing provides and seems to take for granted many positive qualities in her portrayal of Sarah. For example, my students, while faulting Lessing for perpetuating stereotypes about the older woman's discomfort with her body, applauded Sarah's avoidance of sexual liaisons with ill-suited partners. They also pointed out that Sarah is healthy, active, and able to travel. She is engaged in creative/professional work that she enjoys and that earns her the respect of many others—colleagues, financiers, and young actors. She faces her desires honestly, and she is savvy enough to avoid taking actions that would not be appropriate or healthy for her or for her potential romantic/sexual partners. Even though she avoids physical intimacy, she is a good friend to Stephen, a man near her age. Unlike Sarah, he does have sex with a young woman, and his angst is not related to age.

While irritated that Sarah is so enamored of her own younger self that she avoids enjoying her body, I appreciate her vitality. She stands out in contrast to portrayals of older women in many contemporary novels. For example, Ann Lord, in Susan Minot's *Evening*,[12] nearly the same age as Sarah, is dying of cancer and portrayed as bed-ridden, medicated, and reliving scenes of unrequited love from age twenty-one. Or Caroline Spencer in May Sarton's *As We Are Now*,[13] who, having suffered a minor stroke, languishes in a nursing home where she is virtually isolated and ultimately commits suicide at age seventy-six. Nevertheless, although Lessing counters some stereotypes of old women—allowing Sarah to be healthy, to enjoy an exciting career in theater, and to continue to attract male attention—she reinscribes the cultural double standard and leaves unchallenged Sarah's distaste for her body.[14]

In *The Sweetest Dream* Lessing reworks her portrayal of the older woman, allowing Frances—at last—to move slightly beyond the all-encompassing role of nurturer/caretaker so frequently played by Lessing's protagonists. (Think of those pots of homemade soup in *The Good Terrorist*[15] and the need of protagonists from Martha Quest to Jane Somers, from Harriet in *The Fifth Child*[16] to Frances herself, continually to feed hordes of people around large wooden kitchen tables.) In Frances, Lessing portrays a woman who, after putting "the children" first for decades, in a second marriage, at age sixty with blended family, is no longer willing to let children walk all over her. What a relief it is when Frances finally sets a few limits on her previously unlimited nurturing of others. For example, she refuses to prepare the annual Christmas dinner one year, and she sometimes substitutes "take out" for home-cooked meals. She eventually shares with Rupert her flat in the large Lennox family home and redefines what it means to care for children. Frances is honest about her feelings in response to the behavior of Rupert's two children, and the reader knows that these children will be able to count on her reliability while understanding that she will take care of herself as well.[17]

Unlike Sarah, Frances can encounter her mirror, recognize change, alter her hairstyle, or buy a new dress without also yearning for her younger body and denying herself sexual pleasure. Rupert is ten years younger than

Frances, and, perhaps because his former wife left him and is emotionally unstable, Frances does not compare herself negatively with her in spite of their age difference. In her happiness with Rupert, Frances is described as "a large handsome woman, her yellow hair—dyed—in a cut that had cost the earth. She was well dressed: Julia would at last have approved" (*SD,* 333). Julia, her mother-in-law and the person who owns the large family home in which Frances raises her two sons after her divorce, is seen from a distance by her grandchildren as "a kind of old witch, to be laughed at" (70). Frances is awkward and afraid of her for years, noticing her gestures, her out-of-date apparel, and her expensive and romantic association with flowers. Throughout most of the novel, Frances does not *know* Julia, does not *see* her, just as Janna does not initially see old people. Yet perhaps the "maternal" presence of Julia Lennox, considered "the old woman" by everyone in the family, allows Frances to avoid the perceived limitations of that role. Eventually, in a positive nod to the aging active woman, Frances notices that Julia is beautiful in her old age, with erect posture, a slight frame, and elegant clothing and manners, and discovers that, in her seventies, Julia has a debonair and good-looking beau in his eighties who clearly adores her. Romance and affection between Julia and her beau are no less real simply because Frances is not able to recognize or appreciate them in anyone she considers old and out of date. Resisting her own aging, Frances is reluctant to learn from Julia.

Lessing's female protagonists—like those of most novels by women—define themselves over and against their mothers and maternal figures. Mothers and grandmothers serve as sounding boards or mirrors. Even adult female protagonists who have careers and children see the generation of their mothers as beings to avoid or to struggle against, determining never to become such persons. Paradoxically, a daughter may crave her mother's unconditional love and search for it throughout her life in all the wrong places, as she simultaneously determines never to become her mother. While Julia herself is a complex character, she still remains in the role of the traditional nonworking, nonintellectual, feminine hostess, the Mrs. Dalloway role that Frances continually resists. Only after Julia's death can Frances live her own life as an old woman, taking and discarding what is useful from Julia's legacy, and no longer needing to define herself in opposition to her. Frances is Lessing's first complex heroine who works, makes love, thinks about the world with idealism, sees the messes that result from naïve dreams at the personal and global levels, and ages beyond her forties into the decades of her sixties and seventies with grace and a sense of humor, retaining her capacities and interests, and not outgrowing sexual pleasure.

The big bed, rather than the big kitchen table, is now "the emotional center of her life": "She felt as if she had stumbled so late in her life, as in a fairytale, into a glade full of sunshine . . ." (*SD*, 337). She and Rupert "had found [in their second marriage] a happiness they had not expected or even believed in" (338). Frances and Rupert both have "busy outward lives" and "what was at the heart of it was this great bed, where everything was understood and nothing needed to be said" (338). Is it possible that the marital bed replaces the coveted and never realized maternal lap, that place of unconditional love, now realized between adults rather than forever limited to the oceanic amniotic state? And is it possible that it is only when a woman, a daughter, no longer feels like an unloved child that she can accept her adult body and enjoy its pleasures? Perhaps readers, including the feminists Lessing so often denounces, are included in her sweeping remark about Frances and Rupert's realization that "ideology has pronounced their condition impossible and so, people keep quiet" (338). Whether that "condition" refers to married love between a man and a woman, or love at a "certain age," or sex after sixty, Lessing in *The Sweetest Dream* portrays a landscape for the older woman in which she actively embraces life, including responsibility, work, conversation, love, laughter, and sex, well into her seventies.

NOTES

1. Doris Lessing, *Martha Quest*, vol. 1 of *Children of Violence* (1952; repr., New York: Simon and Schuster, 1964).
2. Lessing, *The Diaries of Jane Somers* (New York: Knopf, 1984).
3. Ibid., 237, 21.
4. Lessing, *love, again* (New York: HarperCollins, 1995); hereafter abbreviated *la* and cited in the text. Lessing, *The Sweetest Dream* (London: HarperCollins, 2001; New York: HarperCollins, 2002); hereafter abbreviated *SD* and cited in the text.
5. I develop these ideas in my manuscript, *Garments of the Mind: Clothing and Appearance in the Fiction of Doris Lessing*.
6. See Virginia Woolf, "Professions for Women," in *The Death of the Moth and Other Essays* (New York: Harcourt Brace Jovanovich, 1942).
7. See, for example, Katherine Anne Porter's "The Jilting of Granny Weatherall," in *Flowering Judas* (New York: Signet Classics, 1970); Muriel Sparks's *Memento Mori* (New York: New Directions Books, 2000); and Anita Brookner's *Visitors* (New York: Vintage, 1998).
8. Lessing's female protagonists are primarily heterosexual.
9. Lessing, *The Summer before the Dark* (London: Jonathan Cape, 1973; New York: Knopf, 1973).
10. Lessing, *Under My Skin: Volume One of My Autobiography, to 1949* (London:

HarperCollins, 1994; repr., New York: HarperCollins, 1994); *Walking in the Shade: Volume Two of My Autobiography, 1949 to 1962* (London: HarperCollins, 1997; repr., New York: HarperCollins, 1997).

11. Lessing, *The Memoirs of a Survivor* (London: Octagon Press, 1974; repr., New York: Knopf, 1975).

12. Susan Minot, *Evening* (New York: Knopf, 1998).

13. May Sarton, *As We Are Now* (New York: W. W. Norton, 1973).

14. See Virginia Tiger's analysis of the way that the reader's response to Sarah's sexual frustrations is complicated by the formal complexity of *love, again*'s double-tiered structure in her chapter 7, "*love, again* and *The Sweetest Dream*: Fiction and Interleaved Fictions," in Part Three of this volume [editors' note].

15. Lessing, *The Good Terrorist* (London: Jonathan Cape, 1985; repr., New York: Knopf, 1985).

16. Lessing, *The Fifth Child* (London: Jonathan Cape, 1988; repr., New York: Knopf, 1988).

17. See Robin Visel's discussion of Frances's continuing difficulties with the tensions between being a mother and an artist in her chapter 3, "House/Mother: Lessing's Reproduction of Realism in *The Sweetest Dream*," in Part One of this volume [editors' note].

Bibliography

Abrams, M. H., and Stephen Greenblatt. *The Norton Anthology of English Literature.* 7th ed. New York: Norton, 2000.
Aldiss, Brian. "My Sort of Fairy Tale." *The Guardian,* April 17, 1999, 8.
Allardice, Lisa. "Sniping at Sisters." Review of *The Sweetest Dream,* by Doris Lessing. *Daily Telegraph* (London), September 8, 2001, 6. Custom Newspapers (InfoTrac-Gale) http://find.galegroup.com (accessed September 14, 2006).
Appignanesi, Lisa. "Idealists at Home and Away." Review of *The Sweetest Dream,* by Doris Lessing. *The Independent* (London), September 8, 2001, 11. Custom Newspapers (InfoTrac-Gale) http://find.galegroup.com (accessed September 14, 2006).
———. "Unto Them, a Boy Is Born." Review of *The Cleft,* by Doris Lessing. *Times Online,* January 6, 2007. http://entertainment.timesonline.co.uk/tol/arts_and_entertainment/books/fiction/article1289421.ece (accessed August 13, 2007).
Arendt, Hannah. *On Violence.* New York: Harcourt, 1970.
Armstrong, Nancy. *Desire and Domestic Fiction: A Political History of the Novel.* New York: Oxford University Press, 1987.
Austen, Jane. *Emma.* Vol. 2, *The Complete Novels of Jane Austen.* New York: The Modern Library, 1992.
———. *Northanger Abbey.* Vol. 2, *The Complete Novels of Jane Austen.* New York: The Modern Library, 1992.
———. *Sense and Sensibility.* Vol. 1, *The Complete Novels of Jane Austen.* New York: The Modern Library, 1992.
Balfour, Robert. "Gardening in Other Countries: Schoeman, Coetzee, Conrad." Presented at CSSALL conference, University of Durban–Westville, 1995.
Bancroft, John H. J. "Sex and Aging." *The New England Journal of Medicine* 357.8 (August 23, 2007): 820–22.
Barnacle, H. "On Thin Ice." *Sunday Times,* April 4, 1999, 9.
Barthes, Roland. *The Pleasure of the Text.* Translated by Richard Miller. New York: Hill and Wang, 1975.

Bazin, Nancy Topping. *Virginia Woolf and the Androgynous Vision.* New Brunswick, NJ: Rutgers University Press, 1973.
Beck, Antony. "Doris Lessing and the Colonial Experience." *Journal of Commonwealth Literature* 19.1 (1984): 64–73.
Bedell, Geraldine. "Ancestral Voices." Review of *The Story of General Dann and Mara's Daughter, Griot and the Snow Dog,* by Doris Lessing. *The Observer,* Sunday, July 3, 2005. http://books.guardian.co.uk/reviews/generalfiction/0,6121,1519819,00.html#article_continue (accessed July 28, 2009).
———. "Women and Children First." Review of *The Cleft,* by Doris Lessing. *The Observer,* January 7, 2007. http://books.guardian.co.uk/reviews/generalfiction/0,,1984239,00.html (accessed August 13, 2007).
Bell, Millicent. "Possessed by Love." *Partisan Review* 64.3 (1997): 486–92.
Bentley, Nick. "Doris Lessing's *The Golden Notebook*: An Experiment in Critical Fiction." In *Doris Lessing: Border Crossings,* edited by Alice Ridout and Susan Watkins, 44–60. London: Continuum, 2009.
Boehm, Beth. "Reeducating Readers: Creating New Expectations for *The Golden Notebook.*" *Narrative* 5.1 (1997): 88–97.
Boone, Joseph Allen. *Libidinal Currents: Sexuality and the Shaping of Modernism.* Chicago: University of Chicago Press, 1997.
Brickman, Celia. "Primitivity, Race, and Religion in Psychoanalysis." *The Journal of Religion* 82.1 (2002): 53–74.
Brookner, Anita. *Visitors.* New York: Vintage, 1998.
Butler, Robert N., and Myrna I. Lewis. *The New Love and Sex after 60.* New York: Ballantine Books, 2002.
Byatt, A. S. *A Whistling Woman.* New York: Alfred A. Knopf, 2002.
Canary, Robert H., and Henry Kozicki, eds. *The Writing of History: Literary Form and Historical Understanding.* Madison: University of Wisconsin Press, 1978.
Chaffee, Patricia. "Spatial Patterns and Closed Groups in Lessing's African Stories." *South Atlantic Quarterly* 43.2 (1978): 126–32.
Chennells, Anthony. "Postcolonialism and Doris Lessing's Empires." *Doris Lessing Studies* 21.2 (2001): 4–11.
Chomsky, Noam. *The Culture of Terrorism.* Boston, MA: South End Press, 1988.
———. *9-11.* New York: Seven Stories Press, 2002.
Chopin, Kate. *The Awakening.* Chicago: Herbert S. Stone & Company, 1899.
Clark, Alex. "Growing Pains: Alex Clark Finds Lessing's Sequel as Freakish as Its Hero." *The Guardian,* June 17, 2000. http://books.guardian.co.uk/reviews/generalfiction/0,,332971,00.html (accessed November 15, 2005).
Coetzee, J. M. "The Heart of Me." Review of *Under My Skin,* by Doris Lessing. *New York Review of Books,* December 22, 1994. http://www.nybooks.com/articles/2034 (accessed July 26, 2009).
Collins, J., and R. Wilson. "The Broken Allegory: Doris Lessing's *The Fifth Child* as Narrative Theodicy." *Analecta Husserliana: The Yearbook of Phenomenological Research* 41 (1994): 277–91.
Conrad, Joseph. *The Secret Agent: A Simple Tale.* Edited by Peter Lancelot Mallios. New York: Modern Library, 2004.
Corrigan, Maureen. "Improbably Star-Crossed." Review of *love, again,* by Doris Lessing.

The Nation, May 6, 1996, 62–64.
Crown, Sarah. "Doris Lessing Wins Nobel Prize." October 11, 2007. http://www.guardian.co.uk/books/2007/oct/11/nobelprize.awardsandprizes (accessed July 7, 2009).
Cuddy-Keane, Melba. *Virginia Woolf, the Intellectual, and the Public Sphere*. New York: Cambridge University Press, 2003.
Cunningham, Michael. *The Hours*. New York: Farrar, Straus and Giroux, 1998.
Damasio, Antonio. *Descartes' Error: Emotion, Reason, and the Human Brain*. New York: G. P. Putnam's Sons, 1994.
Dean, S. "Lessing's *The Fifth Child*." *Explicator* 50.2 (1992): 120–22.
de Bertodano, Helena. "Life Is Stronger than Fiction." *Daily Telegraph*, April 11, 1996, 4–6.
Defoe, Daniel. *Moll Flanders*. London: Dent, 1977. Reprint, New York: Dutton, 1977.
Deleuze, Gilles, and Félix Guattari. *Kafka: Toward a Minor Literature*. Translated by Dana Polan. Foreword by Reda Bensmaia. Minneapolis: University of Minnesota Press, 1986.
Denyer, Susan. *African Traditional Architecture*. London: Heinemann, 1978.
Drabble, Margaret. "Doris Lessing: Cassandra in a World under Siege." In Sprague and Tiger, *Critical Essays on Doris Lessing*, 183–91.
Draine, Betsy. *Substance under Pressure: Artistic Coherence and Evolving Form in the Novels of Doris Lessing*. Madison: University of Wisconsin Press, 1983.
DuPlessis, Rachel Blau. "For the Etruscans." In *Feminist Criticism: Essays on Women, Literature, and Theory*, edited by Elaine Showalter, 271–91. New York: Pantheon, 1985.
Dürrenmatt, Friedrich. *The Assignment: Or, On the Observing of the Observer of the Observers*. Translated by Joel Agee. New York: Random House, 1988.
Eliot, T. S. *Selected Prose*. Edited by John Hayward. Harmondsworth, England: Penguin, 1963.
Fand, Roxanne. *The Dialogic Self: Reconstructing Subjectivity in Woolf, Lessing, and Atwood*. Selinsgrove, PA: Susquehanna University Press, 1999.
Fanon, Frantz. *The Wretched of the Earth*. Translated by Constance Farrington. New York: Grove Press, 1966.
Farwell, Marilyn R. "Virginia Woolf and Androgyny." *Contemporary Literature* 16.4 (1975): 433–51.
Fermor-Hesketh, Robert. *Architecture of the British Empire*. London: Weidenfeld and Nicolson, 1986.
Fielding, Henry. *Tom Jones*. Harlow, Essex, England: Addison Wesley Longman, Ltd., 1999.
Fishburn, Katherine. "Teaching Doris Lessing as a Subversive Activity: A Response to the Preface to *The Golden Notebook*." In Kaplan and Rose, *Alchemy*, 81–92.
———. *The Unexpected Universe of Doris Lessing: A Study in Narrative Technique*. Westport, CT: Greenwood, 1985.
———. "Wor(l)ds within Words: Doris Lessing as Meta-Fictionist and Meta-Physician." *Studies in the Novel* 20.2 (1988): 186–205.
Foucault, Michel. "What Is an Author?" In *The Foucault Reader*, edited by Paul Rabinow, 101–20. New York: Pantheon Books, 1984.
Friedman, Ellen G., and Miriam Fuchs. *Breaking the Sequence: Women's Experimental*

Fiction. Princeton, NJ: Princeton University Press, 1989.
Galin, Müge. *Between East and West: Sufism in the Novels of Doris Lessing.* Albany: State University of New York Press, 1997.
Gardiner, Judith Kegan. "Historicizing Homophobia in *The Golden Notebook* and 'The Day Stalin Died.'" *Doris Lessing Studies* 25.2 (2006): 14–18.
Gąsiorek, Andrzej. *Post-War British Fiction: Realism and After.* London: Edward Arnold, 1995.
Gibbons, Fiachra. "Lay off Men, Lessing Tells Feminists": Special Report: Edinburgh Festival 2001. guardian.co.uk (August 14, 2001). http://www.guardian.co.uk/uk/2001/aug/14/edinburghfestival2001.edinburghbookfestival2001 (accessed February 20, 2010).
Golding, William. *The Inheritors.* London: Faber and Faber, 1955.
Goodman, Ellen. "The Doris Lessing Hoax." In Sprague and Tiger, *Critical Essays on Doris Lessing,* 213–14.
Gornick, Vivian. "Opening *The Golden Notebook*: Remembering the Source." Part of PEN Panel Discussion, "Thirty Years of Feminism: Literature and the Movement." November 25, 1991. In *PEN Newsletter* 79 (October 1992): 10–11.
Greene, Gayle. *Changing the Story: Feminist Fiction and the Tradition.* Bloomington: Indiana University Press, 1991.
Grossman, Lionel. "History and Literature: Reproduction or Signification." In Canary and Kozicki, *The Writing of History: Literary Form and Historical Understanding,* 1–40.
Hague, Angela. "Picaresque Structure and the Angry Young Novel." *Twentieth Century Literature* 32.2 (1986): 209–20.
Hanford, Jan. Doris Lessing Web site at http://lessing.redmood.com/biography.html (accessed July 28, 2009).
Hanson, Clare. "Doris Lessing in Pursuit of the English; or, No Small, Personal Voice." *PN Review* 14.4 (1987): 39–42.
Haraway, Donna J. *Simians, Cyborgs, and Women: The Reinvention of Nature.* New York: Routledge, 1991.
Havel, Václav. "The Need for Transcendence in the Postmodern World." Czech Embassy (July 4, 1994). http://dieoff.org/page38.htm (accessed May 30, 2006).
Head, Dominic. *The Cambridge Companion to Modern British Fiction, 1950–2000.* Cambridge: Cambridge University Press, 2002.
Henry, Holly. *Virginia Woolf and the Discourse of Science: The Aesthetics of Astronomy.* New York: Cambridge University Press, 2003.
Hite, Molly. "Doris Lessing's *The Golden Notebook* and *The Four-Gated City*: Ideology, Coherence, and Possibility." *Twentieth Century Literature* 34.1 (1988): 16–29.
———. *The Other Side of the Story: Structures and Strategies of Contemporary Feminist Narrative.* Ithaca, NY: Cornell University Press, 1989.
Hite, Shere. *The Hite Report: A Nationwide Study of Female Sexuality.* New York: Macmillan, 1976.
Hiwad, Farah. "Afghanistan: Tajwar Kakar—Fighting for Women and Freedom (Part 4)." In RFE/RL Newsline. March 5, 2004. http://www.rferl.org/featuresarticle/2004/3/FE443C0B-0B4B-48B8-BEBB-727E653CC158.html (accessed July 12, 2009).
Hobbs, John. "*Love, Again.*" *America* 175.18 (1996): 25–26.

Hussey, Mark, ed. *Virginia Woolf and War: Fiction, Reality, and Myth.* Syracuse, NY: Syracuse University Press, 1991.

Hutcheon, Linda. "'The Pastime of Past Time': Fiction, History, Historiographic Metafiction." *Genre* 20 (Fall–Winter 1987): 285–305.

Ingersoll, Earl G., ed. *Doris Lessing: Conversations.* Princeton, NJ: Ontario Review Press, 1994. Reprint, *Putting the Questions Differently: Interviews with Doris Lessing, 1964–1994.* London: Flamingo-HarperCollins, 1994.

Iser, Wolfgang. *The Implied Reader: Patterns of Communication in Prose Fiction from Bunyan to Beckett.* Baltimore: Johns Hopkins University Press, 1980.

Italie, Hillel. "This Writer Won't Settle Down." *Los Angeles Times: Calendarlive.com.* February 20, 2006. http://articles.latimes.com/2006/oct/20/entertainment/et-lessing20 (accessed February 27, 2010).

Jackson, Shannon M. "Cape Colonial Architecture, Town Planning, and the Crafting of Modern Space in South Africa." *Africa Today* 5.4 (2005): 33–51.

Jones, Ellen Carol. "Androgynous Vision and Artistic Process in Virginia Woolf's *A Room of One's Own.*" In *Critical Essays on Virginia Woolf,* edited by Morris Beja, 227–39. Boston: G. K. Hall and Company, 1985.

Jordan, Judith. "Empathy and Self Boundaries." In Roman, Juhasz, and Miller, *The Women and Language Debate,* 153–64.

Kaivola, Karen. "Revisiting Woolf's Representations of Androgyny: Gender, Race, Sexuality, and Nation." *Tulsa Studies in Women's Literature* 18.2 (1999): 235–61.

Kakutani, Michiko. "Books of the Times; His Weirdness Attracts Types Even More Weird." *The New York Times,* August 8, 2000. http://query.nytimes.com/gst/fullpage.html?res=9A04E2DB103CF93BA3575BC0A9669C8B63 (accessed November 15, 2005).

———. "Books of the Times; Where Millenniums Are Treated like Centuries." *The New York Times,* January 26, 1999: 61. http://query.nytimes.com/gst/fullpage.html?res=9D0DE2DD1539F935A15752C0A96F958260 (accessed November 15, 2005).

Kaplan, Carey, and Ellen Cronan Rose, eds. *Approaches to Teaching Lessing's* The Golden Notebook. New York: The Modern Language Association, 1989.

———. *Doris Lessing: The Alchemy of Survival.* Athens: Ohio University Press, 1988.

Kaplan, Sydney Janet. *Feminine Consciousness in the Modern British Novel.* Urbana: University of Illinois Press, 1975.

Kauffman, Linda S. *Special Delivery: Epistolary Modes in Modern Fiction.* Chicago: University of Chicago Press, 1992.

Keith, Michael, and Steve Pile. *Place and the Politics of Identity.* London: Routledge, 1993.

Kennedy, Dane. *Islands of White.* Durham, NC: Duke University Press, 1987.

Kermode, Frank. "Sensing Endings." *Nineteenth-Century Fiction* 33.1 (1978): 144–58.

King, Jeannette. *Doris Lessing.* London: Edward Arnold, 1989.

Kinsey, Alfred C., et al. *Sexual Behavior in the Human Female.* Philadelphia: Saunders, 1953.

Klein, Carole. *Doris Lessing.* London: Duckworth, 2000.

Koedt, Anne. "The Myth of the Vaginal Orgasm." In *Notes from the First Year.* New York: The New York Radical Women, 1968. http://www.cwluherstory.com/myth-of-the-vaginal-orgasm.html?q=myth+vaginal+orgasm (accessed March 17, 2010).

Kristeva, Julia. *Powers of Horror: An Essay on Abjection.* Translated by Leon S. Roudiez. New York: Columbia University Press, 1982.
LaCapra, Dominick. *Writing History, Writing Trauma.* Baltimore: John Hopkins University Press, 2001.
Laing, R. D. *The Politics of Experience.* New York: Ballantine, 1967.
Latz, Anna. "The Quest for Freedom in *Love, Again.*" *Doris Lessing Newsletter* 18.2 (1997): 3, 6–7, 13–14.
"Leak Reveals Honours Snubs." *BBC News,* December 21, 2003. http://news.bbc.co.uk/1/hi/uk/3338583.stm (accessed July 28, 2009).
Le Guin, Ursula. "Saved by a Squirt." Review of *The Cleft,* by Doris Lessing. *The Guardian Unlimited,* February 10, 2007. http://books.guardian.co.uk/review/story/0,,2009447,00.html (accessed August 13, 2007).
Lessing, Doris. *African Laughter: Four Visits to Zimbabwe.* New York: HarperCollins, 1992.
———. *African Stories.* New York: Simon and Schuster, 1965.
———. Afterword to *The Story of an African Farm,* by Olive Schreiner, 273–90. New York: Fawcett World Library, 1968. Reprint, in *A Small Personal Voice,* edited by Paul Schlueter, 97–120. New York: Vintage, 1975.
———. *Alfred and Emily.* London: Fourth Estate, 2008.
———. "An Ancient Way to New Freedom." In *The Diffusion of Sufi Ideas in the West,* edited by Leonard Lewin, 44–54. Boulder, CO: Keysign, 1972. Reprint, in *The Elephant in the Dark,* edited by Leonard Lewin, 73–81. New York: E. P. Dutton, 1976.
———. *Ben, In the World.* London: Flamingo, 2000.
———. "Bill Moyers Talks with Doris Lessing." By Bill Moyers. *Now* (2003). http://www.pbs.org/now (accessed May 28, 2005); January 24, 2003 (PBS Videotape).
———. "A Book That Changed Me." In Lessing, *Time Bites,* 212–13.
———. "Breaking Down these Forms." Interview by Stephen Gray. In Ingersoll, *Putting the Questions Differently,* 109–19.
———. *Briefing for a Descent into Hell.* London: Jonathan Cape, 1971.
———. "Caged by the Experts." Interview by Thomas Frick. In Ingersoll, *Doris Lessing: Conversations,* 155–68.
———. *The Cleft.* London: Fourth Estate (HarperCollins), 2007; New York: HarperCollins, 2007.
———. "A Conversation with Doris Lessing." Interview by Billy Gray. *Doris Lessing Studies* 24.1 and 2 (2004): 1, 23–30.
———. "Describing This Beautiful and Nasty Planet." Interview by Earl G. Ingersoll. In Ingersoll, *Doris Lessing: Conversations,* 228–40.
———. *The Diaries of Jane Somers: 1 The Diary of a Good Neighbor; 2 If the Old Could. . . .* London: Michael Joseph, 1984. Reprint, New York: Alfred A. Knopf, 1984.
———. *Documents Relating to the Sentimental Agents in the Volyen Empire.* Vol. 5, *Canopus in Argos: Archives.* London: Cape, 1983.
———. "Doris Lessing Provocateur." Interview by Emily Parker. *The Wall Street Journal* online (WSJ.com), March 15, 2008: A11. http://online.wsj.com/article_email/SB120554114603738389-lMyQjAxMDI4MDI1MTUyNDExWj.html (accessed July 28, 2009).

———. "Doris Lessing at Stony Brook." Interview by Jonah Raskin. In Schlueter, *A Small Personal Voice*, 61–76.

———. "Drawn to a Type of Landscape." Interview by Sedge Thomson. In Ingersoll, *Doris Lessing: Conversations*, 178–92.

———. *The Fifth Child*. 1988. Reprint, New York: Knopf, 1988; London: Flamingo, 1993.

———. *The Four-Gated City*. Vol. 5, *Children of Violence*. London: MacGibbon and Kee, 1969. Reprint, New York: Penguin, 1976.

———. *Going Home*. 1957. Reprint, St. Albans, England: Panther Books, 1968.

———. *The Golden Notebook*. London: Michael Joseph, 1962, 1972. Reprint, New York: Bantam, 1971, 1973; London, New York: HarperPerennial, 1990, 1999; London: Flamingo-HarperCollins, 2002.

———. *The Good Terrorist*. London: Jonathan Cape, 1985. Reprint, New York: Alfred A. Knopf, 1985.

———. *The Grandmothers*. New York: HarperCollins, 2003.

———. *The Grass Is Singing*. London: Michael Joseph, 1950. Reprint, New York: Thomas Y. Crowell, 1950.

———. *The Habit of Loving*. New York: Thomas Y. Crowell, 1957.

———. "The Inadequacy of the Imagination." Interview by Jonah Raskin. In Ingersoll, *Doris Lessing: Conversations*, 13–18.

———. "An Interview with Doris Lessing." By Susan Stamberg. In *Doris Lessing Newsletter* 8.2 (Fall 1984): 3–4, 15.

———. Introduction 1993 [to *The Golden Notebook*]. 1994. Reprint, London, New York: HarperPerennial Classics, 1999, vii–ix.

———. *Landlocked*. Vol. 4, *Children of Violence*. London: Panther, 1967.

———. "Learning to Put the Questions Differently." Interview by Studs Terkel. In Ingersoll, *Putting the Questions Differently*, 19–32.

———. *love, again*. New York: HarperCollins, 1995, 1996.

———. *The Making of the Representative for Planet Eight*. Vol. 4, *Canopus in Argos: Archives*. London: Cape, 1982.

———. *Mara and Dann: An Adventure*. London, New York: HarperFlamingo, 1999.

———. *The Marriages between Zones Three, Four, and Five*. Vol. 2, *Canopus in Argos: Archives*. 1980. Reprint, London: Granada, 1981.

———. *Martha Quest*. Vol. 1, *Children of Violence*. London: Michael Joseph, 1952. Reprint, New York: Penguin, 1970; New York: Simon and Schuster, 1964; New York: HarperPerennial, 1995.

———. *The Memoirs of a Survivor*. London: Octagon Press, 1974. Reprint, New York: Alfred A. Knopf, 1975.

———. "The Need to Tell Stories." Interview by Christopher Bigsby. In Ingersoll, *Putting the Questions Differently*, 70–85.

———. PEN/Faulkner reading. Folger Library, Washington, DC, March 19, 2004.

———. "Placing Their Fingers on the Wounds of Our Times." Interview by Margarete von Schwarzkopf in *Die Welt*, May 9, 1981. Translated by Earl G. Ingersoll and Heidrun Neth. In Ingersoll, *Doris Lessing: Conversations*, 102–108.

———. *Play with a Tiger: A Play in Three Acts*. London: Michael Joseph, 1962.

———. Preface [to *The Golden Notebook*]. 1971. London: Michael Joseph, 1972; London: Flamingo-HarperCollins, 2002. Reprint, as Preface to *The Golden Notebook* in *A Small Personal Voice*, edited by Paul Schlueter, New York: Vintage, 1974, 1975, 23–43; as Introduction [to *The Golden Notebook*], New York: Bantam Books, 1971, vii–xxii. Reprint as Introduction 1971 [to *The Golden* Notebook]. New York: HarperPerennial, 1990, 1999, xi–xxvii.

———. *Prisons We Choose to Live Inside*. Montréal: Canadian Broadcasting Corporation, 1986. Reprint, New York: Harper & Row, 1987.

———. *A Proper Marriage*. Vol. 2, *Children of Violence*. London: Michael Joseph, 1954.

———. "The Reason for It." In Lessing, *The Grandmothers*, 131–89.

———. *Re: Colonised Planet 5, Shikasta*. Vol. 1, *Canopus in Argos: Archives*. New York: Alfred A. Knopf, 1979. Reprint, London: Granada, 1980.

———. "A Reissue of *The Golden Notebook*." In Lessing, *Time Bites: Views and Reviews*, 138–41.

———. *Retreat to Innocence*. 1956. Reprint, New York: Prometheus, 1959.

———. *A Ripple from the Storm*. Vol. 3, *Children of Violence*. London: Michael Joseph, 1958.

———. *The Sirian Experiments: The Report by Ambien II, of the Five*. Vol. 3, *Canopus in Argos: Archives*. London: Cape, 1981.

———. "The Small Personal Voice." 1957. In *A Small Personal Voice*, edited by Paul Schlueter, New York: Vintage, 1974, 1975, 3–21; London: Flamingo, 1994, 7–25.

———. *Stories*. New York: Knopf, 1978.

———. *The Story of General Dann and Mara's Daughter, Griot and the Snow Dog*. London: Fourth Estate, 2005.

———. *The Summer before the Dark*. London: Jonathan Cape, 1973. Reprint, New York: Knopf, 1973.

———. *The Sun between Their Feet*. Vol. 2, *Collected African Stories*. 1973. Reprint, London: Flamingo, 1994.

———. *The Sweetest Dream*. London, New York: Harper Collins, 2001. Reprint, New York: HarperCollins, 2002.

———. "Talking as a Person." Interview by Roy Newquist. In Ingersoll, *Doris Lessing: Conversations*, 3–12.

———. *This Was the Old Chief's Country*. Vol. 1, *Collected African Stories*. 1973. Reprint, London: Paladin, 1992.

———. *Time Bites: Views and Reviews*. London, New York: HarperCollins, 2004.

———. *Under My Skin: Volume One of My Autobiography, to 1949*. London: HarperCollins, 1994. Reprint, New York: HarperCollins, 1994.

———. "Voice of England, Voice of Africa." Interview by Michael Upchurch. In Ingersoll, *Doris Lessing: Conversations*, 219–27.

———. *Walking in the Shade: Volume Two of My Autobiography, 1949–1962*. London: HarperCollins, 1997. Reprint, New York: HarperCollins, 1997.

———. "Watching the Angry and Destructive Hordes Go Past." Interview by Claire Tomalin. In Ingersoll, *Doris Lessing: Conversations*, 173–77.

———. "'What Use Are Men?' Asks Lessing." *BBC News/Wales*. June 2, 2007. http://news.bbc.co.uk/2/low/uk_news/wales/6715227.stm (accessed February 9, 2008).

———. *The Wind Blows Away Our Words and Other Documents Relating to the Afghan Resistance*. New York: Vintage, 1987.

———. "A Writer Is Not a Professor." Interview by Jean-Maurice de Montremy. In Ingersoll, *Doris Lessing: Conversations*, 193–99.

———. "Writing as Time Runs Out." Interview by Michael Dean. May 7, 1980, BBC-2. In Ingersoll, *Doris Lessing: Conversations*, 86–93.

Longinus. *On Great Writing (On the Sublime)*. Translated and with an introduction by G. M. A. Grube. Indianapolis, IN: Hackett Publishing Company, 1991.

Luckhurst, Roger. "The Contemporary London Gothic and the Limits of the 'Spectral Turn.'" *Textual Practice* 16.3 (2002): 527–46.

———. "Cultural Governance, New Labour, and the British SF Boom." *Science Fiction Studies* 30.3 (2003): 417–35.

Lyotard, Jean-François. *The Postmodern Explained: Correspondence 1982–1985*. Edited by Julian Pefanis and Morgan Thomas. Minneapolis: University of Minnesota Press, 1993.

Maschler, Tom. *Declaration*. London: MacGibbon and Kee, 1957.

Masters, William H., and Virginia E. Johnson. *Human Sexual Response*. Boston: Little, Brown, 1966.

Maunsell, Jerome Boyd. Review of *The Sweetest Dream*, by Doris Lessing. *The Times* (London), July 27, 2002: 19. Custom Newspapers (InfoTrac-Gale) http://find.gale-group.com (accessed September 14, 2006).

McCarthy, Mary. *Cannibals and Missionaries*. San Diego: Harcourt, 1991.

McCormick, Kay. "The Child's Perspective in *Five African Stories*." *Doris Lessing Newsletter* 9.2 (1985): 12–13.

Melchiori, Barbara Arnett. *Terrorism in the Late Victorian Novel*. London: Croom Helm, 1985.

Michael, Magali Cornier. *Feminism and the Postmodern Impulse: Post–World War II Fiction*. Albany: State University of New York Press, 1996.

Miller, J. Hillis. "The Problematic of Ending in Narrative." *Nineteenth-Century Fiction* 33.1 (1978): 3–7.

Minh-ha, Trinh T. *Woman, Native, Other: Writing Postcoloniality and Feminism*. Bloomington: Indiana University Press, 1989.

Minot, Susan. *Evening*. New York: Knopf, 1998.

Morgan, Ellen. "Alienation of the Woman Writer in *The Golden Notebook*." In Pratt and Dembo, *Doris Lessing: Critical Studies*, 54–63.

Nawa, Fariba. "Afghan Women Debate the Terms of Their Future." In Women's eNews. June 30, 2002. http://www.womensenews.org/article.cfmstory/the-world/dyn/aid/956/context/cover020630/afghan-women-debate-the-terms-their-future (accessed March 17, 2010).

Nicholl, D. J., H. G. Atkinson, J. Kalk, W. Hopkins, E. Elias, A. Siddiqui, R. E. Cranford, and O. Sacks, on behalf of 255 other doctors. "Forcefeeding and Restraint of Guantanamo Bay Hunger Strikers." *The Lancet* 367.9513 (March 11, 2006): 811.

Parkin, David. Foreword. *Locality and Belonging*. Edited by N. Lovell. London: Routledge, 1998.

Patmore, Coventry. "The Angel in the House." In Abrams and Greenblatt, Vol. 2, *The Norton Anthology of English Literature*, 1723–24.

Perrakis, Phyllis Sternberg, ed. *Adventures of the Spirit: The Older Woman in the Works of Doris Lessing, Margaret Atwood, and Other Contemporary Women Writers*.

Columbus: The Ohio State University Press, 2007.

———. "Doris Lessing's *The Golden Notebook:* Separation and Symbiosis." *American Imago* 38.4 (Winter 1981): 407–28.

———. "The Marriage of Inner and Outer Space in Doris Lessing's *Shikasta.*" *Science-Fiction Studies* 17.2 (July, 1990): 221–38.

———."Navigating the Spiritual Cycle in *Memoirs of a Survivor* and *Shikasta.*" In Perrakis, *Adventures of the Spirit,* 47–82.

———, ed. *Spiritual Exploration in the Works of Doris Lessing.* Westport, CT: Greenwood Press, 1999.

———. "Sufism, Jung and the Myth of Kore: Revisionist Politics in Lessing's *Marriages.*" *Mosaic: A Journal for the Interdisciplinary Study of Literature* 25.3 (Summer 1992): 99–120.

Pickering, Jean. "Philosophical Contexts for *The Golden Notebook.*" In Kaplan and Rose, *Alchemy,* 43–49.

Porter, Katherine Anne. "The Jilting of Granny Weatherall." In *Flowering Judas.* New York: Signet Classics, 1970.

Powell, E. "Rivers of Blood." 1968. http://www.sterlingtimes.org/powell_speech.doc (accessed April 23, 2004).

Pratt, Annis, and L. S. Dembo, eds. *Doris Lessing: Critical Studies.* 1973. Reprint, Madison: University of Wisconsin Press, 1974.

Pughe, Thomas. "Reading the Picaresque: Mark Twain's *The Adventures of Huckleberry Finn,* Saul Bellow's *The Adventures of Augie March,* and More Recent Adventures." *English Studies* 77.1 (1996): 59–70.

Punter, David. *Gothic Pathologies: The Text, the Body and the Law.* Basingstoke, England: Macmillan, 1998.

Pye, M. "The Creature Walks Among Us." *The New York Times,* August 6, 2000. http://query.nytimes.com/gst/fullpage.html?res=9D06E4DE163DF935A3575BC0A9669C8B63 (accessed November 15, 2005).

Rapping, Elayne Antler. "Unfree Women: Feminism in Doris Lessing's Novels." *Women's Studies* 3 (1975): 29–44.

Raschke, Debrah. "Cabalistic Gardens: Lessing's *Memoirs of a Survivor.* In Perrakis, *Spiritual Exploration,* 43–54.

———. *Modernism, Metaphysics, and Sexuality.* Selinsgrove, PA: Susquehanna University Press, 2006.

Restuccia, Frances L. "'Untying the Mother Tongue': Female Differences in Virginia Woolf's *A Room of One's Own.*" *Tulsa Studies in Women's Literature* 4.2 (1985): 253–64.

Richardson, Samuel. *Clarissa.* Oxford: Basil Blackwell, 1930.

Roenisch, Rowan. *Encyclopaedia of Vernacular Architecture of the World.* Edited by Paul Oliver. Cambridge: Cambridge University Press, 1997.

Roman, Camille, Suzanne Juhasz, and Christanne Miller, eds. *The Women and Language Debate: A Sourcebook.* New Brunswick, NJ: Rutgers University Press, 1994.

Rooney, Caroline. "Narratives of Southern African Farms." *Third World Quarterly* 26.3 (2005): 431–40.

Rosner, Victoria. "Home Fires: Doris Lessing, Colonial Architecture, and the Reproduction of Mothering." *Tulsa Studies in Women's Literature* 18.1 (1999): 59–89. http://

www.jstor.org (accessed July 17, 2006).

Rubenstein, Roberta. "Fixing the Past: Yearning and Nostalgia in Woolf and Lessing." In Saxton and Tobin, *Woolf and Lessing*, 15–38.

———. *Home Matters: Longing and Belonging, Nostalgia and Mourning in Women's Fiction*. New York: Palgrave/St. Martin's Press, 2001.

———. "*The Marriages between Zones Three, Four, and Five*: Doris Lessing's Alchemical Allegory." In Sprague and Tiger, *Critical Essays on Doris Lessing*, 60–68.

———. "Mar(th)a Still Questing: Reading *Mara and Dann* through *Children of Violence*." *Doris Lessing Newsletter* 21.1 (Winter/Spring 2000): 10–13.

———. *The Novelistic Vision of Doris Lessing: Breaking the Forms of Consciousness*. Urbana: University of Illinois Press, 1979.

Sage, Lorna. *Doris Lessing*. London: Methuen, 1983.

Said, Edward W. "The Essential Terrorist." In *Blaming the Victims: Spurious Scholarship and the Palestinian Question*, edited by Edward W. Said and Christopher Hitchens, 149–58. London: Verso, 1988.

Sarton, May. *As We Are Now*. New York: W. W. Norton, 1973.

Sartre, Jean-Paul. Preface. *The Wretched of the Earth*. By Frantz Fanon. Translated by Constance Farrington, 7–26. New York: Grove Press, 1966.

Saxton, Ruth. *Garments of the Mind: Clothing and Appearance in the Fiction of Doris Lessing*. Unpublished manuscript.

Saxton, Ruth, and Jean Tobin, eds. *Woolf and Lessing: Breaking the Mold*. New York: St. Martin's Press, 1994.

Scanlan, Margaret. *Plotting Terror: Novelists and Terrorists in Contemporary Fiction*. Charlottesville: University Press of Virginia, 2001.

Scarry, Elaine. *The Body in Pain: The Making and Unmaking of the World*. Oxford: Oxford University Press, 1985.

Schlueter, Paul. "Review of *love, again*." *Doris Lessing Newsletter* 18.1 (1996): 1, 6.

———, ed. *A Small Personal Voice: Essays, Reviews, Interviews*. New York: Vintage, 1974, 1975. Reprint, London: Flamingo-HarperCollins, 1974, 1994.

Segal, Hanna. *Klein*. Brighton, England: Harvester, 1979.

Shah, Idries. *The Sufis*. London: Octagon, 1964.

Shakespeare, William. *A Midsummer Night's Dream*. New York: Washington Square Press, 1967.

Shilling, Jane. "Human Engagement." Review of *The Sweetest Dream*, by Doris Lessing. *The Times* (London), October 6, 2001, 20. Custom Newspapers (InfoTrac-Gale) http://find.galegroup.com (accessed September 14, 2006).

Silva, Manoel de Almeida e. "Press Briefing." UN News Centre. May 7, 2002. http://www.un.org/apps/news/infocus/afghanistan/infocusnews.asp?NewsID=174&sID=1 (accessed July 12, 2009).

Silver, Brenda. *Virginia Woolf Icon*. Chicago: University of Chicago Press, 1999.

Singer, Sandra. "Doris Lessing's Fiction and Contemporary Cultural Theorists." PhD diss., University of Cambridge, 1992.

Sizemore, Christine. "The 'Outsider-Within': Virginia Woolf and Doris Lessing as Urban Novelists in *Mrs. Dalloway* and *The Four-Gated City*." In Saxton and Tobin, *Woolf and Lessing*, 59–72.

Smoltczyk, Alexander. "Afghanistan: Operation Freedom." *World Press Review*

50.4 (April 2003). http://www.worldpress.org/article_model.cfm?article_id=1108&dont=yes (accessed July 12, 2009).

Sparks, Muriel. *Memento Mori.* New York: New Directions Books, 2000.

Sprague, Claire. "Doubletalk and Doubles Talk in *The Golden Notebook.*" *Papers on Language and Literature: A Journal for Scholars and Critics of Language and Literature* 18.2 (1982): 181–97.

———. "*The Golden Notebook:* In Whose or What Great Tradition?" In Kaplan and Rose, *Approaches,* 78–83.

———, ed. *In Pursuit of Doris Lessing: Nine Nations Reading.* New York: St. Martin's Press, 1990.

———. "Lessing's *The Grass Is Singing, Retreat to Innocence, The Golden Notebook* and Eliot's *The Waste Land.*" *Explicator* 50.3 (1992): 177–80.

———. "Multipersonal and Dialogic Modes in *Mrs. Dalloway* and *The Golden Notebook.*" In Saxton and Tobin, *Woolf and Lessing,* 3–14.

———. *Re-Reading Doris Lessing: Narrative Patterns of Doubling and Repetition.* Chapel Hill: University of North Carolina Press, 1987.

Sprague, Claire, and Virginia Tiger, eds. *Critical Essays on Doris Lessing.* Boston: G. K. Hall, 1986.

Swedish Academy. Press release. October 11, 2007. http://nobelprize.org/nobel_prizes/literature/laureates/2007/press.html (accessed July 7, 2009).

Taylor, Jenny, ed. *Notebooks/Memoirs/Archives: Reading and Rereading Doris Lessing.* Boston: Routledge and Kegan Paul, 1982.

Thatcher, Margaret. "AIDS, Education and the Year 2000." Interview by D. Keay. *Woman's Own,* October 31, 1987, 8–10.

Tiger, Virginia. "Made from Memories." *Doris Lessing Studies* 22.2 (2002): 1, 8–10, 24.

Townshend, Charles. *Terrorism.* Oxford: Oxford University Press, 2002.

Upchurch, Michael. "Back to Ifrik." *The New York Times,* January 10, 1999. http://query.nytimes.com/gst/fullpage.html?res=9C05E2DD1E3FF933A25752C0A96F958260 (accessed November 15, 2005).

U.S. Census Bureau International Data Base. http://www.census.gov/ipc/www/idb/groups.php (accessed February 23, 2010).

Vlastos, Marion. "Doris Lessing and R. D. Laing: Psychopolitics and Prophecy." *PMLA* 91.2 (1976): 245–57.

Wagner, Erica. "Good on Science." *The Times,* March 25, 1999, 42.

Warnock, Jeanie. "'Soul Murder' and Rebirth: Trauma, Narrative, and Imagination in Shani Mootoo's *Cereus Blooms at Night.*" In Perrakis, *Adventures of the Spirit,* 270–98.

Watkins, Susan. "'Grande Dame' or 'New Woman': Doris Lessing and the Palimpsest." *LIT: Literature, Interpretation, Theory* 1.3–4 (2006): 243–62.

———. "Remembering Home: Nation and Identity in the Recent Writing of Doris Lessing." *Feminist Review* 85 (2007): 97–115.

Waugh, Patricia. *Feminine Fictions: Revisiting the Postmodern.* New York: Routledge, 1989.

———. *Metafiction: The Theory and Practice of Self-Conscious Fiction.* London: Methuen, 1984.

Webber, Jeannette. "Doris Lessing's Prophetic Voice in *Shikasta:* Cassandra or Sibyl?" In

Perrakis, *Spiritual Exploration*, 63–79.

Wharton, Edith. *The House of Mirth*. New York: Charles Scribner's Sons, 1905.

White, Hayden. "The Historical Text as Literary Artifact." In Canary and Kozicki, *The Writing of History: Literary Form and Historical Understanding*, 41–62.

Wilson, Robert Rawdon. *The Hydra's Tale: Imagining Disgust*. Edmonton: University of Alberta Press, 2002.

Woolf, Virginia. "Modern Fiction." 1925. Reprinted in Abrams and Greenblatt, Vol. 2, *The Norton Anthology of English Literature*, 2148–53.

———. "Professions for Women." In *The Death of the Moth and Other Essays*. New York: Harcourt Brace Jovanovich, 1942. Reprinted in *Virginia Woolf on Women and Writing: Her Essays, Assessments and Argument*, 57–63. London: Women's Press Limited, 1979; Abrams and Greenblatt, Vol. 2, *The Norton Anthology of English Literature*, 2214–18.

———. *A Room of One's Own*. New York: Harcourt, Brace, Jovanovich, 1929. Reprinted in Abrams and Greenblatt, Vol. 2, *The Norton Anthology of English Literature*, 2153–214.

———. *Three Guineas*. 1938. Reprint, New York: Penguin, 1977.

———. *To the Lighthouse*. 1927. Reprint, New York: Modern Library, 1937.

Wyatt-Brown, Anne M. "Another Model of the Aging Writer: Sarton's Politics of Old Age." In *Aging and Gender in Literature: Studies in Creativity*, edited by Anne M. Wyatt-Brown and Janice Rossen, 49–60. Charlottesville: University of Virginia Press, 1993.

Wyndham, John. *The Day of the Triffids*. London: Michael Joseph, 1951.

———. *The Midwich Cuckoos*. London: Michael Joseph, 1957.

Yardley, Jonathan. "Lessing Is More: An 'Unknown' Author and the Success Syndrome." In Sprague and Tiger, *Critical Essays on Doris Lessing*, 215–17.

Yeats, William Butler. "Memory." 1919. Reprinted in *The Collected Works of W. B. Yeats*, 168. London: Macmillan Company, 1977.

Yelin, Louise. *From the Margins of Empire: Christina Stead, Doris Lessing, Nadine Gordimer*. Ithaca, NY: Cornell University Press, 1998.

Young, Robert J. C. *Postcolonialism*. Oxford: Oxford University Press, 2003.

Notes on Contributors

SUZETTE HENKE joined the University of Louisville in 1991 as Thruston B. Morton Sr. Professor of Literary Studies. She is author of *Joyce's Moraculous Sindbook: A Study of Ulysses* and of *James Joyce and the Politics of Desire*. With Elaine Unkeless, she co-edited a collection of original essays on *Women in Joyce*. Professor Henke has published widely in the field of modern and contemporary literature, with particular emphasis on feminist interpretation. Most recently, she authored *Shattered Subjects: Trauma and Testimony in Women's Life-Writing* (Palgrave, 2000). With David Eberly, she co-edited *Virginia Woolf and Trauma: Embodied Texts* (Pace University Press, 2007); and, with Jeanie E. Warnock, a special volume of *Doris Lessing Studies* devoted to *Trauma in Doris Lessing's Work* (27: 1–2 [2008]).

TONYA KROUSE is Associate Professor at Northern Kentucky University where she teaches twentieth-century British literature. She has published articles in *The Virginia Woolf Miscellany, Doris Lessing Studies*, and the *Journal of Modern Literature*, and is author of *The Opposite of Desire: Sex and Pleasure in the Modernist Novel* (Lexington Books). Her current book project investigates representations of domesticity in twentieth-century women's fiction. Krouse is the president of the Doris Lessing Society.

PAT LOUW teaches English at the University of Zululand, South Africa. Apart from her research on Doris Lessing's work, she is interested in notions of landscape, place, identity, and ecocriticism in general. She is a member of the English Academy of Southern Africa, the Association of University Teachers of English in Southern Africa, and the MLA. Her most recent publication is a chapter in a Cambridge Scholars text, *Toxic Belonging*.

PHYLLIS STERNBERG PERRAKIS teaches at the University of Ottawa and is editor of *Spiritual Exploration in the Works of Doris Lessing* (Greenwood, 1999) and *Adventures* of the Spirit: The Older Woman in the Works of Doris Lessing, Margaret Atwood, and Other Contemporary Women Writers (The Ohio State University Press, 2007) as well as essays on Lessing and Atwood. A former president of the Doris Lessing Society, she is co-editor of Doris Lessing Studies.

DEBRAH RASCHKE is Professor of English at Southeast Missouri State University, where she teaches nineteenth- and twentieth-century British literature, contemporary literary theory, and myth. Her book Modernism, Metaphysics, and Sexuality was published by Susquehanna University Press (2006). She has also published numerous essays on modernist and contemporary literature, with a specific focus on Lessing, Woolf, Atwood, and Forster. She is former president of the Doris Lessing Society.

ALICE RIDOUT completed a Post-Doctoral Research Fellowship in Contemporary Women's Writing at Leeds Metropolitan University in 2009 and is now lecturing at the University of Salford and Leeds Metropolitan University. She is the UK Book Reviews Editor for the Oxford Journal Contemporary Women's Writing and co-editor of Doris Lessing: Border Crossings with Susan Watkins (Continuum Press, 2009). She has published in the University of Toronto Quarterly, Margaret Atwood Studies, and Doris Lessing Studies. She is currently completing a monograph for Continuum Press titled Contemporary Women Writers Look Back: From Irony to Nostalgia.

ROBERTA RUBENSTEIN is Professor of Literature at American University, where she teaches Modernist fiction, modern and contemporary literature by women, and feminist theory. Her publications include The Novelistic Vision of Doris Lessing: Breaking the Forms of Consciousness (University of Illinois Press, 1979); Boundaries of the Self: Gender, Culture, Fiction (University of Illinois Press, 1987); Home Matters: Longing and Belonging, Nostalgia and Mourning in Women's Fiction (Palgrave/St. Martin's Press, 2001); Virginia Woolf and the Russian Point of View (Palgrave/St. Martin's Press, 2009); and over thirty essays on women writers, including Woolf, Lessing, Atwood, Drabble, Morrison, Kingsolver, and others.

RUTH O. SAXTON, Professor of English at Mills College, co-edited Woolf and Lessing: Breaking the Mold (St. Martin's, 1994); edited The Girl: Construction of the Girl in Contemporary Fiction by Women (Palgrave Macmillan, 1999); and co-edited Teaching Virginia Woolf's Mrs. Dalloway (MLA, 2009). She edited the Doris Lessing Newsletter and co-edited the Doris Lessing Studies issue on aging. Current projects focus on portrayal of the old woman in fiction and a memoir on surviving traumatic brain injury.

SANDRA SINGER, co-editor of Doris Lessing Studies, has published articles on Lessing's novels and other fiction. Her current research on the relationship between trauma and terror in recent literature includes a consideration of Lessing's Children of Violence as well as her 1980s terrorism texts. Recent work includes "Acting Out Justice in 'Courtroom Dramas'" (Canadian Ethnic Studies) and "Ethnographic Memoir" (Sage Encyclopedia of Case Study Research, 2010). She teaches narrative and multicultural literatures in the School of English and Theatre Studies, University of Guelph.

Notes on Contributors

VIRGINIA TIGER, Professor and Chair of English at Rutgers University, Newark, is the author of four books, the most recent being *The Unmoved Target: The Fiction of William Golding* (Marion Boyars, 2003). She has published scholarly articles in such journals as *Contemporary Literature, Modern Fiction Studies, Doris Lessing Studies,* and *Style,* and essays in numerous collections. In the year of Lessing's Nobel Laureate, she was a frequent guest lecturer in various venues, including ones in France and Canada. The co-founder of the Doris Lessing Society, an Allied Organization of the Modern Language Association, she is a former president of the Society and a frequent participant at MLA sessions on Lessing.

ROBIN VISEL is Emeritus Professor of English at Furman University (South Carolina) and Visiting Professor of English at the University of Findlay (Ohio). She has published in such journals as *Doris Lessing Studies, The Journal of Commonwealth Literature, Research in African Literatures, ARIEL,* and *Kunapipi.* Her research areas include Doris Lessing and other colonial and postcolonial writers from Southern and East Africa.

SUSAN WATKINS is Reader in Twentieth-Century Women's Fiction at Leeds Metropolitan University. She is the author of *Twentieth-Century Women Novelists: Feminist Theory into Practice* (Palgrave Macmillan, 2001) and co-editor of *Scandalous Fictions: The Twentieth-Century Novel in the Public Sphere* (Palgrave Macmillan, 2006). Her work on Lessing includes articles in *Feminist Review* and *LIT* and a co-edited symposium in the *Journal of Commonwealth Literature.* Her book on Lessing is shortly to be published by Manchester University Press.

Index

1930s, 6, 69, 165, 180
1940s, 69, 189, 192
1950s, 13, 155–56, 185
1960s, 58, 151, 183, 184; in *Fifth Child*, 154; in *Good Terrorist*, 100; in *The Hours* (Cunningham), 191; in *love, again*, 5; in *Sweetest Dream*, 22, 58, 64–68, 70, 140, 141, 142, 143; Lessing's, 92, 147n39; politics, 95, 100, 151; sexuality in, 154, 190, 198; women's movement in, 1, 15, 187
1970s, 95; in *Good Terrorist*, 99; in *Sweetest Dream*, 23, 140, 143; Lessing's, 11; postmodernism in, 3; readers', 7, 18, 20, 187, 188; sexuality in, 188, 190; women's movement in, 1, 15, 19, 187
1980s, 6, 80, 142, 153; and *Golden Notebook*, 185; in *Fifth Child*, 151, 153; in *Good Terrorist*, 94, 95; in *love, again*, 135; in *Sweetest Dream*, 5, 140, 143; in *Wind Blows Away Our Words*, 92, 94, 103, 106; Lessing's, 12, 92, 94, 109n8, 127n1, 226; politics in, 95, 103, 106, 108n8, 151, 153; readers', 18; women's movement in, 1, 19

1990s, 80, 153, 157, 185
9/11/01, 21, 92, 183, 186, 195. *See also* terrorism; war
21st century, 3, 5, 21, 26–27, 32–35, 45, 58, 70, 134, 135, 143, 149–50, 159, 183–84, 186, 190–92, 195, 197. *See also* relevance

aesthetic: androgynous, 34, 35–38, 40, 43, 46–53, 53n8, 54n16; impersonal, 33, 47; Lessing's, 2, 15, 32–34, 87
Afghanistan, 4, 92–93, 103–6, 108n1, 111n23
African Laughter, 23
African stories, 6, 25, 69, 165, 170–80
aging, 2, 3, 7, 12, 22, 14, 202–9; and creativity, 127n1; and sexuality, 146n10, 203–9; in *love, again*, 133, 134–35, 141, 145, 202–4, 205–7; in *Sweetest Dream*, 134, 140, 141, 202–3, 204, 207–9
AIDS, 60, 64, 67, 142, 186
Alexandrovich, Grand Duke Sergei, 94, 109n10
Alfred and Emily, 21
Alice (Carroll), 4, 97, 101

Index

Alice Mellings (*Good Terrorist*), 93, 94–97, 98–102, 106–7, 108n7, 109n10, 109n13, 109n14, 110n15; forgetfulness, 100–102, 110n16
Al*Ith (*Marriages*), 122
Allardice, Lisa, 62
allegory, 150, 151, 154
Andrew (*love, again*), 135
Andrew Lennox (*Sweetest Dream*), 67, 142, 143
androgyny, 36, 46, 47, 48, 52, 53n8, 54n15. *See also* aesthetic, androgynous
Angel in the House, 3, 52, 59, 63, 64, 65–66, 68, 70, 71, 140
animal, 6, 25, 129n38, 138, 149, 150, 152, 154, 155, 156, 157, 158, 193. *See also* boundaries, of human and animal
Anna (*Play with a Tiger*), 22
Anna Wulf (*Golden Notebook*), 3, 12, 15, 19, 22, 24, 26, 33–34, 49–50, 187; and feminism, 187; and identity, 55n20, 56n68, 115, 128n18; and politics, 11–12, 40, 81, 98, 196; and sex, 13, 36, 44, 188–89; and *Sweetest Dream*, 58–59, 70; and Virginia Woolf, 33, 37, 52–53; as blocked, 15, 27, 34, 37, 50, 52, 59, 194; as Lessing's voice, 27, 37, 43, 84; as mother, 61, 189, 191; as writer, 39, 40–41, 43–44, 45, 47, 50, 56n68, 59, 65, 84, 85, 194; breakdown, 17, 192–94, 199n44; doubled, 136; homophobia, 191–92, 193. *See also* Ella
"Anon," 39–40, 42
anticolonialism, 3, 64, 66, 67, 69, 93, 107, 109n13, 143
apartheid, 69, 70, 107
apocalyptic fiction, 14, 16, 22, 23, 59, 60, 197. *See also* space fiction; speculative fiction
Appignanesi, Lisa, 62, 128n24
Armstrong, Nancy, 61

Austen, Jane, 135, 139, 144
autobiographical links, 70, 74n47, 147n39; with *Children of Violence*, 20; with *Golden Notebook*, 13, 24, 73n41, 84, 187, 192–93; with *love, again*, 7–8, 14, 133, 145, 146n26, 206; with *Martha Quest*, 147n35; with *Sweetest Dream*, 7–8, 68, 85

Balfour, Robert, 175
Balzac, Honoré de, 62, 70
Barthes, Roland, 46–48, 50, 56n55
Beck, Antony, 175
Bedell, Geraldine, 28n10, 118, 127n4
Ben (*Fifth Child*; *Ben, In the World*), 22, 150–57
Ben, In the World, 6, 22, 117, 149, 150, 151–52, 153, 156–57; as satire, 156–57; prolepsis, 161n36. *See also* race; racism
Bentley, Nick, 78
Bert (*Good Terrorist*), 97, 98, 108n7
bhurka, 105, 111n23
Bigsby, Christopher, 77, 85
Bill (*love, again*), 135
binary oppositions, 2, 3, 34, 45, 51–52, 57n73, 58; masculine/feminine, 50; mind/body, 48, 50–51; personal/impersonal, 39, 41–42, 43, 81, 122–23, 140; white/black, 70. *See also* boundaries; individual's relation to the collective
Blakeworthy. *See* Johnny Blakeworthy
bliss, 39, 47, 50, 56n55
Bloom, Harold, 1
body image, 7, 203–9
body of writer in the text, 34, 36, 38–39, 42–43, 45
Boehm, Beth, 196
Boone, Joseph Allen, 191
boundaries, 3, 39, 52, 69, 70, 71, 113, 119–20, 124, 180; of class, 172, 175, 178–79; of country, 125; of gender, 122, 123, 129n43, 174,

176–79; of genre, 154; of human and animal, 34, 51, 117, 150, 155, 156; of indoor and outdoor, 167, 168, 174; of nature and civilization, 157, 166–67, 174–75, 176; of settlers and Africans, 169–80; of self, 115, 124, 126, 194. *See also* binary oppositions; fiction and non-fiction blurred

Brickman, Celia, 157

Briefing for a Descent into Hell, 14, 15, 21, 139

Brontë, Charlotte, 45, 71

Byatt, A. S., 137, 144

Cannibals and Missionaries (McCarthy), 110n15

canon, 19, 32, 33, 34, 42, 45, 54n12, 84, 195, 201n58

Canopus in Argos, 14, 21, 22, 87, 109n14

Carruthers, Major ("Second Hut"), 170

Cartesian. *See* Descartes, René

CCU. *See Good Terrorist*

Celia (*Sweetest Dream*), 63, 67, 144

Chaffee, Patricia, 169, 172

Charles Watkins (*Briefing for a Descent into Hell*), 21

chastity, 42–43, 44

Chennells, Anthony, 149

Chief Mshlanga ("Old Chief"), 170–71, 180

Children of Violence, 12, 13–14, 16, 20, 23, 26, 59, 62, 64, 68; Communism in, 67, 69, 73n40, 79; individual and among the collective, 80; realism of, 68. See also *Four-Gated City; Martha Quest; Ripple from the Storm*

Chomsky, Noam, 93, 109n8, 112n29

Chopin, Kate, 137

clairvoyance, 16, 21, 63

Clarissa Dalloway (*To the Lighthouse*), 65, 71, 208

Clark, Alex, 152

Clark, Suzanne, 185

Cleft, The, 5, 15, 113–14, 116–26, 129n43; gender stereotypes, 113, 116, 117, 120, 121, 129n38; Monsters, 114, 116, 117, 119, 122; mythology in, 121, 129n39

Clever and Zebedee (*Sweetest Dream*), 64, 67, 70

Colin Lennox, 67 (*Sweetest Dream*), 140, 142

"collective," 90n24, 108n7

collective unconscious, 16, 43

collective versus individual. *See* individual's relation to the collective

Collins, J.: and R. Wilson, 154

colonialism, 3, 6, 58, 60, 61, 94, 156–57, 165–70, 180; in Lessing's works, 58, 59, 64, 68–71, 107, 109n13, 124–25, 126, 129n46, 170–80. *See also* anticolonialism; postcolonialism

Communism, 7, 12, 88, 90n24, 95, 97–98, 103, 104, 108n7, 185; in the Czech Republic, 79; in Lessing's works, 3, 40, 58, 61, 64, 65, 67, 69, 79, 80, 81, 83, 84, 86, 87, 90n33, 95, 98, 104, 109n13, 110n18, 140–41, 143; influence on Lessing, 77, 78, 80–82; Lessing's experiences with, 14, 73n40, 78, 83, 84, 89n11, 96, 97; Lessing's rejection of, 82–85, 87, 88, 159. *See also* politics

Comrade Johnny. *See* Johnny Lennox

contraception, 20, 188, 189, 190

Countess Die (*love, again*), 138–39

critical reception, 1, 149, 175; of *Ben, In the World*, 151, 152, 161n36; of *Cleft*, 117–18, 121, 128n24, 129n38; of *Diaries of Jane Somers*, 28n4; of *Fifth Child*, 150, 151; of *Golden Notebook*, 15, 29n19, 32, 133; of *love, again*, 133, 146n19, 146n24; of *Mara and Dann*, 152; of *Story of General Dann*, 28n10; of *Sweetest Dream*, 58, 62–63, 70,

231

Index

71n2
Czech Republic, 79, 86

Damasio, Antonio, 34, 51
Dave (*Play with a Tiger*), 22
"De Wets Come to Kloof Grange, The," 174–76, 180
De Wets, Mr. and Mrs. ("De Wets"), 175–76
Deleuze, Gilles: and Félix Guattari, 150, 153, 155, 158, 159, 192
Descartes, René, 3, 34, 45, 51–52
detachment, 8, 82, 83, 87, 88; and empathy, 113, 114–16, 117, 120; Lessing's, 5, 97, 102, 111n20, 134, 138, 140; characters', 3, 68, 97, 114, 115–16, 119–20, 124–25, 126, 140
"deterritorialization," 150, 154
Diary of a Good Neighbor, The, 14, 22
Diaries of Jane Somers, The, 12, 111n20, 202, 205
Dietrich, Marlene, 139
disaster narrative, 6, 149, 153, 157, 158
dogmatic thinking, 7, 8, 80, 86, 88, 143–44. *See also* political correctness; superiority
Dorothy Mellings (*Good Terrorist*), 96, 99–100, 101, 102, 110n16
doubling, 5, 27, 125, 136, 137, 138, 139, 199n44. *See also* mirroring; reprises
Drabble, Margaret, 11, 14
DuPlessis, Rachel Blau, 188
Dürrenmatt, Friedrich, 108n8

effacement: of self, 37–41, 43–45 47–49, 55n20, 59, 55n20, 89n22; of sex or gender, 34, 36, 40, 43, 44–45
Eliot, George, 62, 70
Eliot, T. S., 56n54, 89n22

Ella (*Golden Notebook*), 19, 43, 44, 55n20, 136, 189–90
Ellington-Smith, Stephen (*love, again*), 135, 139, 207
Emily Cartwright (*Memoirs of a Survivor*), 14
emotion, 47–48, 89n22; and physical pain, 136, 138, 146n26; and sex, 44, 189, 190; damaged, 13, 21, 22, 25, 26, 29n21, 64, 69, 147n39, 184, 191, 193–94, 208; Lessing's, 23–24, 71n2, 108n1, 146n26, 187, 193; personal, 40–41, 45, 47, 81. *See also* empathy; falling in love; grief; homophobia
"empathetic unsettlement," 114
empathy, 114–16, 117, 118, 119, 120, 122, 124, 126, 128n19
Eye/Voice. *See* narrator's voice

fable, 5, 6, 12, 14, 15, 21, 22, 113, 117, 118, 120, 122, 125, 126, 128n33, 150, 151, 152
falling in love, 7, 66, 108n4, 135–39, 146n12, 187, 203–6
Fand, Roxanne J., 41–42, 43
Fanon, Franz, 93, 94
fantasy, 12, 21, 22, 27, 98, 101, 150, 157, 197
Faye (*Good Terrorist*), 97, 99, 100, 101
female subjectivity. *See* subjectivity, female
feminine writing. *See* woman writer
feminism, 39, 45, 51, 52, 80, 187, 188, 190; in Lessing's novels, 3, 34, 46, 58, 59, 64, 65, 68, 70, 134, 143, 144, 149, 183, 186, 187; Lessing's, 84–85, 187; and Woolf, 33, 34, 35, 36, 37, 49, 61, 62. *See also* Lessing, resistance to feminist readings; sex war; women's movement
feminist criticism, 2, 3, 19, 32, 33, 35, 36, 42, 45, 46–47, 49, 51, 209
fiction and non-fiction blurred, 5, 24,

232

73n41, 127n7, 193; in *Cleft,* 114, 116, 117, 119, 120, 123–25. *See also* historiographic metafiction
fiction as truth, 24, 68, 147n35
Fifth Child, The, 6, 22, 108n1, 111n20, 117, 149–51, 153–56, 207
Fishburn, Katherine, 194–95, 196, 200n53
Foucault, Michel, 40
Four-Gated City, The, 3, 14, 16, 20, 21, 23, 58–60, 63, 68, 140, 147n39, 148n40; appendix, 16, 67, 140; ending, 71
Fowles, John, 137
Frances Lennox (*Sweetest Dream*), 3, 7, 23, 59, 60, 63–66, 68, 70, 140–41, 142, 144, 202–3, 204, 207–9; as mother, 61, 64, 65, 141, 204, 207, 208; as writer, 64–65, 204; like Anna Wulf, 63, 64–65, 66, 68; like Martha Quest, 59, 60, 61, 63, 66, 68
freedom fighters, 93, 103, 106; armed guerillas, 93, 94, 106, 107; resistance fighters, 94, 103, 104, 107, 111n21; terrorists, 7, 92, 93–95, 96, 97, 99–102, 103, 106–7, 108n7, 108n8, 109n10, 110n15, 110n18, 111n20, 112n29, 155
"free woman," 19, 33, 42, 44, 63, 71, 136, 187, 189
"Free Women" (*Golden Notebook*), 33, 38, 87, 137, 191, 194
Freudian theories, 188, 189–91, 192, 198n31
Friedman, Ellen G., 52
Fuchs, Miriam, 52
function of the storyteller, 77–78, 80–88

Gale, Major and Mrs. ("De Wets"), 174–76
Gardiner, Judith Kegan, 191, 192
Gasiorek, Andrzej, 62, 159
gendered subjectivity. *See* subjectivity, gendered

global politics. *See* politics, global
Going Home, 23
Golden Notebook, The, 2–3, 12, 20, 22, 26, 33–53, 183–97; 1971 introduction, 5, 18, 29n21, 32, 53n1, 81, 82, 184, 187, 194; 1993 introduction, 73n41; Africa, 186; and *Good Terrorist,* 110n18; as critical theory, 78; as historical record, 26, 27; as journalism, 84, 85; Black Notebook, 38, 56n68, 67, 186; Blue Notebook, 38, 49; compared to *Room of One's Own* (Woolf), 33–53; ending, 71; Golden Notebook, 50, 63, 193; lesson of, 88; politics in, 12, 28n5, 69, 83, 98; realism of, 68; structure, 13, 15, 16–17, 18, 19, 27, 37, 87, 194–96; teaching of, 6–7, 28n5, 183–97, 200n55; Yellow Notebook, 19, 44, 189. *See also* Anna Wulf; critical reception, of *Golden Notebook*; readers' response, to *Golden Notebook*
Good Terrorist, The, 4, 11, 15, 85, 93–107, 108n4, 108n7, 109n8, 109n11, 109n14, 109n15, 111n20, 148n40, 155, 207; and *Golden Notebook,* 110n18; CCU, 95, 96, 97; language in, 96, 97, 98, 109n14; No. 45, 98, 101, 110n15; "shit," 96–97, 109n13, 110n16
Gornick, Vivian, 15
gothic, 6, 157; urban, 6, 149, 153–55
Grandmothers, The, 22, 129n46
Grass Is Singing, The, 24–25, 170, 176, 179
Gray, Billy, 184, 186
Greene, Gayle, 29n23, 49, 199n44
grief, 124, 125, 136, 146n12, 146n26
"groupuscular terrorism," 95, 96, 107, 109n11
Guattari, Félix. *See* Deleuze, Gilles
Guevara, Che, 93, 108n4, 141

Hague, Angela, 155–56

Index

Hal (*love, again*), 135, 144
Hanford, Jan, 29n20
Hanson, Clare, 159
Harare, 23, 24, 142
Haraway, Donna, 34, 51–52
Harriet (*Fifth Child; Ben, In the World*), 150, 151, 153, 154, 155, 207
Havel, Václav, 86–87
Head, Dominic, 62
Henke, Suzette, 6–7, 28n5, 28n7, 55n43, 183–201, 225
historiographic metafiction, 113–14, 117, 118, 119, 121, 123, 127n5, 129n37
home-making, 3, 59, 60, 171, 207; in *Four-Gated City*, 147n39; in *Good Terrorist*, 96, 98; in *Sweetest Dream*, 7, 63–66, 141, 204. *See also* mothers
homophobia, 188, 191–92, 193, 196
homosexuality, 99, 100, 135, 190, 191–92, 193
Horsa (*Cleft*), 124–26
Hours, The (Cunningham), 191
houses, 6, 148n40, 165–80; as gendered, 176–79; cottage, 137; huts, 167, *168*, 170–73, 180; Lessing's, 24, 60–61, 166–67; London, 3, 58, 60, 61, 63, 64, 70, 141–42, 143, 144, 154, 203; play, 177; pole-and-thatch, 60–61, 70; settler houses, 6, 69, 70, 167–70, *169*, 176–77, 178–79; squat, 94–96, 97, 98, 100 ,101, 148n40; verandas, 168, 173–76
Hutcheon, Linda, 113, 119, 121, 123, 127n5, 129n37

the "I." *See* narrator's voice
"I am right, you are wrong," 86, 88. *See also* "you are damned, we are saved"
If the Old Could . . . , 22, 136
Ifrik, 14, 22, 23, 27, 152, 158
imperialism. *See* colonialism

individual opposing the group, 82, 104, 109n14, 173, 192
individual's relation to the collective, 41, 43, 44, 52, 59, 60, 65, 68, 73n40, 80–82, 86–87, 150, 203
interdependence, 121, 125, 126
intergenerational relationships, 30n32, 58, 63, 65, 67, 71, 169, 180
intertextuality, 23; in *Cleft*, 121; in *Golden Notebook*, 13, 191; in *love, again*, 133, 135, 137, 139, 145. *See also* postmodernism
IRA, 95, 98, 100–101
Iran, 17, 93, 103. *See also* Lessing, Doris, in Persia
Iraq, 82, 105, 184, 185, 197
irony, 19, 185; in African stories, 171; in *Cleft*, 121, 125, 126, 128n24; in *Golden Notebook*, 44, 63, 71, 81, 187, 191; in *Good Terrorist*, 94, 95, 98, 110n15; in *love, again*, 138; in *Sweetest Dream*, 3, 68, 141
Iser, Wolfgang, 110n15
Islam, 13, 102, 104, 105, 107, 108n2, 185

Jackson, Shannon, 169
Jane Somers (*Diary of a Good Neighbor*), 12, 14, 22, 207
Janet Wulf (*Golden Notebook*), 189, 191
Janna (*Diaries*), 202, 205, 208
Jasper (*Good Terrorist*), 97, 98–99
Jim (*Good Terrorist*), 96, 97
Jocelin (*Good Terrorist*), 95, 100, 101-2, 110n18
Johnny Blakeworthy ("Non-Marrying Man"), 172–73, 180
Johnny Lennox (*Sweetest Dream*), 63, 65, 66, 67, 140, 142
Johor (*Shikasta*), 118, 128n25
Jones, Ellen Carol, 42
Jordan, Judith, 128n19
Joseph (*Children of Violence*), 60, 63, 64

Index

journalism: in *Golden Notebook*, 84, 85; in *Good Terrorist*, 94; in *Sweetest Dream*, 63, 64, 65, 67, 68, 140, 153; in *Wind Blows*, 93, 94, 102, 103, 105
Julia (*Cleft*), 123–25
Julia (*Golden Notebook*), 19
Julia Lennox (*Sweetest Dream*), 65, 66, 68, 142, 143, 144, 208
Julie Vairon (*love, again*), 134–35, 136-38, 139, 146n12

Kaivola, Karen, 36, 54n15
Kakutani, Michiko, 151, 152
Kaplan, Sydney Janet, 40, 44
Kate Brown (*Summer before the Dark*), 14
Kauffman, Linda, 199n44
Kennedy, Dane, 173
Kermode, Frank, 134
King, Jeannette, 40–41, 78
Kinsey, Alfred, 190
Klein, Melanie, 102
Koedt, Anne, 190, 198n31
Kristeva, Julia, 70
Krouse, Tonya, 2–3, 28n7, 30n24, 32–57, 225

LaCapra, Dominick, 114, 118–19, 120, 124, 127n8
Laing, R. D., 192, 194, 199n44
LeGuin, Ursula, 128n24, 129n38
Lessing, Doris: and Virginia Woolf, 35, 52, 53n9, 56n54, 60, 61–62, 69; annoyance with critics, 18, 19, 79, 133, 147n35, 201n58; as outsider, 17, 60, 62, 156; awards, 17, 29n20; children, 60, 64; and drugs, 191–92; father, 184; in London, 60, 165, 166; in Persia, 17, 93, 108n3, 165; in Rhodesia, 17, 20, 24, 60–61, 69, 93, 108n3, 166, 169, 173; influences, 33; international appeal, 29n21; interruption of novels, 20, 30n28, 30n30; negative critical opinion of, 1, 15; on feminism, 2, 187; on flexibility of the novel, 15, 133; personal interactions with, 79; resistance to feminist readings, 2, 19, 32, 53n9, 81, 84, 186; shortcomings in her craft, 14–15, 28n10, 133, 152; visits to Africa, 23–24. *See also* aesthetic, Lessing's; Communism; emotion, Lessing's; *Golden Notebook*, 1971 introduction; Jane Somers; mothers, Lessing's; Nobel Prize for Literature
London: fictional, 3, 12, 18, 23, 58, 59–61, 63, 64, 66–68, 69, 70, 71, 94–95, 100, 104, 105, 134, 141, 143, 145, 153, 154, 155, 202, 203; factual, 42, 60, 151, 153, 155, 166
London gothic. *See* gothic
Longinus, 54n12
Louw, Pat, 6, 31n42, 72n11, 159n4, 165–82, 225
love, again, 5, 7, 14, 16, 22, 133–40, 141, 144–45, 146n12, 202–4, 205-7; and *Sweetest Dream*, 133–34, 136, 140–44, 202–9; beginning, 138, 139; ending, 144–45; front matter, 139, 145; and *Golden Notebook*, 134, 136, 137, 140, 146n19; plot, 136, 137; structure, 134, 136, 137, 138, 139–40; subsidiary characters, 135–36, 140; title, 139
Luckhurst, Roger, 153, 155, 157, 158
Lynda Coldridge (*Children of Violence*), 16, 21
Lyotard, Jean-François, 4

Maire (*Cleft*), 119, 121, 122, 123
Mann, Thomas, 84, 135
Mara and Dann (*Mara and Dann, General Dann*), 14, 22, 23, 152, 158
Mara and Dann, 6, 14, 15, 22, 23, 129n46, 149, 150, 152–53, 157–58

235

Index

Mark Coldridge (*Children of Violence*), 23
Maronna (*Cleft*), 124–26
Marriages between Zones Three, Four, and Five, The, 22, 122, 125
Martha Quest (*Children of Violence*), 3, 12, 14, 16, 19–20, 22, 23, 26, 59, 61, 64, 67, 69–70, 147n35, 202, 207; and Communism, 67, 69, 79; as mother, 23, 58, 63, 147n39; as outsider, 60, 174
Martha Quest, 59, 60, 70, 139, 174
Mary Turner (*Grass Is Singing*), 25, 179
Massey Lectures, 15, 77, 91n50, 104
Matthew Mungozi (*Sweetest Dream*), 66, 67, 140, 148n41. See also Mugabe, Robert
Maudie Fowler (*Diaries*), 14, 202
Maunsell, Jerome Boyd, 71n2
May Quest (*Children of Violence*), 14, 68, 174
McCarthyism, 7, 185
memoir, 23–24, 114, 126
Memoirs of a Survivor, The, 14, 136, 147n35, 148n40, 206
Michael (*Golden Notebook*), 115, 194
Michael, Magali Cornier, 50
Miller, J. Hillis, 136
Minh-ha, Trinh T., 38, 46, 47
minor genres, 6, 149, 150, 153, 158, 159
mirroring, 25, 37, 208; in *Cleft*, 128n24; in *Golden Notebook*, 13, 15, 50, 187; in *Good Terrorist*, 99; in *love, again*, 145. See also doubling; reprises
mirrors, 7, 145, 203, 206, 207
Molly Jacobs (*Golden Notebook*), 7, 55n20, 187, 196
Molly McGuire (*love, again*), 135
moral certainty, 4, 82–85, 88. See also realism
Morgan, Ellen, 187, 191
Moses (*Grass Is Singing*), 25, 179
Mother Sugar (*Golden Notebook*), 19, 55n20
mothers, 2, 13, 14, 23, 26, 58, 60, 61, 64, 68, 69–71, 98–101, 110n16, 123, 124, 141, 145, 150, 155, 176–78, 204, 208; absent, 62, 136, 203; artist-, 3, 210n17; country, 60, 151, 153, 176; divorced, 204; grandmothers, 22, 63, 203, 208; Henke's, 188; house-, 59, 66, 67, 68, 71, 147n39; -in-law, 7, 23, 65, 68, 142, 204, 205, 208; Lessing, 60; Lessing's mother, 21, 68, 145, 166–67, 206; literary, 33, 34, 40, 52, 68; middle-aged, 202; step-, 142, 204; surrogate, 3, 23, 59, 60, 102, 135, 204; -to-be, 68
Moyers, Bill, 83, 85, 184
Mrs. Ramsay (*To the Lighthouse*), 60, 66
Mugabe, Robert, 66, 67, 69, 142, 148n41. See also Matthew Mungozi
muhjahidin, 4, 92, 102–4, 106, 107, 111n23, 111n24

narrator's persona, 37, 43, 50, 51, 52
narrator's voice, 5, 48–49, 138–40, 142, 157, 205–6. See also point of view
"New Man, The," 178–79, 180
Newquist, Roy, 173
Nobel Prize for Literature, 1, 2, 11, 33, 201n58
nostalgia, 45, 61, 62, 68, 69, 155, 205

objective correlative, 25, 47, 56n54
"Old Chief Mshlanga, The," 25, 170, 180
orgasm, 44, 188, 189–90, 198n31

Pakistan, 93, 103, 106, 111n23, 111n24, 195
Palacky University, 79, 91n62
Parkin, David, 169

Patmore, Coventry, 59, 72
Paul Tanner (*Golden Notebook*), 189, 194
Perrakis, Phyllis Sternberg, 1–8, 27n3, 108n3, 113–29, 159n3, 160n26, 161n29, 225
Persia. *See* Iran: Lessing, Doris, in
phallic, 47, 49, 56n55
picaresque, 6, 149, 151, 153, 155–57
Play with a Tiger, 22
pleasure. *See* orgasm; sexuality; text of pleasure
plot defined, 136
point of view: first-person, 137, 157; free indirect discourse, 97; omniscient, 5, 25, 41, 139, 140, 157; shifting, 139–40, 141, 151; third-person, 66, 97, 102, 122, 137, 151, 154, 157, 158, 173, 180, 202. *See also* narrator's personpolitical correctness, 1, 5, 65, 143, 144, 161. *See also* dogmatic thinking
political demonstrations, 99–100, 141, 184, 188
politics: conservative, 150–51, 153–54, 189, 191, 196; global, 2, 30n32, 134, 184–86; leftist, 3, 61, 66, 97, 98, 142, 149; Marxist, 12, 14, 61, 73n40, 99, 142, 143, 149, 195; personal, 64; sexual, 186–92; socialist, 61, 82, 84, 87, 90n33, 185. *See also* Communism
postcolonialism, 60, 70; critical theory, 28, 93, 149; in Lessing's works, 60, 61, 68, 70, 93, 102, 107
postmodernism, 3–4, 5, 17, 18, 33, 52, 61, 62, 70, 80, 107, 113, 127n5, 159; in *Cleft*, 121; in *Golden Notebook*, 17, 184, 194–96. See also historiographic metafiction; intertextuality
prescience, 2, 11, 16, 18; about aging, 2, 136; about climate change, 129n46; about politics, 7, 143, 196; about psychology, 17; about race, 8, 30n32, 150; about science, 189; about terrorism, 13, 105, 109n8; about war, 21
primitive, 6, 23, 122, 123, 149, 150, 151, 154, 156, 157, 158
Prisons We Choose to Live Inside, 4, 8, 15, 77–80, 82, 83, 85–88, 90n33, 91n50, 104
protean, 1–2, 11–12, 14–16, 18, 24, 26, 27, 126; Kakar, 107
Punter, David, 155

Quest, Mrs. *See* May Quest

race, 6, 21, 93, 149–59; in Africa, 25, 69, 142, 169–80
racism, 6, 69, 150–51, 152–53, 155, 156, 158, 176. *See also* apartheid
Raschke, Debrah, 1–8, 57n73, 108n3, 129n39
readers' response, 12, 17, 19, 20, 134; to *Fifth Child*, 22; to *Golden Notebook*, 7, 13, 18, 20, 27, 29n23, 187, 188, 195, 200n48; to *love, again*, 133, 205, 206–7; to *Prisons*, 78–79
realism, 11, 15–16, 59, 61–63, 67, 68, 82–83, 102, 111n20, 140; and Communism, 73n40; Lessing's movement away from, 4, 78, 83–85, 88, 134, 139; Lessing's return to, 134, 141, 148n40, 159; nineteenth-century, 26, 61, 70, 82–83, 137
relevance, 1, 8, 14, 35, 80, 88, 92, 105, 183, 186, 197
reprises, 20, 21, 22–24, 30n27, 58, 63–64, 204
Retreat to Innocence, 20
Rhodesia, 6, 17, 59, 60–61, 68, 69, 93, 108, 167, 169, 172, 173, 180. *See also* Lessing, Doris; Southern Africa; Zimbabwe
Ridout, Alice, 4, 8, 28n13, 73n40, 77–91, 108n7, 128n20, 159,

161n43
Ripple from the Storm, A, 79, 134
Roberta (*Good Terrorist*), 97, 100
Room of One's Own, A (Woolf), 3, 33–53, 61; Mary Beton, 48, 59, 71; Mr. A, 48–49
Rooney, Caroline, 167
Rose Trimble (*Sweetest Dream*), 67, 140, 143
Rosner, Victoria, 61, 69, 70, 166, 169
Rubenstein, Roberta, 1–2, 11–31, 62, 69, 109n8, 127n2, 197n6, 199n32, 199n44, 226
Rupert (*Sweetest Dream*), 207–9

Sage, Lorna, 78
Said, Edward, 93
Sarah Durham (*love, again*), 5, 7–8, 14, 22, 134–36, 137–39, 141, 144–45, 202–4, 205–7
Sartre, Jean-Paul, 94
Saul Green (*Golden Notebook*), 22, 49, 50, 55n20, 56n68, 115, 187, 193, 199n44, 200
Saxton, Ruth O., 7, 28n7, 31n39, 72n9, 148n45, 202–10, 226; *Woolf and Lessing*, 8n3, 35
Scanlan, Margaret, 109n11, 109n14, 111n18
Scarry, Elaine, 105, 111n22
science fiction, 4, 6, 71, 83, 87, 88, 90n33, 152, 157–58. See also utopias
"Second Hut, The," 170, 171–72, 180
Secret Agent, The (Conrad), 110n15
self-effacement. See effacement: of self
servants, 25, 144, 170, 171, 172, 178–79
sex war, 13, 19, 20, 22, 32, 186, 187
sexuality: women's, 7–8, 28n7, 41, 42, 43, 44, 146n10, 188–91, 203–9. See also homosexuality; orgasm
Shah, Idries, 29n17, 92
Shakespeare, Judith, 42

Shakespeare, William, 43, 135, 145
shape-shifting. See protean
Shikasta, 15, 21, 30n32, 118, 128n25, 128n26. See also *Canopus in Argos*
Shilling, Jane, 62
Sigal, Clancy, 187, 193
Silver, Brenda, 55n18
Singer, Sandra, 1–8, 27n2, 89n11, 92–112, 161n28, 226
Sister Molly (*Sweetest Dream*), 144
Sixties. See 1960s
Sizemore, Christine, 62
"Small Personal Voice, The," 4, 73n40, 77–78, 80–82, 84, 85, 87, 88, 90n24, 156, 159
Somers, Jane. See Jane Somers
Southern Africa, 14, 20, 23, 24, 25, 29n21, 60, 64, 66, 70, 107, *168*. See also Rhodesia; Zimbabwe
Soviet occupation, 14, 92, 102, 103, 105, 106
Soviet Union, 12, 88, 95, 97–98, 185
space fiction, 21, 33, 78, 87, 88, 127n1. See also speculative fiction
speculative fiction, 4, 11, 14, 21–22, 78, 140
Sprague, Claire, 29n21, 30n27, 35, 49, 56n54, 62, 191
Stalin, Joseph, 97, 98, 141, 185, 191
Story of General Dann and Mara's Daughter, Griot and the Snow Dog, The, 14, 22, 28n10, 129n46
"Story of a Non-Marrying Man, The," 172–73
subjectivity: female, 2, 33, 38, 39, 41, 50; gendered, 34, 35, 45, 49, 50; masculine, 49–50
Sufism, 16, 29n17, 92, 108n2, 195
suicide, 26, 95, 100, 101, 110n15, 137, 138, 146n12, 147n26, 185, 207
Summer before the Dark, The, 14, 205
superiority, 122, 123, 158, 167, 175–76. See also "I am right, you are wrong"
Susan Rawlings ("To Room Nineteen"), 26

Sweetest Dream, The, 3, 5, 7, 16, 22–23, 58–72, 85, 147n39, 202–3, 204, 207–9; and *Children of Violence*, 59, 67; and *Four-Gated City*, 58–59, 60, 63, 67, 68, 140; and *Golden Notebook*, 58–59, 68; and *love, again*, 133–34, 136, 140–44, 202–9; critical reception, 58, 62–63, 70, 71n2; ending, 71; realism in, 70, 71, 148n40; title, 143
Sylvia Lennox (*Sweetest Dream*), 23, 60, 63–64, 66–71, 142–43, 144

tables: Frances's kitchen, 3, 7, 63, 64, 65, 66, 67, 141, 143, 144, 207, 209; other, 63, 110n18, 209
Tajwar Kakar (*Wind Blows*), 93, 94, 102, 104–7
Taylor, Jenny, 30n27
Terkel, Studs, 81
terrorism: factual, 4, 11, 21 ,92, 94, 95, 103, 106–7, 109n10, 112n29; fictional, 4, 94–95, 99–102, 108n7, 108n8, 109n10, 110n15, 110n18, 111n20, 155. *See also* 9/11/01; "groupuscular terrorism"; IRA
terrorists. *See* freedom fighters, terrorists
text of bliss, 47, 50
text of pleasure, 46–47, 50
Thatcher, Margaret, 151, 153
Thatcher era. *See* 1980s
theater: in "De Wets," 174; in *love, again*, 7, 134–35, 207, 213; in *Sweetest Dream*, 63, 65, 204
Thompson, Mr. and Mrs. ("Traitors"), 177
Tiger, Virginia, 5, 28n7, 31n39, 63, 68, 133–48, 210n14, 227
To the Lighthouse (Woolf), 60
"To Room Nineteen," 26
Tommy Portmain (*Golden Notebook*), 83, 200, 210
Townshend, Charles, 109n10, 109n11

"Traitors," 176–79, 180
Transit (*Cleft*), 113–14, 116–26, 129n39; is changed, 114, 116, 118, 125–26
trauma, 5, 29n21, 114, 117–19, 184, 186, 193, 194
tribe, 6, 21, 106, 122, 125, 152, 158, 172, 190
twenty-first century. *See* 21st century

Ulysses (Joyce), 134, 190–91, 195
Under My Skin, 96, 110n16, 165
Upchurch, Michael, 152
utopias, 4, 12, 58, 80, 83, 87–88, 90n33, 122, 197; as problematic, 14, 144, 195. *See also* science fiction

Van Heerden ("Second Hut"), 172
Van Rensberg, Mrs. (*Martha Quest*), 174, 202
violence, 4, 93–95, 103, 105, 106, 112n29, 154, 156, 196; bombing, 94–95, 97, 99, 100–102, 103, 104, 105, 107, 108n7, 109n11, 109n15, 110n18, 194, 197; domestic, 99, 114, 117, 119, 120. *See also* freedom fighters; "groupuscular terrorism"; terrorism; IRA
Visel, Robin, 2, 3, 28n7, 31n39, 53n3, 58–74, 147n39, 181n16, 210n17, 227

Walking in the Shade, 133, 147n39
war, 2, 4, 21, 51, 61, 93, 94, 104, 105, 107, 111n22, 144, 196: cold war, 7, 185; nuclear, 60, 63, 65, 67; Vietnam, 66, 184, 188; War on Terror, 8, 21, 80, 106, 185–86, 197n7; World War I, 21, 184; World War II, 184, 192
Warnock, Jeanie, 127n8
Watkins, Susan, 6, 30n36, 149–61,

Index

109n14, 128n22, 129n33, 181n21, 227
Waugh, Patricia, 33, 39
Western media, 104–5, 111n24
Wharton, Edith, 137
whirlpool, 44, 137, 138, 140, 189
White, Hayden, 120, 127n7, 128n23
Wind Blows Away Our Words and Other Documents Relating to the Afghan Resistance, The, 4, 92, 93, 94, 102–7, 108n2, 111n21, 111n23, 111n24
woman writer, 3, 28n7, 33–53, 54n13, 59, 60, 61, 64, 65, 140, 206
women's movement, 19, 20, 27. *See also* feminism; sex war
women who simply get on with it, 5, 68, 144

Woolf, Virginia, 2–3, 32–53, 55n18, 56n54, 60, 61, 69, 70, 71, 203
Wyatt-Brown, Anne M., 127

Yelin, Louise, 150–51, 153, 155
"you are damned, we are saved," 8, 80. *See also* "I am right, you are wrong"

Zeitgeist, 2, 11, 16, 18, 58, 65, 70, 203
Zambesia, 23, 60, 64
Zimbabwe, 17, 23, 24, 67, 68, 93, 108n3, 142, 165, 180. *See also* Zambesia; Zimlia
Zimlia, 23, 60, 63, 64, 66, 67, 68–69, 142, 143, 144

www.ingramcontent.com/pod-product-compliance
Lightning Source LLC
Chambersburg PA
CBHW030134240426
43672CB00005B/128